CW01647607

COMPLETE COMMON WORSHIP

Sermon Illustrations

David Adam

kevin mayhew

kevin
mayhew

First published in Great Britain 2005, 2006, 2007 by Kevin Mayhew Ltd
This edition published 2011
Buxhall, Stowmarket, Suffolk IP14 3BW
Tel: +44 (0) 1449 737978 Fax: +44 (0) 1449 737834
E-mail: info@kevinmayhewltd.com

www.kevinmayhew.com

© Copyright 2005, 2006, 2007, 2011 David Adam.

The right of David Adam to be identified as the author of this work has been asserted by him in accordance with the Copyright, Designs and Patents Act 1988.

All rights reserved. No part of this publication may be reproduced, stored in a retrieval system, or transmitted, in any form or by any means, electronic, mechanical, photocopying, recording, or otherwise, without the prior written permission of the publisher.

Complete Common Worship Sermon Illustrations is extracted from *Searchlights* – Complete Resource Book

ISBN 978 1 84867 341 0
Catalogue No. 1501259

Cover design by Rob Mortonson
© Image used under licence from Shutterstock Inc.
Typeset by Rob Mortonson

Printed and bound in Great Britain

Contents

About the author

David Adam was the Vicar of Lindisfarne, off the Northumbrian coast, for thirteen years until he retired in March 2003. His work involved ministering to thousands of pilgrims and other visitors. He is the author of many inspiring books on spirituality and prayer, and his Celtic writings have rekindled a keen interest in our Christian heritage.

Introduction

The Readings from Common Worship take us through the seasons of the Church year. This is a three-year cycle when we use mainly Matthew in Year A, Mark in Year B and Luke in Year C. St John is used throughout the three-year cycle. Together with the Old Testament and Epistles, this gives us a good variety of readings and takes us through most of the Old and New Testament in three years. In its turn this presents the preacher with parts of the Scriptures that they may not have preached on before and may not have even studied much. All preaching should come out of time spent with God and from meditating on God's Word. Preaching is to come out of our hearts and from our relationship with God. This does not mean that we do not need resources. In fact, the more we seek to understand what the Church has said, what scholars have discovered, the more we can be informed in our preaching.

This book is meant to be a resource book. It provides the readings for each Sunday of the year, a comment, which is usually on the Gospel, and an illustration that is linked to the Gospel. Although the 'Thought for the day' is not just notes, it could not be read out as a sermon; it must be put into your own words and your own experience added to it.

For much of the preparation I have used a way of reading that goes back to the fourth century and the Desert Fathers, the Lectio Divina. The early Fathers knew the words of the Bible needed more than ordinary reading. We have to allow the Word to get into our lives and to touch our hearts. We are not only to know *about* God; we are to *know* God. We are not only to talk about him; we are to introduce others to him. I suggest this pattern for your reading of the Scriptures:

Read (Lectio)

Read the passage aloud and take your time. Read it again in silence thoughtfully and see if there is any event or phrase that stands out for you. But more than anything let the words vibrate in your life. If nothing seems to resonate, it is worth waiting in the presence without anxiety. If still nothing comes, read the words again and at least be able to present your picture of the events to the people. This is the time to use commentaries on the Scriptures and to look at other writers.

Meditate (Meditatio)

Let the words get deep into your being: let them touch your heart as well as your mind. Consider what God is seeking to say to you through the text or phrase. Know this is God's word and he seeks to communicate with you. At this stage I try to bring all my senses to bear on the passage before me.

Pray (Oratio)

Speak to God about this passage and allow God to speak to you. Where possible, let your thoughts be turned into prayer. Preaching develops through our contact with our God.

Contemplate (Contemplatio)

Learn to rest in God's presence. Use the words of the readings to bring your mind back to the presence and love of God. Whenever your mind wanders use a word or two to bring yourself to be still before him.

If you are too busy to spend time before God, you are too busy. Remember that it is God's word you preach on, not your own opinion.

May God greatly enrich you and strengthen you as you seek to proclaim his presence and his power.

David Adam

YEAR A

First Sunday of Advent

Aim

To encourage each other to be aware of Christ's coming to us today.

Readings

Isaiah 2:1-5
Psalm 122
Romans 13:11-14
Matthew 24:36-44

Thought for the day

(Produce an alarm clock and let it ring, then switch it off.) 'I'll just doze for a few more minutes.' (Let the alarm ring again.) 'I'll hit the snooze button. That's better. I like a good sleep – then the rush was on: no time to have proper breakfast, no time to tidy up. I bumped into someone because I did not notice her. I knocked over a bin because I did not even see it. Then when I got there the train had just gone. "You're just too late," said the man on the station. Now I'll be late for school – it would not matter so much if I were not the headmaster!'

Jesus warns us about being too sleepy and not noticing what is going on around us. We must also prepare ourselves for the coming of the Son of Man. We are to be prepared not only for Christmas but also for the coming of Christ to us.

Advent celebrates the coming of Jesus. Jesus has come through being born of the Virgin Mary. Jesus is come – and comes to each of us now today. Jesus will come again in glory. Will he find us ready in his coming to us?

Are we awake to the fact – are we aware – that Jesus comes to us? Hear him say:

> I searched for you and I love you.
> I knocked at your door.
> I called in your dreams.
> I spoke in your life.
> I kept coming to you.
> But you were unaware.

You did not come to me.
You did not open your door.
You were too engaged to hear my call.
You were too busy to respond to me.
I came but you had no room for me.
Yet I will keep coming.
I will call to you,
until you have time to find me.

Illustration

When the devil wanted to ruin the lives of many people he called a meeting of his fallen angels and sought suggestions. 'I will tell them there is no God,' said the first. The devil replied, 'Any sensitive and thinking person knows there is a God and this will not lead them astray.' A second said, 'I will tell them there is no hell.' 'What is the use of that?' asked the evil one. 'Everyone will experience a taste of hell and know that it is a reality.' A third then spoke up and said, 'I will tell them there is no hurry. Put it off until tomorrow – for I know tomorrow never comes.' With this the devil was delighted and this is how most people fail to turn to God.

Pablo Picasso said, 'Never put off today anything that you do not want to leave undone for ever.'

Second Sunday of Advent

Aim

To prepare for the coming of the Lord.

Readings

Isaiah 11:1-10
Psalm 72:1-7, 18, 19
Romans 15:4-13
Matthew 3:1-12

Thought for the day

For a long time there had been no one to whom the Jews would have given the name of 'prophet'. They said that prophecy had been dead for four hundred years. Then suddenly out of the desert of Judea came John. He was dressed in clothing of camel hair and had a leather belt about his waist. This was how Elijah was described in 2 Kings 1:8. As the Jews had a belief that Elijah would return before the Messiah came (Malachi 4:5), John is to be seen as the herald of the Christ. Matthew links John with the prophecy from Isaiah 40:3 and describes him as 'the voice of one crying out in the wilderness, "Prepare the way of the Lord, make his path straight"' (Matthew 3:3). Like the man who went ahead of the visiting king to make sure the road was good and the people were prepared, John came to get people ready for the coming of Jesus.

John sought to bring people not to himself but to God and to make them aware that Christ was coming. John told the people he was not even worthy to carry the sandals of the One who was to come. (Such a task was usually the work of a slave.) John was sure that the Christ was much greater than him.

John challenges us. In this time of busyness and activity when you are preparing for Christmas, are you truly preparing to let the Christ into your life? Are you ready for his coming? John calls the people to 'Repent for the kingdom of heaven has come near' (Matthew 3:2). This is the same as the message we get from Jesus in Mark 1:15. We would do well to hear the call. The word 'repent' means 'turn around': you are looking the wrong way, you are going the wrong way. 'Turn around': you are going in the wrong direction; that is not the way to meet the King. Can we relate this call to much of what we are doing at Christmas and how we are living our lives? Are we truly prepared or preparing to welcome the King? Like going the wrong way down a road, the further you go, the longer the journey back. Have you got your directions right? Today turn to God, turn to Christ. As a preparation for Christmas, turn each day in prayer to the One who comes, and comes to you.

Illustration

Making a journey was not easy in biblical times. An eastern proverb states, 'There are three states of misery: illness, fasting and travel.' Before anyone went on a journey they were advised to 'pay all debts, provide for dependants, provide parting gifts, return all articles under trust, take money and a good temper, then bid farewell to all'. Roads were often in poor condition, full of holes and bumps that made travel difficult if not dangerous. Journeying was never done for pleasure. There were few cared-for roads. Josephus tells us that King Solomon laid a causeway of black basalt stone along the roads that led to Jerusalem 'to manifest the grandeur of his riches and government'. All surfaces and built-up roads were originally built for the king and for his use. Before the king was due to visit an area, the inhabitants were visited and warned to be ready. They had to make sure the road didn't have any obstacles to make the king's journey difficult. They also had to be prepared to welcome him. John the Baptist is to be seen as one who tells us of the need to prepare the way for the coming of the King, of the Christ.

Third Sunday of Advent

Aim

To rejoice in the Christ who comes.

Readings

Isaiah 35:1-10
Psalm 146:5-10 or Canticle: Magnificat
James 5:7-10
Matthew 11:2-11

Thought for the day

The Scriptures never promise and easy life for those who seek to do good. Here is John the Baptist in prison for speaking out against evil. John had dared to speak out against Herod Antipas of Galilee. Herod had dismissed his wife and married his brother's wife, after seducing her. Because John spoke against this he was held prisoner in the fortress of Machaerus up in the mountains near the Dead Sea. John had proclaimed Jesus as the Christ, but there in prison either he or his disciples seem to be having doubts. Perhaps John wanted to point his disciples in the direction of Jesus. John's disciples came to Jesus and asked, 'Are you the one who is to come, or are we to wait for another?'

Jesus does not answer, 'Yes', or explain in words. He does not argue his case but rather asks them to tell what they hear and see. 'Do not tell John what I am saying but what I am doing, what is happening. The blind receive their sight, the lame walk, lepers are cleansed, the deaf hear, the dead are raised, and the poor have the good news brought to them.' Not only are the powers of darkness being defeated but the Scriptures are being fulfilled. (See today's Old Testament Reading, Isaiah 35:1-10.) This is Good News!

Look again at last week's Gospel and the demands of John the Baptist (Mathew 3:1-12). Perhaps the disciples of John were worried about this 'friend of publicans and sinners'. Jesus is not as hard or as judgemental as they would like him to be. This was not a message of destruction for the wicked but one of the love of God. Perhaps John's disciples would have liked a little more severity. Jesus says to the disciples of John, 'Blessed is anyone who takes no offence in me.' We have to accept him as he is and not change him into who we want him to be. In accepting him he will transform our lives as he transformed those of the people he met.

Illustration

When Bede writes about St Aidan he says, 'The highest recommendation of his teaching to all was that he and his followers lived as they taught. He never sought or cared for any worldly possession, and loved to give away to the poor who chanced to meet him whatever he received from kings or wealthy folk. Whether in town or country, he always travelled on foot unless compelled by necessity to ride; and whoever the people he met on his walks, whether high or low, he stopped and spoke to them. If they were heathen, he urged them to be baptised; and if they were Christians, he strengthened their faith and inspired them by word and deed to live a good life and to be generous to others.'

It was the example of a life lived for God that spoke out louder than the words he spoke and backed up what he preached.

Fourth Sunday of Advent

Aim

To show, through the example of Joseph, that God waits upon our obedience to accomplish his work.

Readings

Isaiah 7:10-16
Psalm 80:1-7, 16-18
Romans 1:1-7
Matthew 1:18-25

Thought for the day

There are times when it is as if the whole world waits on the reaction of one person. Today's Gospel is such a moment. Mary is betrothed to Joseph. They may have been promised to each other since Mary was a child. Betrothal is usually for a year and it is when the couple agree to the promises that were made for them. At this stage they are known as man and wife and the relationship is binding. It can now only be terminated by divorce.

Mary has told Joseph she is pregnant and he knows it is not his child. How could he begin to understand when Mary told him of her encounter with the angel?

Joseph's reaction is a natural one. He cares for Mary; he does not want her to face public disgrace, but he feels he must dismiss her. These thoughts obviously disturbed him day and night. But he made up his mind: he knew what he would do. Then he had a dream that changed the course of the world. An angel came and spoke to him: 'Joseph, son of David, do not be afraid to take Mary as your wife, for the child conceived in her is from the Holy Spirit.'

Joseph would never understand this but he could obey God's messenger. Without Joseph's willingness, the whole plan of the birth of Jesus could come to nothing. Often God depends on us for achieving what he wants done in the world. Without our cooperation the kingdom of God cannot come on earth. When we do what God wants us to do, wonderful things happen.

Joseph is told how Mary will bear a son and 'You are to name him Jesus, for he will save his people from their sins.' By naming him, Joseph is accepting Jesus as his own son. By calling him

Jesus, which is Greek for the Hebrew name Joshua and means 'Jehovah is Salvation' or 'God is Saviour', Joseph is to acknowledge what is promised through Jesus.

Matthew is keen to show that the coming of Jesus into the world is God's work, and sets out his credentials from Isaiah: 'Look, a virgin shall conceive and bear a son, and they shall name him Emmanuel', which means 'God is with us'.

God is with us but this reality cannot be achieved without our obedience and cooperation. It is when we say, 'Your will be done' that the possibility of the kingdom of God takes shape in our lives. When Joseph awoke from sleep he did as he was commanded. Through Joseph, as well as Mary, obedience brought the possibility of Emmanuel, God in our midst.

Illustration

Ivan lived under an oppressive regime. If those in power wanted anything, they took it. If they wanted you to do something, you had to do it or your life was at risk. The state police did not knock on doors; they forced their way into people's homes, and if they wanted anything, they took it. Everyone lived in fear and was oppressed. It was during this time that Ivan learnt the Good News of the Gospel. God did not force himself on people. He waited for Mary and Joseph to agree to his plans. In Jesus he did not oppress people but liberated them. Jesus did not burst into lives but said, 'I stand at the door and knock.' Ivan was amazed that so many ignored this loving, saving God. From the moment Ivan heard of such a God he sought to serve in that service which is 'perfect freedom'.

Christmas Day

Aim

To celebrate the birth of Jesus and to give thanks for the presence of God with us.

Readings

Isaiah 52:7-10
Psalm 98
Hebrews 1:1-4 (5-12)
John 1:1-14

Thought for the day

It is not hard to imagine the crowded inn. Friends and relatives have got together and seek to celebrate; the place is packed. Some who are weary are trying to sleep. The place is full to capacity. There is much conversation, perhaps some singing and dancing. There is no room here for Mary who is about to bring forth her son. There was no room at the inn.

How common these words are, though they may be said in different ways: 'Do not disturb me, I am busy'; 'I would like to help but I do not have the time'; 'I like a routine and I don't want anything to interfere with it'; 'I cannot come and see you, I have business to attend to.' And every time we excuse ourselves, we exclude ourselves from certain experiences. Being pre-occupied is a great defence against anything new happening. 'I would have said my prayers but there is too much happening to me.' In such ways we miss the coming of God.

Yet the innkeeper, busy, hard-pressed, found room. He offered a space to Joseph and Mary. Simple accommodation and into it came the Christ child. The innkeeper made room and the Christ was able to come into his place.

Amid all the busyness of Christmas, the activity that threatens to overwhelm us, you have made room. You are here to rejoice that God comes, he comes into the world and he comes to you. We can rejoice in the mystery of the God who seeks to share in our daily life. We celebrate the greatest of miracles that the Word is made flesh and dwells among us. Let us quietly think over these words of St John: 'To all who received him, who believed in his name, he gave power to become children of God' (John 1:12). We will keep a short silence and in it let us give thanks for the coming of Christ into the world and for his coming to us. Let us open our hearts to him and say, 'Come to my heart, Lord Jesus, there is room in my heart for you.'

Illustration

Nan-in was a great Japanese teacher of the art of Zen. One day a university professor came to seek some teaching. Nan-in served the traditional tea to his guest. He poured until his visitor's bowl was full and then kept pouring and the tea overflowed, as there was no room for it in the bowl. The professor watched until he could no longer restrain himself and said, 'It is overfull and no more will go in.' Nan-in said, 'You are like this cup. You are full of ideas and speculations. How can I pour more in unless you empty your cup? You need to make space to learn.'

In the same way we need to make a space in our lives each day for our God who comes to us.

Think upon these words by Angelus Silesius:

Though Christ a thousand times
in Bethlehem be born,
if he is not born in you,
you are still forlorn.

First Sunday of Christmas

Aim

To show that Jesus knows our joys and our sorrows.

Readings

Isaiah 63:7-9
Psalm 148
Hebrews 2:10-18
Matthew 2:13-23

Thought for the day

I like all the glitter of Christmas but we must remember Jesus did not live in tinsel town. Jesus was born into a turbulent world where there was oppression and rebellion, cruelty and evil. King Herod (king from 37–4 BC) typifies the times. Herod was appointed 'King of the Jews' by the Roman Senate and was quite paranoid about anyone who challenged his position or power. Friends, courtiers, priests, nobles were often killed on the suspicion that they might oppose him. That the wise men went to him and enquired about the 'King of the Jews' was unfortunate. This brought about the massacre of the children at Bethlehem. As Bethlehem was not all that large, it would probably amount to 20 to 30 children.

Fortunately, Joseph had another dream of an angel who said, Get up, take the child and his mother and flee into Egypt.' The baby Jesus escaped the tyrant as the baby Moses had escaped Pharaoh. Joseph made the journey into Egypt where long ago another Joseph cared for his family in time of trouble.

When Herod died, the kingdom was divided between his three sons: Archelaus ruled in Judea, Herod Antipas ruled Galilee and Perea, Philip ruled Iturea, Trachonitis and the territory in the north-east.

Joseph had another dream while in Egypt and this time the angel told him to return to Israel because Herod was dead. Joseph once again obeyed but decided that Archelaus was still a danger, so he took Jesus to Galilee and to Nazareth. This was only slightly safer. Herod Antipas was the one who had John the Baptist beheaded. This Herod would meet Jesus briefly at Jesus' trial.

We do not know how long the Holy Family was in Egypt but it would not have been very long. It must have been a great relief to the parents of Mary when they saw her again and found not only was she safe but so was the baby Jesus. From the very beginning Jesus shares in our sorrows as well as our joys. His family are homeless and refugees. It would take a while for Joseph to build up his work in Egypt and again in Nazareth, and without work they would not eat. The shadow of the cross often touched the carpenter's workplace. Let us give thanks that Jesus shares in our humanity and understands our troubles. Our God is not a God who is far-off but a God who loves us and comes among us.

Illustration

There are many stories of how people have been protected by angels; this one is from Vanuatu (the New Hebrides). The Reverend John Paton went as a missionary to the Hebridean Islands. One night a group of hostile natives surrounded his mission and home. Paton prayed for God to protect him. When morning came Paton was amazed to see his attackers leaving. About a year later the chief accepted Christianity and became a believer. The Reverend John asked him why they had not attacked his house and burned it down. The chief in turn asked him, 'Who were those men you had with you there?'

John replied, 'There were no men, only my wife and I.' The chief argued that he saw many men, big men in shining white garments with drawn swords standing guard.

Second Sunday of Christmas

Aim

To rejoice in the mystery of the Word made flesh and in the kingdom of heaven.

Readings

Ecclesiasticus 24:1-12
Canticle: Wisdom of Solomon 10:15-21
Ephesians 1:3-14
John 1:(1-9) 10-18

Thought for the day

St John's Gospel owes its thought patterns to Hellenistic Judaism – that is to both Greek and Jewish ideas. The combination of these two led to the belief that existence has two dimensions. Heaven is the sphere in which God is at work: this would include light, joy, love, peace, grace, spirit and truth. The created world – the Cosmos – is the sphere of Satan and it includes darkness, distress, death, all evil and falsehood. John does talk of heaven above and earth below but he does not seek to imply they are separate; rather, they are different spheres at work in the same space and in the same human being. We have in our lives the potential of heaven and its opposite.

Like God, heaven is not far away but to be experienced in the here and now. The kingdom of heaven is always at hand. Part of the understanding of the at-one-ment – the atonement – is that we are as much in heaven as on earth.

Because we so often live on the level of the cosmos alone, we have blinded ourselves to the reality that heaven is all about us. The call of John the Baptist and Jesus to repentance was a call saying, 'Turn around, you are looking at life and the world in the wrong way. The kingdom of heaven is waiting for you to enjoy it.' To say, 'The Lord is with you,' is a reality we have to make our own. God is not a long-distance phone call and heaven is not 'far, far away'. Heaven is not only somewhere we should be planning to retire to after death but also somewhere we should be entering and living in now.

St John suggests that in Jesus the glory of God is revealed: the very presence of God in an earthly life. Those who see this and believe in him have the power to become the children of God.

Illustration

A woman from County Kerry in Ireland was asked, 'Where is heaven?' She thought for a moment and then replied, 'About one foot and six inches above me.' She wanted to show that God and heaven are always close at hand and not beyond our reach. We have to just stretch ourselves, extend our vision, give the kingdom of heaven some priority in our life to begin to realise we are there. By giving time and attention to God we learn that 'we dwell in him and he in us'.

The Epiphany

Aim

To share in the seeking and the worshipping of the wise men.

Readings

Isaiah 60:1-6
Psalm 72:(1-7) 10-14
Ephesians 3:1-12
Matthew 2:1-12

Thought for the day

The shepherds were lucky because when the angels told them about Jesus their journey to the stable was not really very far. They were given directions and had a good idea where they were going. The wise men were not so lucky because their journey was to be a long one. They were often in the dark and they were not always sure of their destination. To be guided by a star is hardly an exact way of navigation and there is no fixed address they can aim for. Their journey would call for courage and the determination not to give up. It would have been easy to be put off and ask if it was all worth it. It would have been easy to choose comfort and safety, to give up when they met with obstacles. Many people would say, 'Why bother?' But in their hearts they knew they would not be satisfied until they had come before the Chosen One, until they knelt before the Christ child and offered him their gifts and their lives. The wise men knew there was more to life than comfort and security, more to life than possessions or even wisdom. The wise men were searching for a relationship with God. Theirs was a journey of faith. The wise men are an encouragement to all who are seekers and an example of our pilgrimage through life.

In their seeking the wise men went to the wrong place. They went to Herod the king and we know the sad consequence of that mistake. They had assumed a king would be born in a palace and now would have to rethink their ideas. Too often in our search for God we have gone to the wrong people or gone with fixed ideas. But if we continue to seek and do not give up on our journey of faith, we will also be able to come to the Christ and offer ourselves to him. Let us never forget that we are seeking because our God is calling us. He wants us to come before him and to rejoice in his presence.

Illustration

There are many roads to God. God calls each of us and waits for our response. In the wise men we see at least three different roads. Perhaps they travelled alone and on different paths at the outset. Their faith journey brought them together.

Gold is a symbol of all of God's gifts. All things come from God and of his own do we offer. God gives us life and this wonderful world. Many come to God through thanksgiving, through gratitude for all that he gives. Gold is also a symbol of power: wealth helps people to achieve and poverty restricts people.

Frankincense is symbol of awe, of mystery and adoration. If we are sensitive to the wonders of the world and the mystery of creation, this can lead us to God. This in turn can lead us to respect all of creation because it is of God. Frankincense is used in worship and many people learn of God through the worship of others.

Myrrh is a symbol of pain and the need for relief from pain and sorrow. For many it is easy to forget God in the good times. But when we lose a loved one or become seriously ill ourselves, it makes us ask questions about our existence. As mortals we all need the salvation and healing that God gives.

First Sunday of Epiphany
The Baptism of Christ

Aim

To show how Jesus is revealed as God's Son through his baptism.

Readings

Isaiah 42:1-9
Psalm 29
Acts 10:34-43
Matthew 3:13-17

Thought for the day

Throughout the Epiphany season we see how Jesus is revealed to the world. He is visited by the wise men from the East who represent the nations of the world. In today's reading we see at his baptism how the Father gives his sign of approval and how the Spirit comes upon Jesus. Next week we will see how John the Baptist points out Jesus as the Chosen One of God. The following week reveals how Jesus fulfils the prophecies of Isaiah. With Epiphany 4 we will see how the miracle of the water made into wine reveals the power and compassion of Jesus.

John the Baptist's message had four great themes: repentance, confession with baptism, judgement and righteousness. These themes have been the rallying calls of many a revival. But we know there is something more needed. Matthew is a master of understatement when he simply says, 'Jesus came from Galilee to John at the Jordan to be baptised by him' (3:13). After all that John had done, all his preaching, all his preparing the way, Jesus came. Without this, all religion is stern and forbidding, but when Jesus comes and is accepted in a church and in a life, everything changes. There is a new light and a new hope. When Jesus comes on the scene, whatever it is, it is changed.

Sadly there are many good people who are leading righteous and respectable lives who are living BC – before Christ. Even some churches seem to live as if they belonged to the Old Testament rather than the New. They need to allow Jesus into their lives and experience the joy and freedom he brings. This can be well illustrated by Saul and his harsh life before the Damascus Road and his liberated life after it.

Do not live in the BC era. Know the Lord comes and he comes to you. Meet Jesus each day in your prayers and in your daily living. Welcome him into your life.

The revelation of who Jesus is comes as Jesus emerges out of the water. The Spirit comes upon him as a sign that he is now ready for his mission. The voice of God is heard saying, 'This is my Son, the Beloved, with whom I am well pleased.' This tells us from whom he comes and whom he reveals to us. It is worth noting that the Baptism of Jesus is one of the few times the Bible actually mentions Father, Son and Holy Spirit.

Illustration

What a difference Jesus makes. *Miracle on the River Kwai* by Ernest Gordon tells the story of prisoners of war building a bridge. They were overworked, often starving, exhausted and ill. The need to survive made them put themselves first and fail to see each other's needs. Then two men, Dusty and Dinty, began helping others. They put themselves out to care for and respect others. A new spirit began to spread through the camp until the place was transformed, as were its inhabitants. When questioned about their actions, Dusty read from 1 John 4:21: 'The commandment we have from him is this: those who love God must love their brothers and sisters also.' Dusty was a Methodist and Dinty a Roman Catholic, and both were full of the Presence. The lives of the men had been hell. Then 'Jesus came' and what a difference that made.

Second Sunday of Epiphany

Aim

To show the importance of bringing people to Jesus.

Readings

Isaiah 49:1-7
Psalm 40:1-11
1 Corinthians 1:1-9
John 1:29-42

Thought for the day

We continue with the Epiphany theme of the revealing of Jesus.

The day after the baptism of Jesus, John the Baptist saw Jesus coming towards him and declared, 'Here is the Lamb of God who takes away the sin of the world!' John witnesses to Jesus and to what happened at his baptism. John points people away from following him to follow Jesus. He wants people to know that following Jesus is of greater importance because Jesus is the Son of God.

The next day John was with two of his followers, and as he watched Jesus walk by he exclaimed, 'Look, here is the Lamb of God.' To describe Jesus in this way was to build on the promises of the Scriptures. Going right back to Genesis 22:8, Abraham said, 'God will provide a lamb for a burnt-offering, my son.' In doing this and in staying Abraham's hand, God rescued Isaac from death. The Passover Lamb (Exodus 12:1-13) celebrates the gaining of freedom from slavery and from death. (Compare John's statement in John 3:16.) In Isaiah, the Suffering Servant, whom the Christian Church sees as an image of Jesus, is described as 'a lamb led to the slaughter' (Isaiah 53:7).

The effect of the Baptist's words was for two of his followers to leave him and follow Jesus. As ever with seekers, they are met by the one they seek. Jesus turns to meet them. St Augustine said that we cannot even begin to seek God unless he has already found us. When we seek God, we do not go to one who hides from us but to one who has always been seeking us and comes to meet us.

Jesus asks, 'What are you looking for?' This is a good question to ask all of us: is it knowledge, security, meaning, a purpose, peace, or is it a relationship with the living God? When the disciples ask, 'Where are you staying?' Jesus invites them, 'Come and see.' The only real way to truly learn of Jesus is to abide in his presence, to stay with him. Faith is not about believing in facts; it is having a living relationship with Jesus. As an interesting aside, we are told it was about four o'clock in the afternoon. Could it be that the writer of the Gospel remembered this well and that this disciple was John who would witness to Jesus through the Gospel and, in this way, point people to Jesus?

The other disciple was Andrew. The first thing Andrew did after meeting Jesus was to go and tell his brother, 'We have found the Messiah' – that is, the Christ, the Anointed One. Andrew brought Simon to Jesus. Later he would bring the boy with five barley loaves to Jesus. Later still he would bring a group of Greeks to Jesus. Andrew is seen as the first missionary in bringing someone to Jesus. What greater service can you do than to bring someone to Jesus?

Illustration

It is often proclaimed that the Church is suffering from a crisis in the West. There is a shortage of priests, of ministers. Allied to this is a shortage of money. But more money or more clergy will not cure the crisis. The Church needs a dose of Andrews! It needs people who will abide with Christ and then bring others to Christ. The Church is not short of people and it could grow like it did of old if we would learn to abide with Christ and seek to bring others to him.

The Church grew from twelve disciples who were with Jesus and who wanted others to know him. We must learn to bring others to the One we know and love. Just think how quickly the Church would grow if we were all committed to bringing someone else to know Jesus.

Third Sunday of Epiphany

Aim

To encourage people to listen to the call of God and to respond.

Readings

Isaiah 9:1-4
Psalm 27:1, 5-13
1 Corinthians 1:10-18
Matthew 4:12-23

Thought for the day

We continue with Jesus being revealed as the Christ. Perhaps the arrest and imprisonment of John acted as a catalyst in making Jesus take up his ministry. Jesus leaves Nazareth. He leaves his home and goes to live in Capernaum. His life of ministry and his work of salvation now truly begin. This area of Galilee is the most northerly district of Palestine. It was not a large area, only 50 miles north to south and 25 miles east to west. But because it was the most fertile area of Palestine, it was densely populated. Josephus records that there were 204 communities with populations of over 15,000 people. Jesus began his mission where there were the most people likely to hear him. Surrounded by Gentile nations, it was an area open to new ideas and used to change. This would be an area open to the teaching and ministry of Jesus.

Matthew tells us that Jesus began to 'proclaim': the word he uses is that of a herald's proclamation. The herald speaks with a certainty of his message. Preachers cannot tell us anything with certainty if they have doubts themselves. The herald speaks with authority because he speaks on behalf of the king, from a source beyond himself. In this case, Jesus speaks the word of God. True preaching is concerning the word of God and not our own opinions or ideas. The message is: Repent, turn around, turn to God. If you are not looking the right way, you cannot go the right way. Seek God. If you but know it, God's kingdom is near – it is because you look in the wrong direction that you do not see it or enter it.

Jesus now calls his first disciples. It is worth noting in Matthew that the initiative comes from Jesus. This is so often true:

God/Jesus calls but so often we stall. He calls Simon Peter and Andrew as they are casting a net into the Sea of Galilee, saying, 'Follow me.' Immediately they leave their nets and follow him. They do not say, 'Wait until we have finished', or 'Wait until we have sold this fish'; they leave all and follow him. If we do not respond to the call immediately, we are less likely to respond later – though Jesus calls and calls. In the same way, he calls James and John who are in a boat with their father mending their nets. Immediately they leave the boat and their father and follow him. The two sets of brothers give up their security and their homes to follow the Master.

So the ministry of Jesus begins. Jesus travels throughout Galilee, teaching in synagogues, proclaiming the Good News and healing people.

Illustration

There are two stories of Socrates and his calling of disciples. Xenophon met Socrates on the road and the teacher barred his path with a stick. Socrates asked Xenophon simple questions about where certain things were made. Then he asked, 'Do you know where men are made good and virtuous?' 'No, I do not,' answered the young man. Socrates then said, 'Follow me and learn.'

On another occasion a man called Aeschines came to Socrates and said, 'I am a poor man, I have nothing else to offer but myself.' Socrates replied, 'Do you not see that you are giving me the most precious thing of all?'

It is in giving ourselves to God that we truly give.

Fourth Sunday of Epiphany

Aim

To show God meets our lack of resources with his abundant power and generosity.

Readings

1 Kings 17:8-16
Psalm 36:5-10
1 Corinthians 1:18-31
John 2:1-11

Thought for the day

The first miracle recorded by St John is seen as the beginning of the saving works of Jesus, and as a revelation of his glory. The setting for all of this is a country wedding in Galilee.

Jesus' mother prompts the action in this event when she says to Jesus, 'They have no wine.' The celebrations were not meant to end but suddenly the resources ran low. How often this is true of life. We would like to go on but we run out of energy, run out of supplies, and cannot continue. We all experience that as humans our resources are limited. We rarely heed the words of Isaiah when he says, 'They that wait upon the Lord shall renew their strength.' We need to learn that all our powers and resources are gifts from God.

Mary says to the servants, 'Do whatever he tells you.' Throughout the rest of the story they do just that. This is to be seen as a major theme in the story: it is through obedience to Jesus that wonderful things can happen. We are to put our trust in his words.

The stone jars each held about 25 gallons. So the miracle created about 150 gallons of wine – or 682 litres or over 1000 bottles – and that is after they had drunk all the wine that the steward had provided. I know a lot of people who would follow anyone who could do this! But we miss the point if we concentrate on the amount of drink; this is a sign of the superabundant grace of God and how he renews and refreshes us beyond what we can hope for. Our resources are limited but God's are not.

When we scrape the bottom of the barrel or feel totally drained, it is often because we have gone on in our own strength and abilities and have not come to God or sought to do his will. In John's Gospel Jesus says, 'I came that they may have life and have it abundantly' (John 10:10).

We are told that the sign of the water made into wine revealed his glory and the disciples believed in him.

Illustration

Charles was a relatively new Christian. He had a good home, a job and a loving family. Not long before it had been all endangered through Charles drinking too often. He said he could not help it. Whenever his resources were low, whenever he felt tired or exhausted, he turned to the bottle. His family were suffering; they did not have enough income to survive on after Charles's drinking. A friend introduced him to Alcoholics Anonymous and also to his local church. The second had an amazing effect. Charles discovered the power of the love and presence of God. Now when resources were low or when he felt exhausted, he turned to rest in God and to be renewed by him. At a Bible study he expressed difficulty with the miracle of changing water into wine. 'But,' he said, 'I know Jesus can change lives. He can turn wine into food on the table and to clothes on our backs.' Jesus has the power to renew and refresh each of us in our lives.

The Presentation of Christ

(To be used on the Sunday nearest 2 February, if not on the day)

Aim

To let the light of Christ enter our hearts and our lives.

Readings

Malachi 3:1-5
Psalm 24:(1-6) 7-10
Hebrews 2:14-18
Luke 2:22-40

Thought for the day

What Mary and Joseph were doing was what all Jewish parents were required to do. By Jewish Law, Mary could not enter a holy place or touch anything holy until she had given thanks to God for her first-born and offered the accustomed sacrifice. Mary came to be purified and with Joseph to offer two doves. If they were well-off they would have been expected to offer more. The offering of two doves was known as the 'offering of the poor'. This event was being performed every day by couples and their child, and there is nothing unusual about it. When Simeon comes on the scene, however, we enter into something quite different.

Simeon looked for the 'comforting of Israel'. He had been promised he would not die until he had seen the Lord's Anointed One – that is, the Christ. Simeon takes the baby Jesus in his arms and blesses God. He knows he has the Christ in his arms, the one who is to be the glory of Israel. But there is more. The Jews thought upon the Christ as their Saviour; Simeon describes Christ as 'a light for the revelation to the Gentiles'. Jesus would not be the exclusive property of one nation – he came to be the Saviour of the world. Because of this even as non-Jews, we can all say, 'The Lord is my light and my salvation.'

Jesus is revealed as the Light of the World. Later as a grown man and fulfilling his ministry, Jesus will say of himself, 'I am the light of the world. Whoever follows me will never walk in darkness' (John 8:12). To refuse to accept Jesus as our Light is to walk in the darkness of the world. To accept Jesus as our Light is to have our lives filled with his light. Today the Church lights many candles to witness to this fact. The Feast of the Purification is often better known as Candlemas for this reason. Candlemas marks the end of the Epiphany season of the revealing of Christ, and now we turn towards Lent and the suffering of Christ. The Advent candles, if they are still in church, are now taken out. The next time a large candle is brought into church it is the Easter Candle. But today we rejoice in the Good News that the light of Christ is not exclusive – it is for all, it is for you. We can all say, 'The Lord is my light and my salvation.'

Illustration

The night was pitch black as the car drove along a country lane. There were no lights for miles. Suddenly the driver was aware that a rear tyre had a puncture. He would have to stop and mend it. Once out of the car he could see very little. The lights of the car did not give light where he wanted it and he had no torch. This would be a very slow job and he was not sure he could do it in the dark. It was worrying because he was a long way from any houses and it was very late at night. Fortunately, within a few minutes he saw a light coming along the road in front of him. It was a milkman on his early rounds. Though he was busy, the milkman stopped and provided light and what a difference that made. The man no longer worked in darkness but in the light.

Proper 1

Sunday between 3 and 9 February inclusive
(if earlier than the Second Sunday before Lent)

Aim

To look at what it means to be the salt of the earth and the light of the world.

Readings

Isaiah 58:1-9a (9b-12)
Psalm 112:1-9 (10)
1 Corinthians 2:1-12 (13-16)
Matthew 5:13-20

Thought for the day

Matthew seeks to show Jesus as a second Moses. The flight into Egypt echoes Moses' flight into the desert; the killing of the Holy Innocents echoes the infant Moses in danger from Pharaoh. Jesus tempted in the wilderness is like Moses in the wilderness. Moses went up Mount Sinai to convey the Law to the people; Jesus ascends a mountain to teach the people. Jesus says, 'Do not think I have come to abolish the law and the prophets; I have come not to abolish but to fulfil.'

Last week we rejoiced in the Lord as our light and salvation. This week we hear our Lord asking us to be the light of the world. So he is asking us to share in his light and ministry. Jesus asks us to be the salt of the earth and the light of the world. Notice how these qualities are to be for all; they are not restricted to the Jews or to members of the Church. The Gospel is all-inclusive.

Salt was a very precious commodity in the time of Jesus. Sometimes it was used to pay Roman soldiers – the word 'salary' comes from the salt used as wages. The Romans said that salt was the purest of all things because it was made from two pure things: the sun and the sea. The very purity of salt prevents corruption – it stops food going bad. The Christian is asked to be an example: to work to prevent evil and to stop society from going bad. As this can sound negative, we must remember that salt gives taste and zest to food, it brings out the flavour and stops things being insipid. We are called to reveal the joy of living, to show that life has flavour and to stop so much insipid living. A high calling, but it is ours in Christ.

'You are the light of the world.' In the ancient world to keep a light burning somewhere was of utmost importance. If your light went out, you had to go and borrow a light from someone else. All lights receive their light from somewhere. We receive our light from Jesus Christ. The light we give out is a reflected light, a light we have received from Jesus.

Light is to be seen not hidden. We cannot keep our faith a secret but must share it with others and so bring them to the One who is the Light of all. We are called to show the light in the way we live. We are witnesses to the true Light that is come into the world. There is so much darkness and so many dark places that can overcome us without the light of Christ. We are called to bring that light to the world.

Light is often there as a guide, to warn of danger, to lead people to where they ought to be. Those who have received Christ are asked to guide and lead others to him and to the Father of light. Jesus calls us, saying, 'Let your light shine before others, so that they may see your good works and give glory to your Father in heaven' (Matthew 5:16).

Illustration

A man bought a special gift for his wife. It was a musical box that played a tune when you opened it, but it was different because it also glowed in the dark. It was meant to be seen when the days were dark or dull. As it was a present, he kept the box hidden away and all wrapped up. At last he produced it one dark evening and his wife unwrapped it with great excitement. They turned the lights off, but then it could not be seen. It did not glow in the dark, and they were disappointed. Perhaps it was broken. They put the lights back on and discovered a label inside the box that said, 'If you want me to shine all night, keep me in the sun all day.'

There was nothing wrong with the box, and once they left it in the sunlight, it glowed in the dark.

In the same way if we are to be lights in the world, we must spend time each day absorbing the light of Christ.

Proper 2

Sunday between 10 and 16 February inclusive
(if earlier than the Second Sunday before Lent)

Aim

To discover how Jesus wants us to show respect and reverence for each other as a reflection of our reverence for God.

Readings

Deuteronomy 30:15-20
or Ecclesiasticus 15:15-20
Psalm 119:1-8
1 Corinthians 3:1-9
Matthew 5:21-37

Thought for the day

Matthew continues to show Jesus as a Moses figure, so today we hear of Jesus and the Ten Commandments. Jesus does not seek to abolish the Commandments but rather to look at their deeper meaning. Jesus is not challenging the Law but rather extending it to show its implications. Jesus moves from the rules about behaviour to the root cause of that behaviour. This reminds us that our God sees into the heart and mind. Our God is the God 'to whom all hearts are open, all desires known and from whom no secrets are hidden'.

These words from the mountain deserve much attention and thought as they teach us about reverence for each other, for God and for ourselves. In the Jewish synagogue the scrolls of the Law were carried around the congregation at the beginning of each service so that all might show reverence for the Law. Jesus extends that reverence for all people, always. If our relationships with each other are broken or wrong, then it is very unlikely that we have a good relationship with God. There is no cheap grace. We need to look at our lives and our attitudes.

Verses 21 and 22 are concerned not only with murder but also with thinking about murder or harming someone. Evil thoughts towards anyone are forbidden. This involves not only the killing of the body but also what is now called 'character assassination'.

The anger mentioned here is that which is deep-rooted and often nurtured. We are not to treat people as if they were fools or morons. Respect for all is required.

Verses 23 and 24 state that we cannot offer gifts to God if we have bad relationships with others. It is interesting to note how often we use the same attitude towards God as we do to others. If we are not willing to listen to others, it is not likely we will listen to God. The longer we pursue a certain stance against others the deeper the division becomes (25, 26).

Once again Jesus looks at where the trouble begins. Adultery begins with the eyes and the heart. We are easily led astray by our thoughts and our deeds – and we can blame no one but ourselves. To turn away from God's ways is the road to hell (27-30). Broken relationships and loose relationships can show that we have little respect for each other. Those who have little respect for those around them are not likely to respect God (31, 32). The issues of divorce are too complex to be dealt with in a few sentences.

We have to have a reverence for the truth. There should be no need for oaths if our word can be trusted and, if it cannot, an oath is often the belittling of God or ourselves by our words. There is a danger of double standards in our dealings if we even suggest it takes an oath to makes us truthful (33-37).

Illustration

How we think affects all of our lives. It is not what we do but why we do it that has great effect. There is a lovely scene in *Peter Pan* by J. M. Barrie: the children have seen Peter fly and they wish to fly too. They try to fly from the floor and from the bed but fail. 'How do you do it?' John asks Peter. Peter answers, 'You just think wonderful thoughts and they lift you up in the air.'

Too often we do not give enough direction to what goes on in our thoughts.

Proper 3

Sunday between 17 and 23 February inclusive
(if earlier than the Second Sunday before Lent)

Aim

To show how our lives should reflect the love of God because we are made in his image.

Readings

Leviticus 19:1, 2, 9-18
Psalm 119:33-40
1 Corinthians 3:10, 11, 16-23
Matthew 5:38-48

Thought for the day

Once again we hear of words from the Sermon on the Mount. Again Jesus is concerned with our relationships with each other and again Jesus wants us to learn to love as God loves us.

Life under Roman rule was one of violence and the fear of violence. The Jews limited vengeance; Jesus abolished it! Today's teaching is to help people not to react badly and also to learn how to keep cool in heated situations. All of what Jesus suggests today has sometimes been called 'the uncomfortable words'.

The law of 'an eye for an eye, and a tooth for a tooth' (see Exodus 21:23-25) was meant to limit vengeance and to restrain violence. But sadly this often meant that violence was breeding violence, as it often does. We nearly always want to hit back as hard as we can. Jesus is talking about non-retaliation and about having a generous spirit. At the same time, he is saying we should choose our way of doing things and not be forced into wrong actions by the enemy. Do not let the opposition determine how you should act. Marcus Aurelius said, 'The only way to avenge yourself is not to become like the wrongdoer.' Sometime the easiest way of getting rid of an enemy is to make him/her a friend! A generous reaction can often have profound effect.

The advice of turning the other cheek, giving your cloak as well, going a second mile, giving without hope of return, forgiving enemies and praying for those who hate you, may sound impossible but Jesus fulfilled them all in the events leading up to his crucifixion. It is by doing these things that we are seen as the image of God and in this way reflect his love. This is what we are called to do, and in doing this we are counted as 'perfect'.

In no way does this mean we allow ourselves to be a doormat and easily trodden on. It does not mean we allow evil to triumph or have free reign: Jesus never did this. It does mean we do not lower our standards and become like our enemies. Love in this case does not mean the sort of love we have for our nearest and dearest; rather it means we will not allow bitterness and violence to take over our lives. We will not descend to the rule of tit for tat. This is a matter of our will rather than our heart. It is taking a firm stand against evil without joining its methods.

Illustration

One of the Great Masters was painting the Last Supper. The painting was coming along well until he had a violent row with a friend. He went home full of anger and painted on to the canvas his friend as Judas. This would serve to remind him of the row between them; it would keep his anger warm. Now there was little of the painting to finish, only the central character which was the Christ. But the vision would not come. Hand and eye did not work as they should and the canvas was left unfinished. The hatred of the Judas figure was destroying peace of mind and preventing creative work. The anger in the mind left no room for vision. After weeks the canvas was untouched. He met his former friend and now felt ashamed of what he had done. He expressed sorrow to his friend and they were reunited. The artist went home and changed Judas and then painted his friend in the Christ place. The friendship had been restored and so the canvas completed.

Second Sunday before Lent

Aim

To encourage a deeper trust in God.

Readings

Genesis 1:1–2:3
Psalm 136 or Psalm 136:1-9, 23-26
Romans 8:18-25
Matthew 6:25-34

Thought for the day

Do not worry. By saying this Jesus did not mean us to be thoughtless or careless about our future or our world. Jesus was not suggesting a reckless approach to life. But he wants us to live in a trusting and loving relationship with God. Jesus wants us to avoid the anxiety, the angst, that is life sapping, and to enjoy life. Jesus gives us seven reasons not to worry.

Matthew 6:25 – God gives us life and our lives are more than eating and drinking and dressing up. Often we set our sights too low. We are also spiritual beings.

6:26 – Birds do not pile up stores for unknown futures. We are more than the things we amass. We are not measured by what we have but who we are. We are children of God and God loves us.

6:27 – Know that worry does not extend your life – in reality it can reduce it! Be rid of worry; exchange it for trust.

6:28-30 – The lilies of the field are the poppies and the scarlet anemones. Their time is brief but their beauty is worth noticing. Though they are here today and gone tomorrow, God cares for them. Realise how much more he cares for you. Spend time to learn of God's love towards his creation.

6:31, 32 – To centre our lives on things that perish only makes us feel perishable. Jesus calls the worry about food, drink and clothing the worries of the Gentiles – that is, of non-believers. Those who know God know that he will not let them perish John 3:16). Worry about things is often due to a lack of a living relationship with God. This is reflected in a consumer society.

6:33 – Seek God's will for yourself and the world you live in and know that God loves you and is with you. It is only when we are in harmony with God that we can be in true harmony with the world around us.

6:34 – Learn to live one day at a time, to live in the present moment. So much worry is projected fears that never happen. Do not forever plan for tomorrow but live today – this day has enough troubles to occupy us.

If we can learn to live this way, our lives will be greatly enriched.

Illustration

Imagine two people going for a walk together. Both have a difficult task to perform later in the day: a task that will take all their energy and ability.

One man cannot get it out of his mind. He turns it over and over. He does not notice the sunshine or the birds singing. He fails to notice the beauty that is all around him. He may as well be indoors and working.

The other man relaxes for a while in the sunshine. He enjoys the heat of the sun and the sound of the birds. He is aware of the good things around him. He watches a butterfly with delight. This man is being refreshed and restored, ready for the work ahead.

One carried his worries and they wore him down. The other took time off and was refreshed for the job ahead. It is too easy to let worry and anxiety prevent us from enjoying the present moment and steal any energy we have.

Sunday before Lent

Aim

To show that God reveals his glory in his Son Jesus Christ.

Readings

Exodus 24:12-18
Psalm 2 or Psalm 99
2 Peter 1:16-21
Matthew 17:1-9

Thought for the day

The recognition of Jesus as the Christ at Caesarea Philippi and then his telling the disciples of how he must go to Jerusalem to face suffering and death is followed by the Transfiguration. It is as if, before all that happened in Jerusalem, the disciples were given this glimpse of Jesus in his glory to give them hope in the future. Matthew continues to tell the story in a way that compares Jesus to Moses. The Transfiguration happened 'six days later'. In Exodus 24:15-18 we hear of the cloud being on Mount Sinai for six days. The Lord came on Sinai in a cloud (Exodus 34:5). The face of Moses shone after he had been with God (Exodus 34:29). All of these have parallels in the experience of the disciples on the mountain. Matthew draws this out: after telling us that Jesus was transfigured and his face shone, he three times says, 'Behold'. This is seen best in the King James Bible, Matthew 17:3-5:

> '. . . behold there appeared unto them Moses and Elijah' (17:3).
> '. . . behold, a bright cloud overshadowed them' (17:5).
> '. . . behold a voice out of the cloud which said, "This is my beloved Son, in whom I am well pleased"' (17:5).

St Matthew wants us to see not only that the face of Jesus shone like that of Moses but also that Jesus fulfils the law given to Moses and the prophecies as exemplified by Elijah.

The bright cloud is a symbol of the hidden presence of God. Even in the darkest days God is present. The cloud is a bright one to remind us of the presence. This can be compared to the pillar of cloud in the desert (Exodus 13:21, 22); the cloud that descended on the Tent of Meeting (Exodus 40:43); when the Lord came down on Sinai in a cloud (Exodus 24:15-17, 34:5). Psalm 99:7 says of God, 'he spoke to them from a pillar of cloud'. The cloud is seen as a representation of the shekinah, the hidden glory of God which is ever-present.

The voice out of the cloud is the assurance of the presence, and the voice affirms again what was said at the baptism of Jesus: that this is the Son and Beloved of God (see Matthew 3:17). As at the beginning of his ministry, so, as it comes near to a close, Jesus is affirmed by the Father. Jesus is the true icon, the true image of God. St John will write, 'The Word became flesh and dwelt among us, and we have seen his glory, the glory of a father's only son, full of grace and truth' (John 1:14).

Peter would later write, 'We have been eyewitnesses of his majesty. For he received honour and glory from God the Father when that voice was conveyed to him by the Majestic Glory saying, "This is my Son, my Beloved, with whom I am well pleased." We ourselves heard this voice come from heaven, while we were with him on the holy mountain' (2 Peter 1:16-18).

Before this revelation the disciples bowed down in fear. Jesus came and touched them and said, 'Get up and do not be afraid.' Again I prefer the King James Version which says, 'Arise, and do not be afraid', for already there are hints here of the power of the Son of God and his resurrection.

Jesus ordered them, 'Tell no one about the vision until after the Son of Man has been raised from the dead.' Again emphasising not only he is the Christ but the future resurrection.

Illustration

As dark clouds cover the sun, so it is easy to let the dark events of life hide from us the glory and the presence of our God. It is then we need know that, even when we lose our grip, we are in the hand of God and in the heart of his Son who says to us, 'Arise, do not be afraid.'

You might like to affirm the words written by a Jewish prisoner on a wall in Cologne:

> I believe in the sun even when it is not shining.
> I believe in love even when I cannot feel it.
> I believe in God even when he is silent.

First Sunday of Lent

Aim

To show that temptation is the norm if we are truly alive.

Readings

Genesis 2:15-17; 3:1-7
Psalm 32
Romans 5:12-19
Matthew 4:1-11

Thought for the day

Immediately after his baptism Jesus goes into the wilderness. Whenever Jesus had a challenge to face, he spent time alone with the Father. We all need times of stillness and quiet to discover who we are and what we aim to do.

There is a tension in Matthew 4:1 because Jesus is led by the Spirit to be tempted by the devil. The same tension is in all our lives because every moment we can choose to serve God or to turn our back on him. For Jesus the wilderness is where he takes time to sort out his priorities. We need ask ourselves, 'What are our priorities?'

Temptation is nice! If it wasn't, we would not be tempted. 'To tempt' in English usually means 'to lead astray': here in Matthew, 'to tempt' means 'to test' and does not have any connotation of good or evil. We all need times when we test our aims and our priorities or we will just drift from one thing to another. Temptation is not to do with fantasising about what we can do but rather facing up to our own potential and ability and seeing that we use them aright. We are tested, tempted, through our thoughts and our feelings, and there is nothing wrong with this. Temptation shows we are alive! But choice matters. How we use our God-given powers and freedom matters.

The temptations of Jesus are a four-pronged attack. Each temptation is meant to lead Jesus astray. The first temptation is usually not noticed, even though in Matthew it appears twice in this passage (4:3, 6) and again at the crucifixion (27:40). It is contained in the tiny word 'if'. Too often we fail because we are filled with self-doubt and doubt in God – often because we have not spent time getting to know ourselves or God!

The temptation to turn stones into bread is twofold: Look after yourself, bribe people to follow you. If you give people things, you will have a following. Jesus has come to serve and he knows that people need more than food and things: they need to know their Creator. He responds with a quotation from Deuteronomy 8:3.

In the next temptation the devil also uses Scriptures, quoting Psalm 91:11, 12. To quote or know Scriptures is not enough in itself. We need to seek to live by them. Again the temptation is twofold: give people certain assurances and force God to act. Make God do your will by being reckless and foolish and expect him to save you. Now Jesus quotes from Deuteronomy 6:16.

Often thoughts and feeling are liars! The devil offers Jesus the world – it is not his to give (see Psalm 2:8). Turn from worshipping God and worship anything else – be it football or your car – it does not matter. The devil wanted Jesus to compromise and to give in to evil, if only a little. For the moment Jesus chases the devil off with another quotation from Deuteronomy. But he knows the devil will return.

Illustration

One of the Desert Fathers prayed that all his passions should be taken away so that he would not be tempted. He then went to one of the Elders and said, 'You see before you a man who is not tempted and is at rest.' The Elder replied, 'Go and pray that some struggle is stirred up in you for the soul only matures through its battles against evil.' The monk did as he was asked and when temptation came he didn't ask to escape it but instead prayed, 'Lord, give me strength to get through the fight.'

Temptation is part of being alive to what is around us. We will be tempted as long as we live.

Second Sunday of Lent

Aim

To see Jesus as our light and life.

Readings

Genesis 12:1-4a
Psalm 121
Romans 4:1-5, 13-17
John 3:1-17

Thought for the day

Normally we see Jesus working in the daytime and with crowds of ordinary people around him; today's Gospel is about a rich aristocrat who came to Jesus by night for a one-to-one meeting.

Nicodemus was leader of the Jews – that is, he was a member of the Jewish Sanhedrin of which there were only 70 members. The Sanhedrin was the supreme court of the Jews and had religious jurisdiction over all the Jews in the world. One of the things the Sanhedrin did was examine anyone charged with being a false prophet. It is amazing that such a man risked coming to see Jesus. He came at night, perhaps out of caution. Maybe he did not want to be seen with Jesus. Possibly it was because the rabbis taught that the best time to study was at night when one was not disturbed. Perhaps he wanted to see Jesus on his own. Night might also be a symbol of his own darkness, of all the unanswered questions about his life and his relationship with God. He was a believer and a law-abiding person but perhaps he felt that there was more. Religion and law-abiding are not enough. Nicodemus knew there was something else needed. Many churchgoers find themselves in this position: it is the position of needing to move from belief to faith, from religion to the living God.

Nicodemus is courteous and says how he is impressed by the miracles of Jesus. Jesus gently sweeps this aside and comes to the need of Nicodemus. Jesus talks of the need to be born from above. Nicodemus asks if this is possible for an old man. Perhaps we should ask if it is possible for a church that has grown old to be reborn. Jesus says there is need to be born of the Spirit. We are not just earthly beings but children of God and we need to know our Father and that we belong to him. Jesus understands well that Nicodemus knows these things with his head but he has to accept them in his heart and life. Only in this way will the darkness be dispersed with the light and love of God. (See John 3:19-21.) St John wants us to know we can experience this in Jesus from the outset. John says of Jesus, 'in him was life, and the life was the light of all people' (John 1:4).

It is to Nicodemus that Jesus said probably the most famous and well-known words in the Bible: 'For God so loved the world that he gave his only Son, so that everyone who believes in him may not perish but may have eternal life' (John 3:16).

We do not hear of Nicodemus again until after the crucifixion. Joseph of Arimathea, a secret disciple of Jesus, asks to be allowed to take away the body. Nicodemus is also there, bringing a mixture of myrrh and aloes weighing about 100 pounds for the burial of Jesus – two members of the Sanhedrin showing their love and respect for Jesus. The gift is a costly one and one that shows Nicodemus in the daylight.

Illustration

There are many very clever and capable people (they are often also well-off) who feel they are missing out on something of the fullness of life. Listen to the words of Federico Fellini, the Italian film producer: 'Like so many people I have no religion and I just go sitting in a small boat drifting with the tide. I just go on working, cutting, shooting, editing and looking at life and trying to make others see. Today we stand naked and defenceless, more alone than at any time in history. We are waiting for something – perhaps another miracle, perhaps the Martians, who knows?'

Fellini, like Nicodemus, is in the dark, seeking someone or something that will deliver him from the darkness, from nothingness and death. A deliverer, a Saviour, is needed.

Third Sunday of Lent

Aim

To show how Jesus fills our emptiness and our longing for God.

Readings

Exodus 17:1-7
Psalm 95
Romans 5:1-11
John 4:5-42

Thought for the day

Jesus is facing hostility from the Pharisees in Judea. So he decides to leave for Galilee: it is too early in his ministry for confrontation. To reach Galilee he travels through Samaria. In the heat of the noonday sun Jesus rests by Jacob's Well. The disciples have gone to Sychar, about half a mile away, to buy food. Jesus is thirsty but the well is 100 feet deep and he has nothing to draw water with.

Suddenly from the direction of Sychar a woman appears. What is she doing out in the midday sun? This is siesta time. She is either very disorganised or disorientated. It could be that she did not want to meet anyone. A Samaritan, a woman, and someone possibly marginalised. Jews are supposed to have no dealings with Samaritans. Rabbis are not meant to speak to women outside at all. Rabbis had also declared it was not worth teaching a woman. It is also possible that the woman was a sinner and an outcast. Whereas Nicodemus chose to come to Jesus by night, this woman comes in the heat of the day and meets him by chance.

The woman was surprised that a Jew was willing to speak to her, a woman and a Samaritan. Jesus asks for some water and the woman lowers her bucket into the well and gives Jesus a drink.

Jesus asks what brings her out in the middle of the day. 'Thirst' is her reply. Jesus saw beyond what she said and saw she had a thirst she could not quench. Perhaps Jesus learnt from her of the five husbands she had and the man she was now living with. Was her thirst for love? Was it a thirst for acceptance? Was it a need to fill the emptiness within? Maybe nothing would satisfy her for long. She would again feel emptiness, a thirst that needed quenching. Here she was, by chance, at the Well of Life.

Jesus meets her at her own level and says, 'Those who drink of the water that I give them will never be thirsty.' The woman decided to humour Jesus and asked that he gave her such water and then she need not come to the well.

Jesus asks about her husband. From what he says, the woman decides he is a prophet and could solve her problems. Jesus tells her to worship God in spirit and in truth. In response to this, the woman says, 'We must wait for the Messiah to come.' Jesus has now led her to where he wanted and says, 'I am he.'

Because the disciples return, the woman leaves Jesus but then tells the people of Sychar about him. She becomes an apostle! Many Samaritans come and believe because of her testimony.

Today there are many who thirst for life and feel empty inside. So many declare that they are bored. The evangelist Billy Graham likened such people to beautiful cars, with good engines wanting to go – but rusting away with boredom because they have nothing in their tank. They have a thirst for the eternal and cannot be satisfied with less.

Illustration

Bill had tried everything to fill the gnawing emptiness that he felt inside. Whenever there was a time of quiet, the feeling of emptiness and worthlessness came upon him. He sought to escape into never having silence. Music, videos, computer games filled up his emptiness – but he knew it was still there. He tried to escape in thrills, in excitement, in sex and drugs. But underneath, the gnawing feeling was there. He felt alone and empty. One day, listening to the radio, Bill heard a poem by Francis Thompson called 'The Hound of Heaven'. The whole poem seemed to be about him. Certain lines, he said, struck home, especially these:

> 'All things betray thee, who betrayest me.'
>
> 'Naught shelters thee, who will not shelter me.'

And later:

> 'Lo! Naught contents thee, who content'st not me.'

He realised his emptiness was because he had been on the run from God. In tears this big strong man committed himself to God in prayer. He started going to church and became a much more fulfilled and contented person. He came to love the Psalms and in particular Psalms 42 and 43.

Fourth Sunday of Lent Mothering Sunday

Aim

To give thanks for all who care for us, especially our mothers.

Readings

Exodus 2:1-10 or 1 Samuel 1:20-28
Psalm 34:11-20 or Psalm 127:1-4
2 Corinthians 1:3-7 or Colossians 3:12-17
Luke 2:33-35 or John 19:25b-27

Thought for the day

It is very costly to be a mother. Mothers provide free food and shelter for their children. Mothers see their children get what they need and also protect them in times of danger. Mothers spend hours of each day looking after the house, shopping and cooking – it is good when these jobs can be shared. It is very easy to take the love and sacrifice of our mother for granted. It is the love and security she provides that gives us strength for daily life.

Today is the middle of Lent; sometimes it is called Refreshment Sunday. It is a break in the routine of Lent when we stop to give thanks for our homes and loved ones, especially our mother. This is a day when we can show that we appreciate what our mother does for us and when we can say thank you. Let us turn to our mother and say, 'Thank you', or if she is not with us, say, 'Thank you' to God for her.

Today's readings are all about mothers. The mother of Moses hid him from the wicked Pharaoh who would have killed him. To do this meant that Moses' mother risked her life. Even after three months, when she put him in a basket at the riverside, she made sure Moses was safe. She could have been killed just for loving her son.

Hannah did not think she would ever have a child but at last she gave birth to Samuel. When she later gave him to be with the priest Eli, she brought a little robe each year for her boy (1 Samuel 2:19). I am sure she sewed much love into it.

In the Gospel when Simeon met Mary he told her that Jesus would be opposed and how a sword would pierce her heart also. Mothers suffer when they see their child suffering. When one member of a family suffers all feel the pain. Think how Mary suffered when she saw Jesus on the cross.

Let this be a day when we give thanks to God for the love of our homes. It would be best if we showed how much we appreciate what our mother has done for us not only today but every day. It is a good time for families to say grace together at meals and to give thanks for the love of the ones who care for them.

Illustration

In J. K. Rowling's story of *Harry Potter and the Philosopher's Stone,* Quirrell, who is working for the wicked Voldemort, tries to kill Harry but is unable to do so even when he uses all the evil powers available to him. Harry asks Professor Dumbledore why Quirrell couldn't touch him and Dumbledore replies that Harry's mother died to save him, and if there was one thing Voldemort couldn't understand it was love. Love as powerful as hers for Harry left its own mark. Not a visible sign . . . but to have been loved so deeply, even though the person who loved us is gone, will give us some protection for ever.

Fifth Sunday of Lent

Aim

To show Jesus as the resurrection and the life.

Readings

Ezekiel 37:1-14
Psalm 130
Romans 8:6-11
John 11:1-45

Thought for the day

In Lent we meet three events from St John's Gospel. Nicodemus was in the dark and he came to Jesus, the Light of the World. The woman at the well thirsted for life; she met Jesus by chance and found the Living Water. Lazarus was known to Jesus and loved by him but could no longer come to Jesus because he was dead. Jesus came to him and he comes as the resurrection and the life.

In St John's Gospel there are seven miracle stories. The first is Jesus meeting our lack of supplies in the changing of the water into wine. The seventh is when all our human resources are gone and Jesus comes as the resurrection and the life.

Today's miracle is in Bethany, only two miles from Jerusalem. Lazarus is ill. Jesus is beside the river Jordan, teaching and caring for people. A messenger arrives from Mary and Martha and says simply, 'Lord, he whom you love is ill.' There is no request to come because they knew he would come. Jesus continued his work by the Jordan for two days. (Jesus could not be in two places at once as he had the same limitations as any human. It is only after the Ascension that Jesus could be present at all places, at all times.)

Jesus decides to go and says to his disciples, 'Let us go to Judea again.' The disciples are worried about the dangers and Jesus tells them not to worry. Jesus tells them Lazarus is asleep (a euphemism for dead). The disciples misunderstand and say, 'Good, sleep will help him to recover.' Jesus tells them Lazarus is dead and says, 'Let us go to him.' Thomas expresses their fears and the danger when he says to the disciples, 'Let us also go, that we may die with him.'

When they arrive at the outskirts of Bethany, Lazarus has already been in the tomb for four days. Martha hears that Jesus is coming and goes to meet him. Martha says to Jesus, 'Lord, if you had been here my brother would not have died.' Jesus tells Martha that Lazarus will rise again. Martha says she believes in the resurrection on the last day. Jesus wants her to believe not in a future theory but in the reality of the resurrection in him, to believe in him. Faith is to be in the living Lord. Jesus says to her, 'I am the resurrection and the life. Those who believe in me, even though they die, will live, and everyone who lives and believes in me will never die. Do you believe this?' (John 11:25, 26). This is a question we all have to answer. It is a question about our relationship with Jesus and whether we believe in him.

Martha now goes to tell Mary. Jesus waits, possibly hoping they would have a time of quiet together. But the mourners, thinking Mary is going to the tomb, follow her. Mary kneels at the feet of Jesus and says the same as Martha: 'Lord, if you had been here my brother would not have died.' Everyone is weeping and wailing and this disturbs Jesus. Deeply moved, he asks to see where Lazarus is. 'Jesus wept.' (This used to be the shortest sentence in the Bible; it's a pity it is made longer in newer translations.) Again this shows the humanity of Jesus.

Coming to the tomb, Jesus asks that the stone sealing the entrance be moved. Martha questions the wisdom as her brother's body is in a state of decay. Jesus asks about belief. So they move the stone. Jesus now speaks to the Father and then cries, 'Lazarus, come out.' In that moment Lazarus came out in his grave cloths. Jesus says, 'Unbind him and let him go.' It is suggested that this not only means 'loose him' but 'let him go home'. Can we see these as words that Jesus speaks over the grave of each one of us?

John continues to tell us that some believed. Others reported to the opposition, the Pharisees, and they begin to plot to kill him. Caiaphas would say, 'It is better for one man to die for the people.' The crucifixion moves a step closer.

Illustration

An American army chaplain tells how the raising of Lazarus affected one marine. There was a Bible study group on board a troopship returning from Japan. After studying this passage, a marine said, 'Everything is pointing at me.' The marine described how he had led a wild life and got into bad trouble.

No one knew, except God. He felt guilty. He said his life was ruined and he could not face his family. He felt he was a dead man. 'But after reading this chapter, I have come alive again. I know that this resurrection Jesus was talking about is in the here and now, for he has raised me from death to life.' No doubt this man's troubles were not over, but in meeting Jesus he experienced the resurrection and the life.

COMPLETE COMMON WORSHIP

Sermon Illustrations

Palm Sunday

Aim
To join in welcoming Jesus as our Saviour and King.

Readings
Liturgy of the Palms
Matthew 21:1-11
Psalm 118:1, 2, 19-29

Liturgy of the Passion
Isaiah 50:4-9a
Psalm 31:9-16
Philippians 2:5-11
Matthew 26:14–27:66 or Matthew 27:11-54

Let the dramatic readings of the Passion narratives replace the sermon today. Allow the Scriptures to speak for themselves. Use as many people as possible to share in the readings. I have provided ideas for the Liturgy of the Palms rather than comment on the Passion. I hope Holy Week will be used to do that.

Thought for the day
It is near the Passover and the last events in the life of Jesus begin in great drama. Everywhere is crowded. It is estimated that over 2 million people could make their way to Jerusalem to celebrate the Passover. Already there is a plot to take Jesus and put him to death. Jesus must be careful because it is dangerous for him to enter Jerusalem. Let us look at the courage, the claim and the call of Jesus.

We see the courage of Jesus. He was aware of the hostility and the danger. He knew he was likely to be put to death. But he did not go into hiding. He made a public declaration by his entry into Jerusalem. Jesus challenged the authorities – and does to this day. In many ways the riding into Jerusalem was an act of defiance. Yet he was not foolish. When he sent for the donkey and colt, a password is used: 'The Lord needs them.' Matthew alone talks of two creatures, a donkey and colt. He wanted to show how Jesus literally fulfilled what the prophet said: 'Tell the daughter of Zion.

Look, your king is coming to you, humble and mounted on a donkey, a colt, the foal of a donkey' (see Zechariah 9:9). Even in this passage, the double mention of donkey and colt does not imply two creatures but one. It must be remembered that the donkey was considered a noble beast and was sometimes the choice of a king when he rode into a city in peace. To witness to this, the people welcomed him like a king by spreading their cloaks on the road and branches from the trees. Jehu, when he was proclaimed king, was welcomed in this manner by his friends (2 Kings 9:13) and so was Simon Maccabaeus when he entered Jerusalem after a notable victory (see 1 Maccabees 13:51).

So in his entry into Jerusalem we see the claim of Jesus. This is the entrance of a king and of the Messiah. Jesus is the Christ, the One who comes in the name (in the power and presence) of God. It is likely that he is proclaiming to be the cleanser of the Temple as Judas Maccabaeus had done 200 years before. Then people waved branches in the same way and this is the next act of Jesus (see 2 Maccabees 10:7 and Matthew 21:12-14). The cry of the people 'Hosanna' means 'save us now' and is a cry for help. It is a call for deliverance to their Saviour and their King.

The call of Jesus is not one for earthly kingship; it is for the hearts of people. Will we accept him as the Christ, our Lord and Saviour? Will we let him rule in our hearts? His rule is one of peace and love, and yet many still turn away. Will you acknowledge-ledge his claim and hear his call to you?

Illustration

In a time when in some areas even the wearing of a cross is forbidden, and when the media are often pro-other faiths and anti-Christian, one Anglican bishop made a telling comment. He was asked why the Christians did not threaten with bombings and reprisals as some did. The bishop replied simply, 'We are not allowed to react like that: we follow the Prince of Peace.'

Easter Day

Aim

To enter into the wonder and joy of Easter.

Readings

Acts 10:34-43 or Jeremiah 31:1-6
Psalm 118:1, 2, 14-24
Colossians 3:1-4 or Acts 10:34-43
John 20:1-18 or Matthew 28:1-10

Thought for the day

In these few verses from Matthew is an earth-changing event. Nothing can be the same once you know the risen Lord.

He begins by telling us two Marys go to the tomb, no doubt to pay their respects to the dead. One was Mary Magdalene and the other was Mary the mother of James (see Mark 16:1). We are told that these two women were present at the death (Matthew 27:56) and burial of Jesus (27:61). Their faithfulness brings them to the empty tomb.

Matthew tells of the earth shaking and the appearance of an angel. The guards shake with fear. But the two Marys are told, 'Do not be afraid; I know that you are looking for Jesus who was crucified. He is not here; for he has been raised.' They are not to look for the living among the dead. Jesus is alive. 'Come, see the place where he lay.' They are asked to believe and to go and tell the disciples, 'He has been raised from the dead.'

Now they leave the tomb with awe and wonder and great joy. They run to tell the good news. On their way Jesus meets them and says, 'Greetings.' The word Jesus used for 'greetings' is 'chairete', which means 'rejoice'. How can you do other than this if you have met the risen Lord! Knowing the risen Lord fills our lives with hope and joy.

The women worship him and hold on to him. Jesus then tells them, 'Do not be afraid; go and tell my brothers to go to Galilee: there they will see me.'

Jesus is not just a figure in history; he is the living Lord. He is not just a memory but is alive and seeks a relationship with us. Christians are not those who know about Christ but those who know him, meet with him and talk with him.

The sequence of this Gospel is: come and see, believe and tell. Note how they meet Jesus and worship him before they tell the Good News. Outreach and mission can only arise out of our own personal encounter with Christ. Know that the Lord is risen. The Lord is with you. Alleluia.

Illustration

1066 is a date we all know: the Battle of Hastings. Did you know the Normans nearly lost the battle?

The English were behind a stockade. The Normans twice tried to break through. The second time they were repelled, it was rumoured that their leader was dead. The troops immediately began to lose heart. Soon they would be in headlong flight. William pulled off his helmet and rode among his troops shouting, 'I am alive. I am still alive.' The result was immediate: new courage, new strength of heart and purpose. This time they burst through the stockade and victory was won.

How like the state of the disciples after Good Friday. They had seen Jesus die; they had lost heart. And then, on that Easter morning, Jesus said to Mary, 'Tell them I am still alive.' What a difference his appearing would make to them and to the world.

Second Sunday of Easter

Aim

To continue to rejoice in the presence of the risen Lord who comes to us.

Readings

Acts 2:14a, 22-32
Psalm 16
1 Peter 1:3-9
John 20:19-31

Thought for the day

Last week's Gospel ended with the two Marys going to tell the disciples they had seen the Lord. They had a message of joy and hope. Today's Gospel starts on the evening of the same day. Ten disciples are locked in for fear of the Jews, frightened to go out or to let anyone in. Closed doors do not hinder Jesus. He comes and gives them the typical Jewish greeting: 'Shalom' – 'peace and well-being be yours'. As it is a common greeting, Jesus is almost saying, 'Hello, I'm back!' Jesus shows them his hands and his side that still have the wounds of the crucifixion. The disciples are full of joy in his presence.

As God sent Jesus, now Jesus sends out his disciples. To enable them to go boldly, Jesus again offers them his peace. Then he breathes on them and says, 'Receive the Holy Spirit.' Just as God breathed life into Adam and Eve, Jesus breathes life into his new creation. Just as the Spirit gave life to the dry bones in the valley, and God gave hope to the people of Israel (Ezekiel 37), so Jesus gives new life and courage to his disciples.

Thomas was not there. When he returns he hears what has happened and sees the excitement of the disciples but refuses to accept their word only. Thomas wants to see Jesus – seeing is believing!

It is worth noting:

1. Thomas stayed with those who had the experience; he remained with the disciples. He listened to what they had to say. He prayed with them, ate with them and no doubt

questioned them. It is through the believing community that most people encounter the risen Lord.

2 . Thomas was not afraid to express his doubt – for that is how he really feels. But he did not depart from the disciples because he was truly seeking. The surest way to belief is to mix with real believers. It may be doubt but it was not rejection. Thomas kept an open mind.

There lives more faith in honest doubt,
believe me, than in half the creeds.
In Memoriam, Tennyson (1850)

Jesus comes again and once more says, 'Peace be with you.' How often do we let the peace of the risen Lord enter our lives and hearts? We believe it, but do we give it the opportunity to ha pen?

Thomas is now invited to reach out and put his finger in the nail holes and his hand into the wounded side. Thomas needs no more proof and says to Jesus, 'My Lord and my God.' Here, almost at the end of St John's Gospel, is the declaration that Jesus is God. Jesus is not just a good man; Jesus is a man but Jesus is also God.

There are many who have not seen Jesus – but they are blessed by their belief in him. This belief is a relationship with the unseen yet ever-present Christ.

Illustration

As a result of an explosion a small group of miners were trapped underground in a confined area. The phone to the surface still worked and they indicated they were all alive but they feared there was not enough air. It was realised that they would die without help – instant help. There was not much hope of getting them out alive. There were tons of earth to be removed and it was calculated it would be too late by the time it was done. With a special drill the rescue team bored a hole to where the men were and then pumped air into the cavern. Though it took another three days to get to them out, the men were found to be well and in good spirits. When one of them was asked what it was like he replied. 'A bit like the resurrection. We were sealed in a tomb unable to get out. Then we were given new air, the breath of life from the air pumped in to us. And then we were rescued and raised into the light.'

Third Sunday of Easter

Aim

To show that we meet Jesus the risen Lord in various ways.

Readings

Acts 2:14a, 36-41
Psalm 116:1-3, 10-17
1 Peter 1:17-23
Luke 24:13-35

Thought for the day

This is yet another appearance of the risen Lord on Easter day.

Cleopas and his companion – perhaps his wife – were making for Emmaus, seven miles west of Jerusalem. They were walking towards the setting sun at the close of day. They were a sad couple, having seen the death of a loved one, Jesus. In his dying they had lost hope; they were very much in the dark. (Compare the people of Israel in the valley of dry bones in Ezekiel 37:1-10.) As they were talking to each other, Jesus came near and went with them along the road. Jesus asked them to tell him what they were talking about.

They said how they were talking about the crucifixion and death of Jesus. They also told how they were astounded by the women who had reported that Jesus was alive. They told of the empty tomb. All of this was not enough to raise their hopes; they needed more than other people's stories and empty tombs.

Jesus walked with them and talked with them. He shared the Scriptures with them and helped them to understand about the suffering of the Messiah. Jesus the risen Lord can make sense of our experiences of life.

Jesus did not force himself upon them. He walked ahead as if going on. He turned back because they invited him: 'Stay with us, because it is almost evening.' Jesus is often passing by but will only stay if invited. God has given us a most wonderful and dangerous freedom called free will. The choice is ours. We can choose to ignore him, reject him, squeeze him out of our life, or we can invite him in, ask him to abide, share with him, put our faith in him and put our hopes on him. Jesus passes by not only in church but in every encounter, in 'mouth of friend and stranger'.

Now Jesus is revealed to them in the breaking of the bread. In our Holy Communion, Jesus is revealed; and in our communion with each other. Jesus is in church but he is also at home in our homes. At an ordinary meal, in an ordinary home, Jesus is there.

The two realised how their hearts 'burned' in his presence. Darkness had been replaced with light, sadness with joy and despair with hope. They were no longer on the sunset road but facing the dawn of a new life. They turned to Jerusalem in the direction of the rising sun, wanting to share the Good News. This is the way the Good News grows – in sharing it. It grows in us and in the world. In sharing we discover, like them, that people have had similar experiences and others know the risen Lord, not as a figure in a book but as the living Lord.

Illustration

The Church in the Outer Hebrides rejoiced in the living Lord who could be met on the road and in the guise of a stranger. The following is an old poem from the Hebrides and now used by the Iona Community:

> I saw a stranger at yestere'en.
> I put food in the eating place,
> drink in the drinking place,
> music in the listening place,
> and in the sacred name of the Triune
> he blessed myself and my house,
> my cattle and my dear ones,
> and the lark said in her song,
> 'Often, often, often,
> goes the Christ in the stranger's guise;
> often, often, often,
> goes the Christ in the stranger's guise.'

Fourth Sunday of Easter

Aim

To know we have life and eternal life through Jesus Christ our Lord.

Readings

Acts 2:42-47
Psalm 23
1 Peter 2:19-25
John 10:1-10

Thought for the day

The uplands of Judea were more suited to rearing sheep and goats than to growing crops. The shepherd was a familiar figure and was seen as a strong rugged character. Life for the shepherd was not easy. He had to make sure his sheep did not get lost and this kept him alert and watchful. He cared for his sheep and had to give account to the owner for them. Out in the country there was always danger from wild animals; wolves and hyenas prowled at night. There was the added danger from thieves and robbers who were always ready to rob a flock.

To protect the sheep, they were often penned in a sheepfold. This was usually a stonewall structure with briars on the top of the wall. The entrance was a single opening. There was no gate on the entrance but the shepherd acted as gatekeeper and stayed across the entrance to protect the sheep. In a sense no one could enter except going through the shepherd. Anyone trying a different way was obviously not to be trusted. So when Jesus describes himself as the 'gate' and the 'shepherd', this is one and the same person.

Often flocks were mixed together so that the shepherds could have strength in fellowship. When the sheep then had to be sep rated, the shepherd would call his and they would follow him. There were often one or two leaders of the flock that encouraged the others to follow. The shepherd knew his sheep and they knew him. They actually had a relationship with each other. Note how the shepherd in Judea does not drive his sheep; he leads and they follow.

Jesus came to a world of darkness and despair. People 'erred and strayed like lost sheep'. There were those who had got the selves trapped and could not free themselves. Others were in danger of being robbed of their well-being, their joy and even their life. Jesus came that we might have life and have it abundantly; that we may have eternal life – that even death could not rob us of our being. He would descend to all the troubles we experience. He would be betrayed, deserted, rejected, crucified and buried for our salvation. He would give his life for us.

He knows us and wants us to get to know him. He will not force himself upon us but calls each of us by name. He is the gate to life and to eternal life. Salvation is through Jesus. We come to the fullness of life through Jesus. We enter into eternal life through Jesus Christ our Lord.

Illustration

There is an old Jewish legend about why God chose Moses to be a leader of his people. When Moses was in the wilderness and caring for the sheep of his father-in-law, Jethro, a young lamb strayed away and got lost. Moses searched for it until he came to a deep dark ravine where it had gone down to find water. When Moses got to it he said, 'I did not know you ran away because you were thirsty. Now you must be very tired.' He took the lamb and put it on his shoulders and carried it back to safety. God said to Moses, 'Because you have cared for and brought back one of a flock belonging to man, you shall lead my flock Israel.'

Fifth Sunday of Easter

Aim

To show Jesus is with us on the journey of life and prepares the way for us.

Readings

Acts 7:55-60
Psalm 31:1-5, 15, 16
1 Peter 2:2-10
John 14:1-14

Thought for the day

There are dark days ahead. The disciples are in the Upper Room. Judas has gone out to betray Jesus. Jesus has told Peter how he will deny him. A world of darkness, fear, sadness and chaos is soon to come upon them. They will lose hope and lock themselves in. Jesus did not promise them an easy time. Now he calls on them to trust in God the Father and in himself, to hang on by putting their faith in him and their hand in his.

'In my Father's house are many dwelling places.' This can mean resting places on our journey where we will find refreshment and comfort. Such places help us to progress and develop. God's world is not static, nor is the kingdom of heaven.

'Many dwelling places' can simply mean there is room for all. The world may close its doors, society may lock us out, but God has room for us. 'If it were not so, I would have told you.'

Jesus says, 'I go to prepare a place for you.' He goes on ahead for us to follow. He goes before us to make the way easier. He is like a trailblazer who goes on ahead to make sure it is safe for us to go down that road. Jesus is like a pilot boat that goes before to guide a vessel into the safe harbour: he leads us into the fullness of God's kingdom. He goes to prepare a place for us. That is like us saying we have a reserved seat with our name upon it: there is a place in heaven that is specifically for us.

Jesus will come to us and take us to himself so that we are one with him and his kingdom. This is not a put-off but for us a present reality. It is expressed well in this affirmation:

I am in the heart of Jesus.
Jesus is in my heart.
Jesus is in heaven.
Heaven and where I am, are one.

This idea of a Way into the kingdom is confusing to Thomas (and to many of us!). Thomas seeks clearer directions. Jesus tells Thomas he is the Way to God. He could have given complex directions on how to find God – like getting directions in a strange area. Someone says, 'Turn right, then left, then second right, last exit at the second roundabout and across the third.' By now you feel well and truly lost. Then someone else says, 'I am going that way. I will show you and go with you.' Jesus says, 'I am with you always', and he says, 'I am the way'. He is our companion on the journey and through him we come to life eternal.

Illustration

Often when we are feeling lost it is because we have wandered from him who is the Way. More than any book of directions, we need to know God is with us on our journey.

And I said to the man
who stood at the gate of the year:
Give me a light
that I may tread safely into the unknown.
And he replied:
Go out into the darkness
and put your hand in the Hand of God.
That shall be to you better than a light
and safer than a known way.

(From *Desert* by Minnie Louise Haskins, 1908, and quoted by King George VI in his Christmas broadcast, 25 December 1939.)

Sixth Sunday of Easter

Aim

To show that the love of God asks for our response in actions.

Readings

Acts 17:22-31
Psalm 66:7-18
1 Peter 3:13-22
John 14:15-21

Thought for the day

St John's Gospel is about the love of God as revealed in Jesus Christ (John 3:16). God has created us out of his love, by his love and for his love. God wants us to love him as he loves us. But he will not force himself upon us. We have the freedom to ignore God and go against him if we so choose. The Christian way of life is one of love rather than law. We seek to do what is right not because of a set of rules but out of love. If we do not love, we are not likely to walk in the ways of God. Devotion comes before obedience. This is what Jesus is telling the disciples when he says, 'If you love me, you will keep my commandments.'

St Augustine of Hippo understood this when he said, 'Love God and do what you will.' He knew that in our love for God we would do nothing to offend him or cause him sorrow. We cannot say we love a person if we cause them constant heartache, grief or anxiety. If we are inconsiderate or unkind towards someone, then we do not truly love them. If we use someone for our own ends and are with them for what we can get out of them, that is not love. We should never take the love of our loved ones for granted. Love demands sensitivity, a willingness to give and even a willingness to serve. This service or obedience is what is described as the 'perfect freedom' because it is what we do out of love. This type of loving service is seen in the sacrifices and work that loving parents do for their children and for each other.

Love is God's gift of himself to us and our response is to love him in return, and in this way our love grows. 'They who have my commandments and keep them are those who love me; and those who love me will be loved by my Father, and I will love them and reveal myself to them' (John 14:21).

Faith is not a set of beliefs or keeping a book of rules; it is a living loving relationship with Father, Son and Holy Spirit. In today's Gospel we hear mention of the Father, Son and Holy Spirit and how the Spirit of God abides in us. We are not alone in the world, for the Spirit is with us and Christ comes to us. We must learn to be aware of and to rejoice in their presence and their love.

Illustration

How often do we fail to realise the cost of love in our homes? How our parents spend much of their lives giving themselves and what they have to us? Many of the household chores that are done for us are done not out of compulsion but out of love. But we should never take this for granted and the only way to respond to such love is to love in return. This, of course, would mean taking our share in the household tasks! Love is expressed in action. We do not do it because we have to – or because it is a rule of the house; we do it out of love for each other. True devotion is taking on some of the routine of caring for our home. Our failure in this work shows a lack of sensitivity and personal response to love.

Ascension Day

Aim

To affirm that the presence of the ascended Lord is always with us.

Readings

Acts 1:1-11* or Daniel 7:9-14
Psalm 47 or Psalm 93
Ephesians 1:15-23 or Acts 1:1-11
Luke 24:44-53

* *The reading from Acts must be one of the readings for the day*

Thought for the day

From Easter Day onwards the disciples not only rejoiced in the presence of the risen Lord but actually saw him in various places. The women saw Jesus in the garden. The travellers on the road to Emmaus found that he walked with them and was made known to them in the breaking of the bread. Jesus appeared in the room to ten disciples and a week later was seen again when Thomas had joined them. Jesus shared a meal with them by the Sea of Galilee. He walked and talked with Peter and John. Finally he is with them on the mountain of the ascension. The disciples were learning that he was with them wherever they were and whatever they were doing.

The ascension brings us to a change. Jesus enters into the cloud and is gone from their sight. But we know that this is no ordinary cloud. This is the cloud that represents the hidden glory and the hidden presence of God, who is unseen yet ever near. In returning to the Father, Jesus leaves our sight but not our presence. St Matthew's Gospel captures this in the last words of Jesus, and the last words of his Gospel: 'Jesus says, "And remember I am with you always, to the end of the age"' (Matthew 28:20b).

The longer ending to St Mark's Gospel tells of the abiding presence in this way: 'So then the Lord Jesus, after he had spoken to them, was taken up into heaven and sat down at the right hand of God. And they went out and proclaimed the good news everywhere, while the Lord worked with them, and confirmed the message by the signs that accompanied it' (Mark 16:19, 20).

The disciples were in no doubt they were not left alone but, as he had promised, Jesus was with them and worked with them and through them. The great message of the ascension is this: 'The Lord is here; his Spirit is with us.'

Illustration

If the disciples were asked after the ascension, 'Where is Jesus now?' their reply would be very like the one that Longinus made to the wife of Pilate in John Masefield's *The Trial of Jesus*. Procula asks, 'Do you think he is dead?' To which Longinus replies, 'No, lady, I don't.' When asked, 'Then where is he?' Longinus replies, 'Let loose in all the world, lady.'

In the ascension we come to know that the Jesus who was limited by time and space is now able to be with all peoples at all times and in all places.

Seventh Sunday of Easter

Aim

To show that eternal life comes from abiding in God and knowing he abides in us.

Readings

Acts 1:6-14
Psalm 68:1-10, 32-35
1 Peter 4:12-14; 5:6-11
John 17:1-11

Thought for the day

Like Moses (see Deuteronomy 31–33), Jesus prays at the end of his earthly life. This prayer is a 'last will and testament' that shows certain key ideas. Jesus prays in the typical Jewish fashion, eyes open and looking towards heaven.

In the first part of his prayer Jesus asks that his 'hour' will glorify the Father. In St John's Gospel the 'hour' is not one event but is made up of the life, death, resurrection and the appearances of Jesus. 'Glory' and glorification echo the Old Testament idea of glory as revealing God's power. To see God is to experience his power and his will (see Exodus 16:10; 24:7). When God's glory is revealed through people, it is because they do his will and manifest his power. Jesus reveals the hidden glory of God.

More than this, Jesus has the power to give eternal life. Through Jesus we have life eternal. The way to eternal life is to know God and to know Jesus Christ. Let us be aware that eternal life does not mean a quantity so much as a quality. Eternal life is a certain quality of life. It is life lived in awareness of the presence and power of God and of his Son Jesus Christ. This would make St John say, 'Whoever has the Son has life; whoever does not have the Son of God does not have life' (1 John 5:12). The Old Testament understood well about the relationship of knowing God and life: 'by knowledge the righteous are delivered (Proverbs 11:9). Wisdom is 'a tree of life to those who lay hold of her' (Proverbs 3:18). Hosea hears God saying, 'My people are destroyed for lack of knowledge' (Hosea 4:6). Amos is aware of this when God says, 'Seek me and live' (Amos 5:4). Habakkuk dreamed of a time when 'the earth will be filled with the knowledge of the glory of the Lord, as the waters cover the sea' (Habakkuk 2:14).

Though it is very necessary to know with our minds, this knowledge of God demands of us an intimacy of the deepest sort of relationship with him. It is to know him in a way that we become one with him (see Genesis 4:1). The fullness of life depends on maintaining a relationship with the Father and the Son. If we break with that relationship, we are in danger of no longer having eternal life. God does not break that relationship with us, and if we turn to him, he will welcome us home. Our joy is to know we can abide in him and he abides in us – and in this is eternal life.

Illustration

In his diary for 1922 Shackleton writes of his Antarctic expedition:

> When I look back on those days, with all their anxiety and peril, I cannot doubt that our party was divinely guided both over snowfield and across storm-swept sea . . . I know that during that long racking march of thirty-six hours over unnamed mountains and glaciers of Southern Georgia it seemed to me we were not three but four. I said nothing to my companions on the point but afterwards Worsley said to me, 'Boss, I had a curious feeling in the march that there was another person with us.'

Do we affirm in our lives that our Lord is with us and travels with us wherever we go?

Pentecost

Aim

To proclaim and enjoy the fact that 'his Spirit is with us'.

Readings

Acts 2:1-21* or Numbers 11:24-30
Psalm 104:25-35, 37
1 Corinthians 12:3b-13 or Acts 2:1-21*
John 20:19-23 or John 7:37-39

* *The reading from Acts must be used as the first or second Reading*

Thought for the day

Pentecost is 50 days after the Passover. As the Passover is usually in April, Pentecost comes in June. Because the weather is better then, it is possible there are more pilgrims from other countries at Pentecost than there are in April. The disciples are also in Jerusalem. Their number is now made up to twelve again as they have appointed Matthias in place of Judas Iscariot. The disciples are doing what Jesus asked them: they were waiting in Jerusalem for the power of the Holy Spirit (Acts 1:4-8).

The disciples were all together in one place when suddenly from heaven there came a sound like the rush of a violent wind. Tongues of fire seemed to rest upon each of them and they were all filled with the Holy Spirit.

We will never know quite what happened at Pentecost but the results are seen in the change that came over the disciples. At one moment they were hesitant, frightened, unable to speak out, and they probably felt drained and powerless; then, they were ready to go out, bold and courageous, ready to proclaim the Good News, full of the Holy Spirit and his power.

In the first thirteen chapters of Acts there are more than 40 references to the Holy Spirit, empowering, moving and guiding people. The Acts of the Apostles has been rightly called the Gospel of the Holy Spirit. The longing that Moses expressed in Numbers 11:24-30 is fulfilled, for the Lord has poured his Spirit on his people.

The symbolism used is to help us realise the presence of the Spirit in the lives of the disciples, although their own actions are the true testimony.

The wind is the hidden presence of God, not seen but felt. It is the same word that is used for 'breath' and for 'spirit'. Whatever happened at Pentecost, new life was breathed into the disciples. Fire is a symbol of the presence, as in the burning bush. It is a sign of a strong power at work and a sign of enlightenment. At Pentecost the disciples were given new vision and power.

That same Spirit is offered to us, is with us, but can only work if we respond to his coming. Let us celebrate that the Lord is here and his Spirit is with us.

Illustration

For a long time the flute seemed to lie around the house. It was not played and it gathered dust. Occasionally, someone would get it out and struggle to play a tune. It was decided that is was not a good instrument, perhaps useless and should be got rid of. This was mentioned to a friend of the family when he came to dinner. He asked that he might be able to handle it and play it. Mother had to dust it down before she gave it to him. Somehow it looked special as soon as it was in his hands. Once he started to play, the family were amazed at the beautiful sounds and music. This was a wonderful instrument and responded beautifully in the master's hands. It was just waiting for the touch of the master.

In many ways the disciples were like this until they were filled with the Spirit.

Trinity Sunday

Aim

To encourage everyone to be Trinitarian in their faith and their prayers.

Readings

Isaiah 40:12-17, 27-31
Psalm 8
2 Corinthians 13:11-13
Matthew 28:16-20

Thought for the day

The word Trinity does not appear in the Bible. Even so, the experience of God as Father Creator, as Son Redeemer, as Spirit Guide and Strengthener can be known and shared. At the baptism of Jesus there is the voice of the Father and the descent of the Spirit. The Trinity is there to be experienced.

When Jesus tells of his return to the Father, he promises the coming of the Spirit of God. Once again this is mention of Father, Son and Holy Spirit.

At the very end of Matthew's Gospel, the risen Jesus comes to the eleven disciples. There is his presence to be experienced. He tells of his power, his authority.

He gives the disciples a purpose, a commission. They are to 'Go and make disciples of all nations, baptising them in the name of the Father, and of the Son and of the Holy Spirit.' Here again we have the Trinity.

We must remember this is not a formula to be used at a service but a way of life. The reality of God as a Trinity – Three Persons in One God – is there for us to experience and to share with others. We are asked to immerse people in the Trinity, in the power, in the presence and in the peace of Father, Son and Holy Spirit. We are to know for ourselves and to encourage others to be aware that our lives are lived in this Triune presence.

At the end of his second letter to the Corinthians, St Paul has those words we often use: 'The grace of the Lord Jesus Christ, the love of God, and the communion of the Holy Spirit be with all of you' (2 Corinthians 13:13). We are not to see this as a request but as a reality, a reality that we need be aware of and live. If these words are used at the end of a service or a meeting, they are to remind us that we are in the presence of the Trinity and we go out and live in that presence. Remember today and each day that you are immersed in the Holy Three.

Illustration

In the Hebrides, the islands off the west coast of Scotland, it was often difficult for a priest to get to some of the communities to baptise a new-born child. It became the tradition for the midwife to do a form of baptism that was known as the 'birth baptism'; later the child would be baptised in church and this was known as the 'great baptism' or the 'church baptism'. One such midwife said, 'When the image of the God of life is born into the world I put three little drops of water on the child's forehead. I put the first little drop in the name of the Father, and the watching-women say, "Amen." I put the second little drop in the name of the Son, and the watching-women say, "Amen." I put the third little drop in the name of the Spirit, and the watching-women say, "Amen." . . . All the people in the house are raising their voices, with the watching-women giving witness that the child has been committed to the blessed Trinity.'

Here is part of such a baptism prayer:

In the name of God,
in the name of Jesus,
in the name of the Spirit,
the perfect Three of power.

The little drop of the Father
on thy little forehead, beloved one.

The little drop of the Son
on thy little forehead, beloved one.

The little drop of the Spirit
on thy little forehead, beloved one.

To aid thee, to guard thee,
to shield thee, to surround thee.

Proper 4

Sunday between 29 May and 4 June inclusive (if after Trinity Sunday)

Aim

To encourage the building of a relationship with our God.

Readings

Genesis 6:9-22; 7:24, 8:14-19
or Deuteronomy 11:18-21, 26-28
Psalm 46 or Psalm 31:1-5, 19-24
Romans 1:16, 17, 3:22b-28 (29-31)
Matthew 7:21-29

Thought for the day

Today's Gospel is the end of the Sermon on the Mount. The words that precede today's Gospel are 'you will know them by their fruits' (Matthew 7:20). Words are not enough; our relationship with God is shown in the way we live. No amount of religious acts or fine words can replace the doing of God's will. If we want to be part of the kingdom, we have to live by the rule of its king. We need notice every time we pray the Lord's Prayer that we say, 'Your kingdom come: your will be done.' God's kingdom will only come in us if we do his will.

Some of the toughest words in the Gospels are 'I never knew you'. Jesus is saying we need a relationship with him. This is the foundation of the kingdom and this is the way to eternal life – a relationship with Jesus. This is not just saying prayers and saying his name; it is having a living vital relationship with him. Jesus compares the person who does his will to a wise builder who builds on the rock. Throughout the Old Testament the 'rock' is a symbol for God's protecting presence, God's sheltering. The wise person builds their life not only on the knowledge of God but on a relationship with him. This is far-sighted and means that whatever happens the person will survive in God.

The foolish person lives for quick results and for ease. Such a person does not have far-sighted vision but lives short-term. There is no building of a deep relationship with God. Life is measured by wealth, possessions, popularity, personal achievements, health and strength. All these are good things but not safe or lasting foundations. The danger for such a person is one day to hear the words, 'I never knew you.'

We all need to think about our future, our long-term future. This is in no way life-restricting but in fact life-enhancing. None of us want to live in a rickety, falling-apart structure when we can have a house of firm foundations.

Illustration

In the last century the cathedral at Winchester had restoration troubles. Great cracks were appearing in the structure. Experts suggested building buttresses to hold the cathedral up; others suggested great metal tie-bars to be placed across the cathedral to stop its walls falling outwards. One man insisted that they were only dealing with the symptoms of the trouble and the real cause was much deeper: he wanted to look at the foundations. He sunk a shaft into the ground and looked. He discovered the cathedral was built on a peat bog. The builders had laid tree trunks over the watery land and the cathedral was built on these. Due to improved drainage in the city the peat had dried out and shrunk. In many places there was a space between the cathedral and the ground below it. A man was employed for five and a half years to work underground in the removing of peat and putting in its place concrete blocks. Even a cathedral is only as firm as its foundations.

Proper 5

Sunday between 5 and 11 June inclusive (if after Trinity Sunday)

Aim

To look at the power and love of Jesus

Readings

Genesis 12:1-9 or Hosea 5:15–6:6
Psalm 33:1-12 or Psalm 50:7-15
Romans 4:13-25
Matthew 9:9-13, 18-26

Thought for the day

In today's Gospel we see various facets of the power of Jesus at work. Jesus is able to call people from all walks of life, if they will respond. Matthew is so unlikely and he is working in an unlikely place. Matthew belonged to a priestly family but had preferred to make money and work for the enemy who occupied the country. Matthew was a collaborator. Because of his work as a tax collector, Matthew was hated by many and banned from the synagogue. Yet no matter how Matthew filled his pockets with money, he still felt an inner need. Matthew was not at ease or at peace with himself. Jesus had the power to see this and to call Matthew from his work to follow him. Jesus saw the potential of the man who could keep the accounts, and in time Matthew would give us a fine account of the life of Jesus. Matthew was changed through the power of Jesus.

The leader of the synagogue was desperate. He had tried every way he could to bring healing to his daughter but no one had been able to help. The little girl should have been entering into the fullness of life but her life was ebbing away. The leader came to Jesus as a last resort but he at least acknowledged that Jesus could do something. He believed that Jesus could restore life. Jesus saw the faith of the man. We shall see that Jesus has the power over life itself. While Jesus was going to the house the little girl died. But Jesus had the power and took her by the hand. With her hand in his she arose.

While he had been going to the leader of the synagogue's house, a woman interrupted his journey. This woman thought she could steal a cure from Jesus by touching one of the tassels on his cloak. She should not have been there because of her illness. Because she was suffering from haemorrhages she was counted as unclean – and anyone she touched would be counted as unclean. She was rather superstitious thinking she could steal a cure. But she recognised that Jesus did have power. Jesus had the power to restore her life to its fullness. Because of her faith in him Jesus healed her and so revealed his power.

If we truly believe in Jesus, we will respond to his call. We will allow him to enrich our lives and transform us by his power.

Illustration

Jim had all the money he needed. It seemed whatever he did turned to gold. He had a great home and a lot of friends. He was able to spend a good deal of time enjoying himself. But Jim had an emptiness that nothing could fill. The more he tried to fill it with action, things or parties, the more it gnawed at him. He told a friend and the friend introduced him to a poem called 'The Hound of Heaven' by Francis Thompson. The line that worried the rich man was 'All things betray thee, who betrayest Me'. The friend had the sense to tell him that he need not worry, for the hunger that he felt was none other than the calling of God in his life. 'Listen to God, respond to God and you will soon feel different.' Jim did as advised, he did not change his way of life or his friends, but he turned to God each day, started to worship each Sunday at his local church. He did not change but God changed him and he was now a far richer man than he had ever been.

Proper 6

Sunday between 12 and 18 June inclusive (if after Trinity Sunday)

Aim

To show that those whom Jesus calls he also sends out.

Readings

Genesis 18:1-15 (21:1-7) or Exodus 19:2-8a
Psalm 116:1, 10-17 or Psalm 100
Romans 5:1-8
Matthew 9:35–10:8 (9-23)

Thought for the day

Today's Gospel shows Jesus going about doing his daily work: he is teaching, proclaiming the good news and healing the sick. Jesus is aware of how harassed and helpless so many people are – you can see it in their faces and in their actions. Look at people in any street and you can see the same distress and stress on their faces. Jesus feels for them; he had compassion for them. He sees that they are like sheep without a shepherd, wandering with no one to guide them or protect them. He wants to help all of them. Jesus is aware of the great harvest to be won and says to the disciples, 'The harvest is plentiful but the labourers are few; therefore ask the Lord of the harvest to send out labourers into the harvest.' Such a prayer should come with a health warning, for the reply from God is, 'Whom shall I send?' and the answer should be, 'Here am I, send me.'

Jesus calls his twelve disciples to him, to learn of him, to be with him, to love him, but also to send them out. Jesus gives of his power to his disciples but for them to give to others. Here in Matthew 10:2 we see the other title of the chosen: they are 'Apostles', those who are sent by him. Jesus sends them to be heralds and healers, to proclaim the good news and to care for the distressed. Jesus needs his disciples to continue his work. Jesus warns them of the dangers: the task will not be easy an there will be opposition. But they will have the power of the Spirit so they are not to worry.

In Matthew's Gospel the last words of Jesus are still saying, 'Go': Jesus sends all whom he calls. Let it be said, though, he does not send out before he calls people to him. We cannot speak in his name if we do not know and love him. Coming to him and then going out in his power into all the world is what makes us the true Church of God. It is then we are seen as

the one (united in him)
holy (belonging to God)
catholic (for all people, at all times and in all places)
and
apostolic (sent out by him in the power of the Spirit)
Church (called by him and answering his call).

Our God is a calling God, seeking a response from each of us: he is a sending God. In Jesus we hear the command, 'Go, therefore, and make disciples of all nations, baptising them in the name of the Father and of the Son and of the Holy Spirit.' With this sending is the promise, 'I am with you always' (Matthew 28:19, 20).

Illustration

Picture yourself coming to your own community and all the lights are out. The only light is coming from the church. You go to see where the light is coming from. It is coming from near the altar, so you approach the light. You see it is coming from a man sitting in a chair. You are about to ask him what he is doing and you see it is the Christ. You kneel before him. He does not move because he is a captive. He is tied to the chair, a prisoner. You ask him, 'Why are you tied, what has fixed you here?'

He replies, 'I am stuck here because my people will not reach out in love. My people do not proclaim the good news. My people do not help in the healing of the nations. They have fastened me in the building.'

'Lord, how can I set you free?'

'By going out in my name and working with me in all the world.'

You offer yourself to his service, saying, 'Here I am, send me.' At that moment the Christ is freed and the lights begin to come on again.

Proper 7

Sunday between 19 and 25 June inclusive (if after Trinity Sunday)

Aim

To show how God cares for us, and how this should drive away fear.

Readings

Genesis 21:8-21 or Jeremiah 20:7-13
Psalm 86:1-10, 16-17
or Psalm 69:8-11 (12-17), 18-20
Romans 6:1b-11
Matthew 10:24-39

Thought for the day

It is worth remembering that Matthew is a Jewish Christian. He sees Jesus as the fulfilment of the Jewish hopes and Scriptures, as a link with their history. It is likely that the Gospel was written after AD 70, after the destruction of Jerusalem and its Temple. Because of the rebellion of the Jews, the Roman general Titus reduced the city and the Temple to ashes and rubble. It was so completely destroyed that a plough was drawn across the city. This was a time of tribulation when people's faith was deeply challenged. It was a time when Christians were being persecuted for their faith and needed words of encouragement. By the time the Gospel was written Jesus had not only been scorned and rejected, crucified, dead and buried, but he had risen again. This is the context in which to read today's Gospel.

Jesus talks about the relationship between him and his disciples. A disciple cannot hope for an easier life than Jesus. If Jesus had been maligned and called 'Lord of the dung' (one understanding of Beelzebul), the disciples could not hope to escape. Jesus does not promise an easy life but he does offer life eternal.

Now we come to one of the great themes of the Bible. Jesus says, 'Have no fear, do not fear.' In a world of darkness and trouble it is easy to fear and to lose hope but we are not left alone because our Lord is with us. In this passage fear is mentioned four times.

Do not fear them (10:26, 27). Jesus tells us that nothing goes unnoticed, nothing is hidden or secret; God will triumph. Jesus tells us to speak out without fear. Jesus is there even in the dark.

Do not fear those who kill the body but cannot kill the soul (verse 28). No matter how much people seek to destroy us, Christ gives us the gift of life eternal. We are more than mere bodies. Our human bodies are forever dying but we as a person survive. For the Christian death is not fatal! We shall not perish but have everlasting life (see John 3:16).

But rather fear him who can destroy both body and soul in hell (28). The Jews well understood that 'the fear of God is the beginning of wisdom'. This is not terror but awe, not being afraid but having great respect for. Because it sounds like a threat, the following words are important (29-31): God values each of us, cares for all his creation, so 'Do not be afraid'. Learn that God loves you and cares for you. Then you may know that 'perfect love casts out fear'.

Illustration

Because Jesus says we need to fear God, he adds the balance of the fact that God values us and loves us. He talks of the sparrows. He says in Matthew's Gospel, 'Are not two sparrows sold for a penny? Yet not one of them falls to the ground without God noticing.' St Luke gives this in a slightly different form: 'Are not five sparrows sold for two pennies? Yet not one of them is forgotten in God's sight.' It would seem if the buyer was willing to buy four sparrows for two pence, a fifth was thrown in for free. It was as if the sparrow had no value at all! But God noticed and cared; God cares for all his creation.

When Jesus talks of one falling to the ground, it is easy to think of its death, and most people would not notice. But it may just mean land on the ground, to descend from flying. If God notices the small action of the sparrow, will he not all the more care for us?

Proper 8

Sunday between 26 June and 2 July inclusive

Aim

To show how through hospitality Christ can be proclaimed and accepted.

Readings

Genesis 22:1-14 or Jeremiah 28:5-9
Psalm 13 or Psalm 89:1-4, 15-18
Romans 6:12-23
Matthew 10:40-42

Thought for the day

Jesus is still talking about mission when he talks about the disciples being welcomed. Jesus has previously been talking about the hostility they will experience; now he talks of hospitality. If all had been hostile to the Gospel, the disciples would not have survived to tell the message and Christianity would not have grown. But many people were longing for the Good News and readily welcomed the disciples. We need to be on our guard and not express hostility towards people when we can extend hospitality and welcome.

Hospitality was a characteristic of the Middle East. Among the Jews it was typified by Abraham and Sarah who welcomed the three strangers and found they had welcomed angels: they had welcomed God (Genesis 18). The writer to the Hebrews say show we should be hospitable when he says, 'Do not forget to show hospitality to strangers, for in so doing some have entertained angels without knowing it' (Hebrews 13:2). The meeting of people also involves the 'shekinah', the hidden presence of God.

Hospitality was often a sign of a relatively secure community. From the Hebrides comes a lovely statement:

> I saw a stranger at yester'en.
> I put food in the eating place,
> drink in the drinking place,
> music in the listening place,
> and in the sacred name of the Triune

he blessed myself and my house,
my cattle and my dear ones,
and the lark said in her song,
'Often, often, often,
goes the Christ in a stranger's guise.'

The disciples are to go out in the name of God. They are to be his representatives, his image, his icon to the world. The Jews believed that to receive an envoy of the king was to receive the king. To welcome a messenger of a friend is the same as welcoming the friend. Not all doors are closed to Jesus; many long to hear the Good News. We are his disciples and if we do not take the message, how will people hear?

Illustration

The Selfish Giant banned the children from his garden. He built a wall around it and put up a notice saying:

TRESPASSERS
WILL BE
PROSECUTED

From that time spring did not come to the giant's garden; it remained in winter. By keeping himself to himself, there was no warmth in the place.

Only when the children sneaked back did spring return with them. It was then that the giant realised his hostility to the children had kept him in the cold.

(Read the full story of the Selfish Giant in *The Happy Prince* by Oscar Wilde, Puffin Books.)

Hostility brings about isolation. Hospitality opens us to the warmth of relationships.

Proper 9

Sunday between 3 and 9 July inclusive

Aim

To encourage people to respond to the welcoming call of Jesus.

Readings

Genesis 24:34-38, 42-49, 58-67 or Zechariah 9:9-12
Psalm 45:11-18 or Song of Songs 2:8-13
or Psalm 145:8-15
Romans 7:15-25a
Matthew 11:16-19, 25-30

Thought for the day

Jesus talks about how poor some people are at responding; in fact, they are often perverse in their unwillingness to react. There were obviously some days when he thought that he was in a poor reception area. Jesus said people were sometimes like petulant children who refused to cooperate, they were given music and invited to dance but they refused; so they were called to join the mourners and show sadness, and they refused this also. Because John the Baptist came fasting and out of the desert, they called him a mad man. When Jesus shared in their eating and drinking, they called him a glutton and a drunkard. People avoided being moved by either man. But those who excused themselves from the company of Jesus excluded themselves, and so it still is today. Jesus sends out an invitation: 'Come to me, all you that are weary and are carrying heavy burdens, and I will give you rest' (Matthew 11:28).

> Come to me, enjoy my presence, my company.
> Come to me and receive my power and peace.
> Come to me and know of my healing love.
> Come to me, on whom your life depends.
> Come, all who labour, in field or factory,
> in shop or office, in school or sweatshop.
> Come, all who labour in vain and for nothing.
> Come, all who are carrying heavy burdens,
> with personal problems, with fear, with doubt,

with debt, with guilt and sin.
Come to me and I will give you rest.
Come, let me revive you, refresh and restore you.
Come and learn to be resurrection people.

The invitation stands; it is for you, but will you accept it? Think seriously about these words from a hymn:

What a friend we have in Jesus,
all our sins and griefs to bear!
What a privilege to carry
everything to him in prayer!
O what peace we often forfeit,
O what needless pain we bear,
all because we do not carry
everything to God in prayer!

Illustration

From *The Pilgrim's Progress* by John Bunyan:

He ran . . . till he came to the place somewhat ascending and on that place stood a cross . . . Just as Christian came up . . . his burden loosed from his shoulders and fell from off his back . . . I saw it no more.

Then Christian glad and lightsome said with a merry heart, 'He has given me rest by his sorrow and life by his death' . . . it was very surprising to him that the cross should ease him of his burden . . . Then Christian gave three leaps for joy, and went on singing,

'Thus far did I come laden with my sin
nor could ought ease the grief that was within
till I came hither: what place is this,
must be here the beginning of my bliss,
must here the burden fall from off my back,
must here the strings which bound it crack.
Blest Cross! Blest Sepulchre! Blest rather be
the man who was put to shame for me.'

Proper 10

Sunday between 10 and 16 July inclusive

Aim

To encourage more receptivity in our hearing and receiving of the Word.

Readings

Genesis 25:19-34 or Isaiah 55:10-13
Psalm 119:105-112 or Psalm 65:(1-8) 9-13
Romans 8:1-11
Matthew 13:1-9, 18-23

Thought for the day

Matthew introduces us to a turning point in the ministry of Jesus. Up to this point Jesus has been teaching in the synagogues; now he is teaching on the seashore. The doors of the synagogues are beginning to close, even though the ordinary people want to hear him. Some minds and hearts are shutting Jesus out. At this stage Jesus begins to use parables, good earthly images that challenge us and ask us to go deeper into their meaning. Jesus wants us to ask, 'What does that mean for me? Is this a story about me?'

At the point where some are refusing to hear him, Jesus tells the parable of the Sower. He had already warned his disciples that life would not be easy. No doubt there was a danger they would feel it was all a waste of time. Yet Jesus told them that there was also a welcome awaiting them in many places. Maybe some labour is lost but the harvest is still bountiful. No farmer expects every seed to germinate – some are blown away, some eaten and some choked by weeds – but the majority grows and produces a harvest. It must be said, of course, if there is no sowing, there will be no harvest.

In our lives we need to look at what is needed for the Word of God to grow. We are not the seed of this parable but the soil. The seed is the Word of God and this will grow in us, given the opportunity.

The seed must be able to get in. If it is denied entry, it will not grow. Closed minds and closed doors, the unwillingness to listen and prejudice all prevent the entry of the Word. If we cannot listen and give our attention, then we will not hear. The footpath of the parable is caused by the regular passage of feet; it is hardened and unreceptive, and in the same way regular habits can prevent us from hearing properly.

The rocky ground is shallow ground. Shallowness is a greater danger of our age. We know about many things but of little in depth. We do not stay long enough with a thing to learn of it. Like butterflies we flit from one thing to another. To grow we need good roots.

Then there are the thorns that choke out the life of the growing seeds. The seed needs room to grow. Busyness, hyperactivity, crowded lives, cares, anxieties – yes, and having so many things – can fill our days and leave no room for the Word of God. We all know this but do we learn from it?

But if the Word is allowed entry and given some depth, it will grow. If we give space and room, it will produce fruit. We will be greatly enriched and be part of the great harvest of God.

Illustration

In India 150 years ago, in the area of Dornakal, there was a man called Venkaya who could neither read nor write. He heard from a friend about a new religion that was of a God that loved everyone. One day as he watched the Hindu pilgrims bathing in the river he was asked by one of their leaders why he was not bathing. He said he no longer believed enough in the Hindu ways. The leader asked if he was a Christian and Venkaya said, 'No, but I would like to be.' The leader told of an English Christian preacher who could help him. Venkaya sought out Mr Darling who was a missionary with the Church Missionary Society. At that moment Mr Darling was deeply distressed: he had spoken of Christ for eight years and had not had one convert. Now, amid much opposition, Mr Darling taught and then baptised Venkaya and sixteen other outcasts. The seed was beginning to grow. In his old age and quite blind, Venkaya sat by the roadside to tell others the Gospel story. Through his preaching 500 converts were baptised. His work continues to bear fruit.

Proper 11

Sunday between 17 and 23 July inclusive

Aim

To show that, although good and evil are woven into our lives, we must at some stage weed out the harmful.

Readings

Genesis 28:10-19a or Wisdom of Solomon 12:13, 16-19
or Isaiah 44:6-8
Psalm 139:1-11, 22, 23 or Psalm 86:11-17
Romans 8:12-25
Matthew 13:24-30, 36-43

Thought for the day

This story of the field with good seed and weeds is only in St Matthew's Gospel. Here Jesus is talking about the problem of evil in the world and how it is difficult to get rid of it. If you have ever done any gardening, you will feel for the person who asks, 'Where, then, did these weeds come from?' A friend of mine gave me some useless advice: 'If you want to find out which are weeds, pull everything out and wait: the weeds are the ones that will come back.'

In the parable, Jesus suggests it is an enemy that has sown the weeds. The weeds are tares and the trouble is they look like wheat. This is because it is a degenerate sort of wheat: it is wheat that has gone wrong.

The Jews had a legend that said the tares, also known as 'bearded darnel', had their beginning in the time of wickedness before the flood. It was a time when all creation went astray and brought forth things contrary to their nature. This was a time when perverse and wicked things happened. This is when the tares came into existence. It is for this reason the Jews often called tares 'bastard wheat'.

In their early stages of growth wheat and tares look very alike. It is only when they mature, when they have headed out, that you can distinguish them. Tares must not be left with the wheat because they are poisonous. They produce a narcotic that cause dizziness and sickness. Yet if pulled out too early, you may pull out the wrong plants. There is a right time to do it and it often takes patience and then discernment.

There is certainly much about life in this little story. All of us are a mixture of good and evil. It is not the way God wants us to be. Wickedness in individuals and society needs to be rooted out. We all know that one bad apple can spoil them all. But we do need sensitivity in dealing with people – for all have some good in them. Think how the early Church nearly rejected Saul. Because of his record in persecuting Christians people were rightly cautious. But, as Paul, the convert had a wonderful record in spreading the Good News. Early judgements are often in danger of being rash. There is a danger we will get rid of the lively and the adventurous in early judgements. It all takes discernment. We must learn to discern and, when the time comes, to separate out, just as we do to the weeds in our gardens. Corrupt people corrupt, and perverse people cause perversity. It matters what we do and who we mix with, and, remember, if we are careless, evil triumphs.

Illustration

They were known as the terrible twins at school. They were disruptive in class and caused no end of bother in the playground. They were encouraging other children to be disruptive too. Staff meetings talked about them, offered ideas to help them, but all were determined to keep them in the class if possible. Teachers used their skill and discernment in dealing with them. It was only in the third year that it became obvious that it could not go on. By then it was also obvious it was not both of them but just one who was the real trouble. They were put in separate year groups. Now one settled down and worked hard. The other continued to be trouble at school and at home. The school finally had to remove the disruptive one from the normal class. They were reluctant to do so but it needed doing. Though they were twins with apparently equal opportunities, one caused trouble all his life; the other became a doctor and a healer.

Proper 12

Sunday between 24 and 30 July inclusive

Aim

To show how we need to sow, to search for and to sift out the kingdom.

Readings

Genesis 29:15-28 or 1 Kings 3:5-12
Psalm 105:1-11, 45b or Psalm 119:129-136
Romans 8:26-39
Matthew 13:31-33, 44-52

Thought for the day

In today's Gospel we are given five parables about the 'kingdom of heaven'. The first is the parable of the mustard seed, which is a symbol of smallness and yet grows into the greatest of shrubs. This tiny seed grows so much that the birds are able to nest in its branches. Not only is this a sign of growth from small beginnings but also of hospitality. Every kind of bird is a symbol of all the nations. Though the kingdom is hidden and starts from what appears to be small beginnings, its growth potential is there – though we do need to sow it.

It is the same way with yeast. It is amazing how a small amount of yeast can transform dull and heavy dough. The contrast between unleavened bread, which is hard like a water biscuit, and leavened bread, which it soft and light, is due to the transforming power of the yeast. Do we see the joy of sharing in the transforming power of the kingdom? Yeast in the ancient world was usually added from a former batch of bread. Do we see how in each generation we have to hand on the transforming power of God? Let us remember the yeast is a disturbing element in the dough; it will not let it lie low but makes it rise and be active. There are times when we are called to disturb a situation that has become too dull and settled.

The hidden quality of the kingdom is shown in the next two parables. The treasure hidden in a field was lying there waiting to be discovered. It has the possibility of enriching life beyond the wildest dreams of the finder. He is willing to sell all that he has for it. Do we realise that it is well worth trading the temporal for the eternal? There is little use in treasure if we have lost our soul in the gaining of it.

The treasure was stumbled upon but the pearl was sought after. How much time do we spend seeking to enrich our lives with things of God? Is not some of the great discontent of our age due to the loss of our awareness of God's love and abiding presence? Surely we should be happy to give up minor treasures and beauty for the greatest beauty and treasure of all. Are you aware that many of our deepest longings are related to the call of God?

Like fishermen, we are always hauling into our lives things both good and bad. Once ashore, the fishermen sort out their catch and the bad is thrown out. This takes discernment and practice. Sometimes in our daily living we seem to have no discernment at all; we take on board the good and the bad and carry them around with us. To be part of God's kingdom we have to begin to get rid of all that is destructive or against the life in the kingdom.

Jesus asked, 'Have you understood all this?' They answered, 'Yes' (Matthew 13:51).

How about you?

Illustration

Every so often we hear of someone finding a great treasure. These days metal detectors are often used to go over fields and ancient sites to turn up all sorts of wonderful things. Sometimes it is the work of archaeologists who patiently, carefully and slowly remove piles of debris before they get to the treasure they are looking for. In 1947 a Bedouin shepherd boy was looking for a sheep that had strayed. Spying a cave in the cliff face, he decided to come back with a friend and explore. In the cave they found large earthenware pots with scrolls inside wrapped in linen. They were treasure indeed, for they were the Dead Sea Scrolls and the place was Qumran. In time the scrolls were sold and the boy compensated. All the caves in the vicinity were searched and more scrolls were found. A sect of Jews around the time that Jesus lived had written the scrolls. Many insights into the world that Jesus lived in have come from the deciphering and reading of these scrolls – they are a treasure indeed.

Proper 13

Sunday between 31 July and 6 August inclusive

Aim

To show that the compassion of Jesus can reach out to others through our willingness to give and share.

Readings

Genesis 32:22-31 or Isaiah 55:1-5
Psalm 17:1-7, 16 or Psalm 145:8, 9, 15-22
Romans 9:1-5
Matthew 14:13-21

Thought for the day

Today's Gospel is set in times of trouble. John the Baptist has been beheaded. Jesus withdraws to the wilderness. The wilderness is often a symbol of chaos. Suddenly, in a life where all seems to be going well, chaos breaks in. But Jesus also chose the wilderness because it would give him space to think and commune with God.

We need to remember that when chaos seems to take over, God does not leave us. God was with the Israelites in the wilderness and provided them with manna, with refreshment and with his presence (Exodus 16:13-35). God fed Elijah, a widow and her son (1 Kings 17:8-16). God supplied Elijah with food and his presence when he felt he wanted to die (1 Kings 19:1-18). God fed a hundred people with only twenty barley loaves and a few fresh ears of grain (2 Kings 4:42-44). Matthew sees that the people are in wilderness times. The feeding of the five thousand wants us to recognise that God is able to transform the wilderness. As in the days of Moses, even so now God provides for his people.

By blessing the bread, Jesus reminds the people of the divine presence. The words Jesus used were most likely the same as every Jew used before meals, 'Blessed are you, Yahweh, our God, King of the Universe, who brings forth bread from the earth.' Let us remember every time we say grace we are acknowledging not only the goodness of God but his presence with us. When Matthew says that Jesus took the bread, blessed it, broke it and gave it, he wants us to think also of the Last Supper (Matthew 26:26).

By the feeding, Jesus shows his concern for the welfare of the people. Though Jesus had sought solitude, he is ready to help those who have come out to find him. His compassion is for those who have sought him out and are in danger of fainting through hunger. Hunger is not what God wants for his people. The faithful are called to relieve hunger out of their resources, even though those resources may be small. God wants to help us but first we need to make the moves we can out of what he has already given us. In giving they are to trust in God (cf. Matthew 25:34-40). Jesus challenges his disciples to give, and when they do, he gives to them and they then give to others. Jesus does his work through his disciples, through us. He waits for us who have received to help him to give to the hungry.

It is wonderful to hear that they gathered up what was left over. God gives to us richly but he does not want us to waste what he has given us. This has much to say to our modern world.

Illustration

This is the story of the 'long spoons'. Someone was given a vision of what life is like. She went into a room where there was a lot of food to be eaten but only by a long spoon. The spoon was so long that the people could not get it to their mouths and food was being spilled and wasted. Everyone looked frustrated and hungry. It looked like a picture of hell.

Then she went into another room where there were still long spoons and the same system. Here everyone was feeding someone else. They were reaching out and feeding a neighbour. Here there was much laughter and fellowship. It felt more like heaven than hell.

She thought long on this and realised that there is enough in the world for everyone's need but not for their greed.

Proper 14

Sunday between 7 and 13 August inclusive

Aim

To show that our God cares and is with us in the storms of life.

Readings

Genesis 37:1-4, 12-28 or 1 Kings 19:9-18
Psalm 105:1-6, 16-22, 45b or Psalm 85:8-13
Romans 10:5-15
Matthew 14:22-33

Thought for the day

Jesus has been with the five thousand plus, caring for them and feeding them. He has been pouring out himself in caring for them, and now he needs to have the quiet time to be alone with God. It is for this he came into the wilderness. He sends the crowds away, back to their homes. He sends the disciples off in their boat and he goes up a mountain to pray. We need to keep contact with God especially when our lives are at their busiest. We need time for rest and renewal or we face trouble.

Jesus was alone in the evening, meeting God in the stillness. In contrast to this, the disciples were now caught up in a storm; they were being battered by waves and the wind was against them. It is amazing how in a short distance we can find we have moved out of peace and into trouble. There are many storms that can so easily overtake us. In this frail craft that we call life there is always the danger of being overwhelmed.

In the hour of their need Jesus came to them. No doubt he had realised the wind had suddenly become fierce and the disciples could be in difficulty, so he came to them. There is no way we can easily explain this. Some believed Jesus walked along the shoreline and in the surf; others that Jesus walked on water. Whatever, you need be aware that in the storms of life Jesus is there and ready to help. What wonderful words to hear in the midst of a storm: 'Take heart, it is I; do not be afraid.'

There is that lovely picture of Peter acting on impulse as ever, seeking to come to Jesus over the waves and Jesus saying, 'Come.'

With eyes on Jesus, he steps out but soon he notices the wind and waves and begins to sink. Is not this the story of many of our lives? Peter calls out, 'Lord, save me.' Jesus is as ready as ever and reaches out and Peter is saved.

The image of a boat on a stormy sea is an ancient image of the Church in the world. It is the logo for the World Council of Churches. Today's Gospel is meant to reassure us in times of storm and trouble. Our faith may be small but it is in a great God and he always stands by ready to help.

Illustration

At lifeboat stations there is usually a record of rescues and of the wonderful bravery of those who went out in the storms to help others. Sometimes, instead of a record of rescue, it simply says, 'Standing by'. That is when the lifeboat was there and ready to help if needed. The crew were keeping a watch and were ready to come to the aid of a troubled vessel if called to do so. How often our God is like that – 'standing by', always ready to help those who call upon him.

Julian of Norwich lived through stormy times. It was the time of the Black Death, the Peasants' Revolt, the battles of Crécy, Poitiers and Agincourt. She saw four kings sit on the throne of England. As a young woman she had nearly died, but she could write:

> He did not say, 'You shall not be tempest-tossed; you shall not be work-weary; you shall not be distressed.' But he did say, 'You shall not be overcome.'

Julian was deeply aware that God is 'our maker, our lover and our keeper'. Amidst the storms of life, Julian was aware of the presence, the love and the power of God.

We need to learn to put our hand into the hand of God who never leaves us or forsakes us.

Proper 15

Sunday between 14 and 20 August inclusive

Aim

To show that God's love is not exclusive but is offered to all people, in all places and at all times.

Readings

Genesis 45:1-15 or Isaiah 56:1, 6-8
Psalm 133 or Psalm 67
Romans 11:1, 2a, 29-32
Matthew 15:(10-20) 21-28

Thought for the day

The exclusiveness of the Jews could not portray the inclusiveness of the love of God. The Jews would restrict God's love; Jesus would show its wideness. Jesus had been talking about how it is not foods that make a person unclean. Now we find him among the Gentiles and he is showing that contact with them does not defile anyone.

This is the only time we hear of Jesus outside Jewish territory. He is in the land of the Phoenicians who were great sailors and traders. The Phoenicians were the first to navigate by the stars. They traded with the whole of the Mediterranean and it is likely they made their way to Britain to get tin from Cornwall.

Jesus was here to avoid the hostility of the Scribes and Pharisees and of Herod. He was also avoiding the wrong kind of popularity that the crowds were bestowing upon him. This is an attempt the escape trouble for a while so that he can prepare himself and his disciples.

Here a Canaanite woman comes to Jesus for help. To converse in public with a woman who was also a Gentile was breaking the regulations of the Jews twice over. The woman comes out of love for her afflicted daughter. She has heard somehow that Jesus is a healer. She does not just ask, she shouts. She shouts, 'Have mercy on me, Lord, Son of David, my daughter is tormented.' She obviously has some faith in Jesus. It may be small, it may be poor, but it is in his ability and power. It does not matter how small our faith is if it is in a great God. Not only does she have faith, but she is persistent, she is not easily put off. (Compare the nagging widow and the judge, Luke 18:1-8.) She begins by following and shouting, and she ends on her knees, kneeling and praying.

From the beginning the disciples wanted Jesus to help her only in order to get rid of her. But Jesus wanted to open her awareness of him and his power. Jesus rebuffs her on her approach. He says it is not right to throw the children's bread to the dogs. The Jews called the Gentiles dogs as a disrespectful way of speaking of them. Probably our nearest is to call someone a bitch. But Jesus, though making a point of how he was sent to the Jews, speaks more kindly than it sounds. The word he uses is the diminutive word that means puppy or house dog. The woman, possibly still on her knees, answers that even the dogs are allowed the crumbs from their master's table. This witty reply seems to delight Jesus. Although he was for the Jews first, that was because he had to start somewhere. Jesus is for all people, in all times and at all places. Jesus rejoices in the faith of this Gentile woman. In her is a sign of the universality of the love of God as revealed in Jesus. Only at the end of the Gospel, when he has completed his mission to the Jews, does Jesus send the disciples out into all the world (Matthew 28:19, 20).

Illustration

We may hate what a person does but we need to learn not to hate the person. It is said that God hates sin but loves the sinner. The more exclusive we become in our dealings, the smaller our world and our heart. God's love is not exclusive.

There is a story of a young man who tried to join a famous London club. He had tried for months and was refused entry for one reason or another. The club was determined to be exclusive. The man's background, place of schooling, position in society did not suit. He was a good man but firmly kept out. In his prayers he asked why this was so. Then, in a vision one night, Jesus came and spoke to him and said, 'I would not worry, you have tried for months to get in; I have tried for years and they have kept me out!' See Matthew 25:45. Consider Edwin Markham's words:

> He drew a circle that shut me out –
> Rebel, heretic, thing to flout.
> But love and I had the wit to win –
> We drew a circle and brought him in.

Proper 16

Sunday between 21 and 27 August inclusive

Aim

To show that Jesus is the Christ, our Saviour.

Readings

Exodus 1:8–2:10 or Isaiah 51:1-6
Psalm 124 or Psalm 138
Romans 12:1-8
Matthew 16:13-20

Thought for the day

As in last week's Gospel, Jesus is outside Galilee (and Herod's jurisdiction). He is about 25 miles north of the Sea of Galilee and in the area of Caesarea Philippi. At this stage Jesus is still avoiding conflict. There are already those who are plotting and planning to kill him. He needs time to be sure the disciples know fully who he is and to be prepared for what lies ahead. Before he sets out for Jerusalem and the cross, he needs to be sure of the awareness of the disciples.

You can imagine them sitting by a campfire in the evening and in a pagan area. Jesus asks them who people say that he is. A few answers tumble out. 'Some say John the Baptist come back.' Perhaps they put this one first because it is a bit hilarious: some of the disciples knew both John and Jesus. They were well aware of them at work at the same time.

Elijah was the next in people's minds. This could be far more likely and had to be looked at. It was believed that, before the Christ came, Elijah would return. Malachi declared the promise of God: 'Lo, I will send you the prophet Elijah before the great and terrible day of the Lord comes' (4:5). These are almost the last words in the Old Testament and to this day the Jews look forward to the coming of Elijah before the Christ comes.

'Jeremiah,' said some. This may sound strange to us but there was a tradition that, before the coming of the Messiah, Jeremiah would return. It was believed that Jeremiah had hidden the ark and the altar of incense that were in the Temple before the exile.

He had hidden them in a cave. Before the Christ came, Jeremiah would come and produce the goods.

All of these were precursors of the Christ. The people were not yet aware enough. Jesus then asked the disciples the big question, 'But who do you say that I am?' Jesus does not want to know what they have been told; he wants to know about their own relationship with him and their vision of who he is. For the Christian it is not enough to know about Jesus; we need to know him, to have a relationship with him. Faith is not so much about belief but about a living relationship with Christ.

It is good to look at the first three Gospels and hear the response of Peter:

> You are the Messiah, the Son of the living God. (Matthew 16:16)
>
> You are the Messiah. (Mark 8:29)
>
> The Messiah of God. (Luke 9:20)

The word Messiah is the same as Christ, and both mean the Anointed One. Kings are anointed when they enter into their position. The Messiah is God's Anointed One, the appointed one, who is King over all.

This was something that Peter said for himself, and no doubt for the disciples. Jesus is the Christ. Although it may be a small start, it is upon this that Jesus can build. At the moment they only know in part. They are hardly ready to accept that the Christ will suffer. But it is a start and on this beginning their faith will grow. It is when we make the affirmation of faith in Jesus, and seek a living relationship, that Jesus can build his Church in us and through us. It is no use just reciting what we have been told. Jesus wants to know what we think about him personally. For many of us the Gospel grows when we try to put it into our own words.

For the moment Jesus wants his disciples to tell no one. They do not yet quite fully understand and the people would also misunderstand. It was because of wrong ideas about the Messiah that Jesus had to keep out of Galilee. But the day would come after Easter and Pentecost when the disciples would go out into all the world.

Illustration

Many people ask 'What do you believe in?' but for Christians it is not what but whom. We believe in the living Christ. We believe that Jesus is the Son of God and is our Saviour. We seek a living relationship with him.

Not what but whom

Not what, but whom, I do believe
that in my darkest hour of need
hath comfort that no mortal creed
to mortal man may give;
not what but whom!
for Christ is more than all the creeds
and his full life of gentle deeds
shall all the creeds outlive.
Not what I do believe but whom!
Who walks beside me in the gloom?
Who shares the burden wearisome?
Who all the dim way doth illume,
and bids me look beyond the tomb
the larger life to live.
Not what I do believe but whom!
Not what, but whom!

John Oxenham

COMPLETE COMMON WORSHIP

Sermon Illustrations

Proper 17

Sunday between 28 August and 3 September inclusive

Aim

To show that we are to seek the will of God

Readings

Exodus 3:1-15 or Jeremiah 15:15-21
Psalm 105:1-6, 23-26, 45b or Psalm 26:1-8
Romans 12:9-21
Matthew 16:21-28

Thought for the day

The Gospel follows on from last week when Peter confessed that Jesus is the Christ. This is certainly seen as a high moment and turning point in the first three Gospels. It is also a turning point in every life when we discover for ourselves that Jesus is the Christ and our Saviour. It is a very exciting and important moment. It is for this reason we need to be sure we get it as right as possible.

Jesus is pleased with the answer of Peter. He can now build on this. On this awareness of him there is hope for the future. But there are dangers. There are so many false ideas of the Christ. Even now some wanted Jesus to become their king and drive out the Roman army. This danger would arise again when he entered Jerusalem. With all the joy of recognition, Jesus had to prepare the disciples for what lay ahead. Jesus told them how he must return to Jerusalem and the conflict. He warned them that he would be taken and killed. He even spoke of the resurrection.

The reaction of Peter must have been the same for all the disciples. They did not want this to happen. It would be better for them to stay where they were. Jesus being human must have been tempted: he did not look forward to conflict and death. But Jesus also knew it was for this he came. Only this way could he reveal the deep love of God. For a moment he sees Peter as the Tempter and says, 'Get behind me, Satan.' Peter's target is too low; it is not seeking the will of God but rather the saving of his skin. We can have great sympathy with Peter. He wanted to protect his friend from any troubles. Sadly, in the desire to protect us our friends sometimes prevent us doing what God asks of us.

Jesus then had to tell them clearly of what lay ahead and that this involved the denial of themselves and the taking up of the cross. They could escape this but it was those who laid down their lives for the sake of Christ who would enter into life. Jesus gave them something very hard to think about when he said, 'For what will it profit them if they gain the whole world but forfeit their life? Or what will they give in return for their life?' (Matthew 16:26) This is a question we should ask of ourselves!

Illustration

When the devil cannot get at us directly he will seek to lead us astray by our friends. It is sad how many people are led astray by friends and family. Sometimes our loved ones are only seeking to protect us but in so doing they stop us risking for God.

Columbanus was born in Ireland about 540 AD. He was of noble birth, strong and intelligent and destined to be a ruler of people. Columbanus heard the call of God and decided to dedicate his life to God in a monastery. His poor mother was heartbroken. He could have such a wonderful career and he was hardly ready to leave home. She tried to stop him, at first holding on to him and then lying down across the doorway sobbing. It was very difficult for Columbanus but he had set his sights on serving God. He stepped purposefully over his mother and set out for the monastery. If he had stayed at home, we would never have heard of him, but in time he became one of the greatest missionaries and teachers in Europe.

Proper 18

Sunday between 4 and 10 September inclusive

Aim

To look at forgiveness and the presence of Jesus.

Readings

Exodus 12:1-14 or Ezekiel 33:7-11
Psalm 149 or Psalm 119:33-40
Romans 13:8-14
Matthew 18:15-20

Thought for the day

Today's Gospel is a difficult reading in that it does not sound like Jesus: it is more like statements from a committee! Jesus could not have said it in its present form because the Church did not as yet exist and the passage assumes an organised Church. It suggests that Gentiles and tax collectors are outcasts, but this was not the way of Jesus who was known as a friend of tax collectors and sinners. There is a danger: there are limits set on forgiveness. Next week's Gospel on forgiveness (Matthew 18:21-35) seems to be in contrast with the statement here. Much seems to have been lost in translation from the words of Jesus to these statements.

At its simplest, it is about the breakdown of relationships and their rebuilding. Here the advice is relatively simple.

Speak about your hurt or grievance rather than let the resentment or anger simmer until it boils over. Those who do not speak about anger often go around like unexploded bombs.

Meet up and talk it out. See if you can come to some sort of agreement.

If this fails, get help from friends.

If this still fails, try and deal with it within the community. There is a feeling that litigation and any legal proceedings only spell trouble. What underlies it all is that we are to seek to love and to forgive and that we are in the presence of God. Our God is always ready to help but we cannot ask God to heal broken relationships if we have made no effort ourselves. This is true of every request in prayer. God will work with us but not instead of us.

The passage ends with Jesus saying, 'Where two or three are gathered in my name, I am there among them' (Matthew 18:20). When we meet as the Church we need to spend time rejoicing in the presence and in the peace of our Lord. We do not come for sermons or hymns, good as they may be, but to rejoice that the Lord is here, that his Spirit is with us. Whenever we meet up and share with others we need to rejoice that the Lord is with us: he is in our homes, our schools and in all places. We can turn to the Lord whenever we want and he is there to help and protect us.

Illustration

In the story *Great Expectations* by Charles Dickens, Pip has dealt badly with Joe the blacksmith who cared for him in his early days. When Pip is ill and in debt, Joe comes to care for him. Joe stayed by him, gave him cooling drinks.

> At last, one day, I took courage, and said, 'Is it Joe?'
>
> And the dear old home-voice answered, 'Which it air, old chap.'
>
> 'Oh Joe, you break my heart! Look angry at me, Joe! Strike me, Joe! Tell me of my ingratitude. Don't be so good to me.'
>
> For Joe had actually laid his head down on the pillow at my side and put his arm around my neck, in his joy that I knew him.
>
> 'Which dear old Pip, old chap,' said Joe, 'you and me was ever friends. And when you are well enough to go out for a ride – what larks!'
>
> After which Joe withdrew to the window and stood with his back towards me, wiping his eyes. And as my extreme weakness prevented me going to him, I lay there penitently whispering, 'O God bless him! God bless this gentle Christian man!'

Proper 19

Sunday between 11 and 17 September inclusive

Aim

To show there are no limits to God's love and forgiveness.

Readings

Exodus 14:19-31 or Genesis 50:15-21
Psalm 114 or Exodus 15:1b-11, 21b
or Psalm 103:(1-7) 8-13
Romans 14:1-12
Matthew 18:21-35

Thought for the day

Peter was a practical sort of man and to go around with Jesus was not always easy. Peter felt there was a need for what we would now call damage limitation. He felt generosity was important, but surely forgiveness needs to have some limits. The Jewish teaching was quite simple: if someone sins, forgive them, once, twice, three times, but after that enough is enough; a sinner must be made to face consequences. That is sensible enough. Peter saw that Jesus was going beyond this and asked how often he should forgive. Seven times? Surely this was as far as anyone should go; it was more than reasonable. Jesus refused to put a limit on forgiveness and suggested 70 x 7 – in other words, without limit. There can be no limit to love and forgiveness.

Jesus then told a story about two debtors with whom the King wished to settle accounts. One was brought owing ten thousand talents. This is an extraordinary amount of money – it was greater than a king's ransom. It was more money than the revenue from all of Samaria and Galilee put together. It was an amount no one could pay. Yet the King forgave him this debt out of mercy, out of care for his wife and children.

This man, forgiven such an enormous debt, then attacked a fellow slave who owed him a hundred denarii – the sort of money that could be carried easily in a pocket. He was not merciful; he had the slave put into prison for his debt. He was a hard man. He demanded what was his by rights.

Fellow slaves were distressed by this and reported it to the King. The King was very angry and had the unforgiving slave put in prison until he could pay the debt, which he would never be able to do.

This tells us of the danger of an unforgiving heart. The unforgiving heart is damning. Hatred, vengeance, resentment can all poison our lives. God cannot forgive the unforgiving. It seems forgiveness cannot be poured in if forgiveness is not given out. As we receive, so we must give. Forgiveness, like love, grows only by our giving it out. We cannot claim forgiveness if we are unwilling to forgive others. We must all pray the Lord's Prayer with caution when we say, 'Forgive us . . . as we forgive'.

Illustration

When John Wesley was sailing to America he witnessed the keel-hauling of a member of the crew for an offence on board ship. This was a particularly cruel form of punishment as it meant being tied to a rope, thrown overboard, drawn under the vessel and out the other side. There was always the chance you would drown or perish in some other way. The captain said to John Wesley as they watched, 'You see, Mr Wesley, I never forgive.' It was not for John Wesley to question the captain's power of command but he could and did question that statement. He replied, 'Then, sir, I hope that you never sin!'

Proper 20

Sunday between 18 and 24 September inclusive

Aim

To show how caring and generous God is.

Readings

Exodus 16:2-15 or Jonah 3:10–4:11
Psalm 105:1-6, 37-45 or Psalm145:1-8
Philippians 1:21-30
Matthew 20:1-16

Thought for the day

The parable about the labourers in the vineyard is really more about the owner and employer than the labourers. It would be better to call it the parable of the generous employer. The Jews were used to such stories for they had many featuring a beloved father, *abba,* and a beloved son, *amon,* all relating to work in the vineyard. The vineyard is often used as a symbol of the people of God (see Isaiah 5:7).

Each time the owner goes out he finds workers idle in the market place – 'early', 'about nine o'clock', 'about noon', 'about three o'clock', and 'about five o'clock'. These are people thrown out of work by economic conditions. This is still a familiar sight – day-workers and immigrants waiting for someone to give them a day's employment. Usually they are paid below the 'going rate'.

At the end of the day all the labourers are given a normal day's wage. This is in keeping with the Torah, which said, 'You shall not keep for yourself the wages of a labourer until the morning' (Leviticus 19:13). Simply because they are so poor they need this money to survive.

That all are given the same rate would bring many a union worker forward to object. But no one is underpaid. The ones who worked the longest get a fair wage. The owner could have given the others less but he is generous towards all of them. This parable tells us about God's grace and generosity and how he gives bountifully to all. If we received from God what we deserved, most of us would be in a sorry state, but God is generous in giving himself and his love to us. Our relationship with God is not about rights and rewards but about grace and generosity on the part of God. There is a great lesson here to a society that is always chasing after its 'rights'. We need a fair and just society but rights alone are not enough; we need grace and generosity or life becomes tough and the survival of the fittest.

The parable expressed something about the care of Jesus for the marginalised and outcasts of society.

Illustration

Theo kept strange accounts. He gave equally and generously to all who worked for him. He did not count one worth more than another. All who were willing and able to work were given a whole day's pay whether they had been asked to work all day or only for an hour. It was the same with his relationships: he cared for all equally. Some thought that they clocked up a bigger balance for reward and expected to receive more. But Theo loved all equally. Some grumbled about this but in truth they were trying to buy his love and affection when it is freely given to all. There are always people who grumble. The only people Theo could not help were those who chose to turn away from him. Even these he gladly would give to if they allowed him to. Theo kept strange accounts.

Proper 21

Sunday between 25 September and 1 October inclusive

Aim

To look at making choices and practising what we profess.

Readings

Exodus 17:1-7 or Ezekiel 18:1-4, 25-32
Psalm 78:1-4, 12-16 or Psalm 25:1-9
Philippians 2:1-13
Matthew 21:23-32

Thought for the day

At the beginning of Matthew 21, Jesus enters Jerusalem to a welcome of palm-waving by the people. He then proceeds to drive out the money changers from the temple. The chief priests and elders ask Jesus, 'By what authority are you doing these things, and who gave you the authority?' (21:23): this group will constitute the primary antagonists throughout the Passion narrative. They were the aristocracy and not like the many priests who came into Jerusalem to serve at the temple. The chief priests and elders are those who worked in collaboration with Rome and had vested interests in keeping the status quo. They are compromised leaders who will not challenge the ruling authority. Jesus obviously disturbs them. They question Jesus but in turn he questions them and they dodge an answer. Out of this situation comes the parable of the two sons.

Remember that the vineyard is an image of the Israel of God, an image of the Church. The first son refused to work in the vineyard saying, 'I will not.' There seems little respect for the father here. But later he changes his mind and goes. The second answered the father with respect and said, 'I go, sir', but he did not go. Neither son is perfect. Neither seemed truly willing. One professes but does not practise; the other does not appear willing but in the end does what the father wants. If you had to choose, which of these two imperfect sons did the will of the father? The answer would have to be the son who did what the father wanted.

Jesus now takes this a stage further and says to the priests and elders, 'tax collectors and prostitutes will enter the kingdom of God ahead of you'. It may be worthwhile to note that tax collectors and prostitutes also served Rome. Jesus did not say, '*instead* of you', but '*ahead* of you'. As long as they live, each has the potential for change. If we profess something, we should show we believe it by the way we live. Words without deeds are of little worth. This is all about promises and performance, words and deeds. It remains true, of course, that love, care, respect for the world and for each other can often be found in those who do not profess to serve God in any way.

Illustration

In a community there was a group of people who were always ready to say, 'Yes, sir. Three bags full, sir.' They appeared to be willing to take on anything that was asked and always talked with respect. They appeared only too willing, ready and able. But when it came to the crunch they were too busy, too tired, couldn't be bothered, or had just forgotten what they had promised. When they were needed they did not turn up.

There was another group who always seemed reluctant. They did not particularly want to get involved. They had other things to do. Yet when they were aware of the need they had a change of heart and waded in. They would not profess to be part of any system, but out of love and care they got on and did what was needed.

It was hard to depend on either group but in the end the second group was more likely to get things done.

Proper 22

Sunday between 2 and 8 October inclusive

Aim

To appreciate all that God has given us.

Readings

Exodus 20:1-4, 7-9, 12-20 or Isaiah 5:1-7
Psalm 19 or Psalm 80:7-14
Philippians 3:4b-14
Matthew 21:33-46

Thought for the day

Once again Jesus talks about a vineyard and so the chief priests and scribes would be aware that Jesus was talking about the people of God (Isaiah 5:7, Psalm 80:8). There is a protective hedge around the vineyard, winepress and tower. This was a vineyard that was well provided for and protected. This is about privileged people.

The action of the owner was quite common in Palestine. The owner let the tenants have use of the vineyard and in return they paid him a portion of the harvest in kind or in money. Even the reaction of the vine growers was not unusual as there was much unrest and discontent in the land and tenants were feeling rebellious.

God gives us the world for our benefit, but God does want some response. It is still God's world. God gives his protection and provides for us. He then gives us the freedom to get on with our lives. God does not keep making demands. He trusts us and seeks a faithful relationship. In all his dealings God is patient, even when we ignore him and his messengers. God gives us chance after chance but this cannot go on for ever. If we ignore him, that has its own consequences. It is not that God turns away from us; we have turned away from God and not given him his due. We have misused our freedom and for this we are answerable to him. We are answerable to God for the way we use the world and how we live our lives. The privileges we have, come with responsibilities: privileges are meant to be used to the benefit of others and to the glory of God.

Through this parable it is easy to pass judgement on the House of Israel. This avoids the issue that we are often in the same position. Do we heed God's messengers? Do we give God his due? Are you certain you show respect for his world? Before we point at anyone else, we need to look at our own relationship with God and with his Son. It would seem that human attitudes are always repeating themselves. This is what makes the Scriptures so meaningful and relevant to us. By our actions do we exclude ourselves from the presence of God and the benefits of his kingdom?

Illustration

The group was given a new hall through the generosity of others and through national grants. But from the start they did not appreciate it. The walls were daubed with graffiti, the floor was covered with litter; inside the building they ran riot. Though people tried to care for them, they rejected any offers of oversight or help. In time the hall looked derelict and no one dared to go and look after it. Windows were broken and toilets were vandalised.

Sadly after all the efforts of some the hall was shut down. Those who were given it were causing too much trouble. It became a liability. The idea had been a good one but the group did not appreciate this. Finally it was dismantled and the land given to others.

Proper 23

Sunday between 9 and 15 October inclusive

Aim

To encourage awareness that we are invited to share the joys of the kingdom in the presence of the King.

Readings

Exodus 32:1-14 or Isaiah 25:1-9
Psalm 106:1-6, 19-23 or Psalm 23
Philippians 4:1-9
Matthew 22:1-14

Thought for the day

The readings for today are full of joy. Isaiah and Jesus both talk about a feast. Isaiah says how God will wipe away all tears. In Psalm 23 the psalmist rejoices in the presence and protection of God who is compared to a shepherd. St Paul asks us 'to rejoice in the Lord always' and, to emphasise it, he repeats, 'again I say rejoice'. To be invited to come to God or to be a Christian is not a gloomy life-restricting event; it is life-extending and joyful. Jesus compares it to being invited to a wedding banquet. It is a joy to be invited into God's presence and we miss out on this if we refuse to come. Those who excuse themselves exclude themselves. God has given us an open invitation; if we do not come, the fault lies in ourselves.

It is interesting to look at the excuses because they are not bad things in themselves. People miss out by going about their daily work and doing that alone. Many of us allow the call of earthly things to deafen us to the heavenly. We spend a good deal of time on that which is passing away and ignore that which is eternal. Like Esau in the Old Testament, we trade our birthright for a bowl of food. We are in danger of seeing to our bodies and neglecting our souls. Because God does not force us, it is easy to have prayer and even God himself low on our agenda. But if so, it is we who miss out.

Jesus is not threatening us with punishment but rather telling us that we are in danger of missing out by the way we are living. It is very sad when we realise too late what we have missed. We often miss out by being unwilling to learn the disciplines so that we might then have the joy of playing an instrument, for example, or taking part in a sport.

In the parable, those from the highways and byways had no call on the King. You could not say they were worthy of an invitation. We see God's grace and goodness at work in the invitation he sends out to everyone. All are welcome, including you and me. We are called to enjoy God's presence and to feast on all that he offers us.

Matthew 22:6 sounds very like the parable from last week's Gospel and is a follow-on from it. There is a warning that all are invited, but if you reject the invitation, be it on your head. It is you who have made your choice. Verse 7 sees the fulfilment of that warning in the destruction of the Temple and Jerusalem by the Roman army in 70 AD. Many would say this was caused by the attitude of the Jews at the time.

Illustration

Richard and Judy were invited to the palace to meet the King to enjoy sharing in the beauty of the surroundings and to take part in a banquet. It was a most generous invitation and they wondered what they had done to deserve it. In fact, it was sent out because of the love of the King. They showed lots of people the invitation with pride. They put it where it could be seen in their house.

Most days they looked at it and said how wonderful it was. They had advance warning of the date and slowly it came near. One day Judy looked at her calendar and said, 'Oh, I am supposed to get my hair done today – what shall I do?' Richard replied, 'That's OK. Just go ahead. I fancy doing some gardening.' For all their talk and show, they counted the invitation of little value. By excusing themselves, they excluded themselves.

Proper 24

Sunday between 16 and 22 October inclusive

Aim

To show how we are meant to be concerned for the world as well as for God.

Readings

Exodus 33:12-23 or Isaiah 45:1-7
Psalm 99 or Psalm 96:1-9 (10-13)
1 Thessalonians 1:1-10
Matthew 22:15-22

Thought for the day

The Romans had tax systems that are not dissimilar to our own – and, as you would expect, they were not welcome. They had 'ground tax', which meant you had to pay 10 per cent on all grain and 20 per cent on oil and wine that you produced. This was paid in kind or in money. There was income tax at 1 per cent of your earnings. There was poll tax on every adult male from 14 to 65 and every female from 12 to 65. Obviously the women matured earlier! This tax was one denarius and was known as the 'tribute to Caesar'. The Roman coinage itself was offensive to the Jews for each coin not only depicted the head of Caesar but also gave him divine status. To carry such money was to accommodate oneself to imperial rule.

The Pharisees and Herodians were trying to lay a trap for Jesus by asking if it was right to pay tribute to Caesar or not. Matthew suggests they are doing this out of malice and describes them as hypocrites. They had presented Jesus with a real 'Catch 22' situation. Not to pay tribute would be a rebellion against the empire. For this Jesus would be reported for preaching sedition. If he said it was right to pay, Jesus would be discredited in the eyes of many of the ordinary people.

Jesus asks for a denarius and asks, 'Whose head is this and whose title?' When they answered, 'The Emperor's', Jesus replied, 'Give to the emperor the things that are the emperor's and to God the things that are God's.'

There is great wisdom in this answer – or you could say it is no answer at all. Who are we to give to? The answer is not either one or the other but both. It is a mistake to separate one from the other. The sacred and secular are not independent of each other; they are so intertwined that we cannot divide them, just as we cannot separate the human into body and soul. Both are woven together. God made the world, God loves the world and God is present in his world. The Christian who says that we must not get involved in politics does not realise what Christianity is about. We cannot hope for a new heaven and a new earth unless we work towards it happening. It is no use praying for peace if we do not help to bring it about. We give to the state – even if only by law – for our own benefit.

And we give to God – what? Does God get the priority he is due in our life? Do we respond to him in praise and thanksgiving? Do we seek to do his will? You must ask what do you render to God – and this is far bigger than talking about money.

Illustration

Some of the greatest witnesses to giving God his due were the early Christian martyrs. Catherine, who gives her name to the 'Catherine Wheel' firework, was born of a noble family and lived in the fourth century. The emperor was attracted to her and wanted to marry her. Catherine refused because she was already a 'bride of Christ'. She is said to have disputed with 50 philosophers whose job it was to convince her of her error and she defeated them. Because she refused to do as commanded by the emperor she was tortured by being fastened to a large wheel and driven around the arena – but the wheel broke. Finally she was beheaded.

Proper 25

Sunday between 23 and 29 October inclusive

Aim

To encourage us to love God with our whole being.

Readings

Deuteronomy 34:1-12 or Leviticus 19:1-2, 15-18
Psalm 90:1-6, 13-17 or Psalm 1
1 Thessalonians 2:1-8
Matthew 22:34-46

Thought for the day

Every Jewish service starts with the same words: 'Hear, O Israel: The Lord is our God, the Lord is one. You shall love the Lord your God with all your heart, with all your soul, and with all your might.' The words continue by telling them to teach their children these words, to bind them to their hand, fix them on their forehead and write them on the door posts of their house. These words are called the 'Shema', which means 'Hear', and they ask people to listen and obey. Jews recite these words in the same way that Christians say the Creed. As commanded, these are the first words Jewish parents teach their children from the Scriptures. They put these words in little leather boxes, called phylacteries, and bind them on their wrists so that they may think of God in all their actions. They also fix them to their heads so that God may be known in their thinking. Then in a little cylinder, called a mezuzah, they fasten them to the doorpost of their houses and touch them as they go out and in, to remind them that God is with them in their going out and their coming in. All this is to encourage an awareness and deep love of God.

When Jesus was asked what the greatest commandment was, everyone would have agreed with him when he replied, 'Love God'. Love God with all your heart, and with all your soul, and with all your mind. Love God with your whole being. Every Jew would agree with that. Later St Augustine would say, 'Love God, and do what you like.' By this he meant if we love God, we will do nothing to hurt or go against him.

Jesus then added, 'And a second [commandment] is like it: "You shall love your neighbour as yourself." On these two commandments hang all the law and the prophets.' This can be found in the Old Testament in Leviticus 19:18. Jesus put the two together to make a Summary of the Law. Our love for God is to be reflected in our love for each other. Only when we love God are we able to love others as we ought, yet in a strange way we can only love God when we have learnt love from others. Through the love of our homes and our loved ones, God reveals his love to us. When we know love, we can love. We also learn to love ourselves and accept ourselves because we are counted worthy of the love of God and of others.

In the words of the song, 'All you need is love' – love God and love one another.

Illustration

'Christmas wouldn't be Christmas without any presents,' Jo had grumbled as she waited with her three sisters until their mother returned from church . . .

> 'Merry Christmas, Marmee! Many of them!'
>
> 'Merry Christmas, little daughters! But I want to say one word before we sit down. Not far away from here lies a poor woman with a little newborn baby. Six children are huddled into one bed to keep from freezing, for they have no fire. There is nothing to eat over there, and the oldest boy came to tell me they are suffering from hunger and cold. My girls, will you give them your breakfast as a Christmas present?'
>
> They were all unusually hungry having waited nearly an hour, and for a minute no one spoke – only a minute, for Jo exclaimed impetuously, 'I am so glad you came before we began!' '
>
> 'May I go and help to carry the things to the poor children?' asked Beth eagerly.
>
> 'I shall take the cream and the muffins,' added Amy, heroically giving up the articles she most liked.
>
> Meg was already covering the buckwheats, and piling the bread into one big plate.
>
> 'I thought you would do it,' said Mrs March, smiling as if satisfied. 'You shall have bread and milk for breakfast and make up for it at dinner time.'
>
> They were soon ready, and the procession set out.

Fortunately it was early and they went through the back streets, so few people saw them, and no one laughed at the queer party.

A poor bare miserable room it was with broken windows, no fire, ragged bedclothes, a sick mother, wailing baby and a group of pale, hungry children huddled under one old quilt to keep warm.

How the big eyes stared and the blue lips smiled as the girls went in!

'Ach mein Gott. It is good angels come to us!' said the poor woman crying for joy.

Louisa May Alcott, *Little Women* (1868)

COMPLETE COMMON WORSHIP

Sermon Illustrations

All Saints' Day

1 November or Sunday between 30 October and 5 November inclusive

Aim

To show how the blessed share in the eternal.

Readings

Revelation 7:9-17
Psalm 34:1-10
1 John 3:1-3
Matthew 5:1-12

Thought for the day

Today's Gospel is known as the Beatitudes: the word 'Blessed' is used nine times in three groups of three. Blessed means happy but much more besides because it also means not being subject to fate or circumstance. To be blessed means to have an imperishable quality. For this reason many Jewish prayers begin with the words 'Blessed are you, Lord our God'. For God is imperishable, God is eternal – our blessedness can only come from God. We show our blessedness by living the way God wants us to live.

The first three 'Blesseds' are about our attitude to the world around us. The poor in spirit are those who are not grabbing and seeking to get all the time. They are able to let go and live simply. Those who mourn are people with feelings: they have passions and have not become hard-hearted; they feel for others. When you say, 'good grief', you mean such people. The meek are those who do not force others but are gentle in their dealings.

The next three are about relationships. To hunger and thirst for righteousness is to seek to live in right relationships with people and to strive for justice. The merciful do not demand their rights but are forgiving and kind towards others. The pure in heart are the single-minded who seek to live God's way.

The third group concerns our position in a difficult world. Those who seek peace are those who seek to bring harmony and balance to the world and they are seen to be children of God as his image is seen in them. Those who endure persecution for righteousness show themselves to be followers of Jesus who died for us and they shall inherit the kingdom. Then there are those who do not let persecution get the better of them but stand firm in the faith. Those who remain loyal will not lose out. Even if they lose their life, they will have life eternal.

These are the qualities that make a saint: they show the people who are striving to serve God. The saints were not perfect but they sought to live the life of the blessed and they have given us an example to follow.

Illustration

The word 'blessed' comes from the Greek word 'makarios' and is used to describe the gods. Jesus uses it to describe those who do God's will. The Greeks called Cyprus the 'blessed island' or the 'happy island' because it was such a rich and fertile land with a good climate, rich in minerals and natural resources. Fruit and grain and flowers could grow in abundance. It was a place where people should be perfectly happy. It should be a place of peace and harmony. In the same way, those who lived the beatitudes would find peace and harmony in God's presence and God's love.

Fourth Sunday before Advent

Sunday between 30 October and 5 November inclusive; for use if the Feast of All Saints was celebrated on 1 November and alternative propers are needed

Aim

To show that our God cares for us in all our troubles.

Readings

Micah 3:5-12
Psalm 43
1 Thessalonians 2:9-13
Matthew 24:1-14

Thought for the day

Today the Church's yearly cycle takes on a new dimension: we begin to look towards the preparation for Advent and Christmas. This period is kept as the 'Kingdom Season': we look at the kingdoms of the world and the kingdom of Christ.

Jesus grieves for Jerusalem and the Temple. It could be that some of the followers of Jesus had never seen another building like the Temple. The white marble of the Temple and the gold leaf made it look radiant. At the corners of the Temple were stones that were 20 to 40 feet in length and weighed up to 100 tons. You would imagine they were unmovable. It was a very spectacular building when most people lived in small houses made of mud bricks. It looked as if it would last for ever – and because it was God's house they thought it would.

Jesus realises that the prophecy of Micah is about to come to pass. God is not condemning Jerusalem. The people are bringing the trouble upon themselves. The disciples are horrified when Jesus says that the Temple will be destroyed.

It is only when they are alone on the Mount of Olives that they question Jesus and ask to know more. Jesus then talks of the unrest not only of people but the earth itself. People will be led astray by false-Christs, there will be wars and rumours of war, with nation rising against nation. Along with this there will be famine and earthquakes. It sounds a real picture of doom and yet it is something that is always happening to the world and temporal powers. Many kingdoms have come and gone. It is easy to despair. But Jesus does not want us to concentrate on the troubles, only to be aware that they come.

Jesus does not want us to be led astray by false claims. He wants us to stay loyal to him because all the troubles are like birth pangs. A new kingdom is coming in with Christ as King. God has not abandoned his world. For all its troubles, God still loves the world. God still cares for his creation. God seeks to redeem the world and to free it from captivity.

Jesus was well aware of the mounting opposition to him and therefore to his disciples. Jesus does not promise a good time. In this world there will be all sorts of persecution. People will lose faith and fall away. False prophets will mislead many, and lawlessness will increase. In all this love will appear to die because people will harden their hearts. Can we not see much of this going on in our society today?

That is the bad news. The Good News is that these are signs of the coming of Christ. His kingdom is near. Christ the King will bring in the age of peace. We are not left on our own in all this trouble. For us the end is not the end because Christ is our Saviour and he brings us into his kingdom. All our troubles are to be looked upon as birth pangs and the bringing in of the new age, where the kingdoms of the world are the kingdoms of Christ and of God. We are not promised a journey without storms but are promised we will not be alone and at the end of the journey we will arrive into the fullness of his kingdom.

Illustration

When we have dark or bad days we need to remind ourselves that God is with us and cares for us. Here is a prayer from the Hebrides which you may find helpful:

> Though the dawn breaks cheerless on this Isle today,
> my spirit walks in a path of light.
> For I know my greatness.
> Thou has built me a throne within thy heart.
> I dwell safely within the circle of thy care.
> I cannot for a moment fall out of the everlasting arms.
> I am on my way to thy glory.
>
> Alistair Maclean, *Hebridean Altars* (1937)

Now that is Good News, whatever the day!

Third Sunday before Advent

Sunday between 6 and 12 November inclusive

Aim

To show how we need to keep ourselves aware that Jesus comes to us.

Readings

Amos 5:18-24 or Wisdom of Solomon 6:12-16
Psalm 70 or Wisdom of Solomon 6:17-20
1 Thessalonians 4:13-18
Matthew 25:1-13

Thought for the day

It is amazing how many people are willing to pray 'your kingdom come; your will be done', but then put it all off to another day. Jesus wanted us to know the kingdom of heaven is at hand (Mark 1:15) and we should be entering into it. In this 'Kingdom Season' we look at another parable of the kingdom. The parable of the ten bridesmaids is full of warnings. There is no doubt they are all invited; they are all given the opportunity to share in the joy of the wedding. They are all excited about it. There is no suggestion that the foolish ones were wicked or evil, only that they had neglected certain things that were required of them. It was a small matter to make sure they had oil and light – they could have done it but they never bothered. How often have we made excuses for not saying our prayers and welcoming God into our homes? There comes a time when it is too late. The night comes and the time for getting oil is past. The time for meeting the King passed; the time for entering the banquet passed – and all for the want of a little oil, a little thought and preparation. The artist Pablo Picasso said, 'Never put off today anything you do not want to leave undone for ever.'

To live our lives without due care and proper attention courts disaster. We ignore the things of God at our peril.

The words of the bridegroom to those clamouring to come in are a terrible statement: 'I never knew you.' Often we ask, 'Do you two know each other?' Have we taken the time and made the effort to know Jesus, to be friends with him, or have we been too preoccupied? Can Jesus say to us, 'I never knew you'? God does not exclude us from his kingdom. He has given us an open invitation. Only we can exclude ourselves by excusing ourselves.

Illustration

John could have learnt much more at school but he was always fooling around or thinking about what he was going to do after school. He never listened. He was there in body but not in mind or spirit.

Jean knew it was no use talking to her father while he was watching a football match on the television. He was in the same room but he was not really where she was and he would not hear.

There is a danger that we are never really aware of our Lord's coming and we miss the wonderful relationship that is offered to us: we miss the moment even though it is offered to us more than once. Too often Jesus finds we are 'not there' when he comes. He seeks us out but we do not give him any attention. Think of Jesus saying:

> I called your name but you were out or preoccupied.
>
> I came to you in the night but you did not notice.
>
> I knocked on your door and your heart but they remained closed.
>
> I asked for your help but you were too busy.
>
> I wanted to know you, to give my love to you, but you were otherwise engaged.

Second Sunday before Advent

Sunday between 13 and 19 November inclusive

Aim

To encourage the awareness that we all have talents to share and develop.

Readings

Zephaniah 1:7, 12-18
Psalm 90:1-8 (9-11) 12
1 Thessalonians 5:1-11
Matthew 25:14-30

Thought for the day

Today's parable for the Kingdom Season tells how we are trusted by the King to do something with our lives and not just waste them. Each of us is expected to work according to our ability and talents.

We are told of a man leaving his property in the trust of his slaves. He gives them varying quantities of resources. To one he gives five talents, to another two and to another one. They are not all the same; each has different gifts. They are not equal in talent but they all need to make an effort with what they have. It is not how many talents you have that counts but how you use them.

The talent Jesus talks about was not money but rather an ingot of gold, silver or copper. The most common was silver and in today's value would be well over £2000, when a working man was only getting a penny a day! There is no doubt all could do something with such talent.

Two of the slaves show a profit. It is not about money but about not wasting or failing to use what you are given. If we do not use our God-given talents, we are in danger of losing them. This is what happens to the third slave. He was afraid to risk or be adventurous: he did not invest the talents. In fact, he did nothing at all: he hid the talent. This angered the master because he wanted the talents to be used. The talent was taken from this man and given to another.

Because we are all unique human beings, we all have something to offer that no one else can offer – even if that offering is only of our self and our time. No one is without something to offer. Yet we all know that if talent is not used, it atrophies and dies. For talent to grow and develop we need to use it. We need to use our lives for the benefit of the King and the kingdom.

Illustration

Millie was now quite old but she always had a strange attitude to gifts. If she was given a present, she would thank the person profusely and say how kind it was of them to give her a gift. She said she would treasure it. Then without unwrapping it she put it away in a drawer for another day. When a niece came to help her to move she discovered many unused gifts, still wrapped. There were biscuits and cakes that had moulded away; there was jars of things that had long passed their sell-by date; there were clothes that now would no longer fit Millie. Drawer after drawer of gifts were put out in the bin. Because she did no use them she lost them; she never had the benefit of them.

In the same way we will lose our local small shops unless we use them. We will lose bus services unless we use them. We will lose our God-given gifts and talents unless we use them. The thing we need understand is 'Use it or lose it'.

Christ the King

Sunday between 20 and 26 November inclusive

Aim

To make people aware that Christ comes to us in our encounter with others and in the needs of the poor.

Readings

Ezekiel 34:11-16, 20-24
Psalm 95:1-7a
Ephesians 1:15-23
Matthew 25:31-46

Thought for the day

For the last Sunday in the Kingdom Season we have a vivid parable that tells us what will happen when the Son of Man comes in glory. Christ the King will separate the sheep from the goats. He will welcome the sheep on his right hand and offer them the kingdom that has been prepared for them since the creation of the world. This in itself is a wonderful thought: there is a place that has been reserved for you from the beginning. There is a place that is just yours, it has your name on it and no one else can take it. We need to be aware, however, that there is a judgement and it is about love. If we have expressed love, we need have no fear.

> Listen to what the King says:
> I was hungry and you gave me food.
> I was thirsty and you gave me something to drink.
> I was a stranger and you welcomed me.
> I was naked and you gave me clothing.
> I was sick and you took care of me.
> I was in prison and you visited me.

When the people ask when was this the reply is:

> Just as you did it to the least of these who are members of my family, you did it to me.

Time and again we will learn that the way we deal with others is the way we deal with God. If we do not listen to others, we are not likely to listen to God. If we are mean towards others, we have a mean relationship with God. If we only like people who will obey us, we will seek a puppet God. Our faith is not one that is out of this world; our faith is reflected in our relationships with each other as well as with God.

As God is in each person, though sometimes so hidden that he is hard to find, we have to treat everyone with reverence and respect. There is no one single person who does not have God hidden within, even though they may live in total disobedience to God. The tramp and the criminal have no less of God than the archbishop or saint.

Illustration

Christopher wanted to serve the King. He wanted to go to the palace and give himself to serve the King. But he was held up. First he had to look after ageing parents. When he set off he had a gift for the King but he met a poor family who had been robbed of their belongings and he gave the gift to them. Later on he met a family whose cart had stuck deep in the mud. He stayed to help them and got sprayed with mud. Now he had no gift and his fine clothes were filthy. He felt he could not journey on but something encouraged him – words he had heard long ago. When he finally reached the palace, he received a royal welcome. He was about to apologise for the state he was in but the King said, 'You have been a great help to me over the years, in the way you cared for your parents, in the way you gave to the poor and when you helped those in need. I was there and it was me you gave your help and love to. Welcome to the fullness of the kingdom which you have served for a long time.'

YEAR B

First Sunday of Advent

Aim

To make people more aware that Christ comes to them today.

Readings

Isaiah 64:1-9
Psalm 80:1-7,17-19
1 Corinthians 1:3-9
Mark 13:24-37

Thought for the day

Happy New Year! This is the first Sunday in the Church Year. We celebrate the Church's New Year by lighting a candle. It is called an Advent candle. Advent is about the coming of God into the world.

Isaiah sees God's coming as something that is frightening, because we have not been looking for our God; in fact, we have been ignoring him. God has been coming to us and we have not let him into our lives. But because God has made us and loves us, he will have mercy upon us. We may annoy our parents, we may ignore them, but they still continue to love us and care for us. We are not alone in the world; if we seek God he comes to us.

Psalm 80 has the refrain 'Show us the light of your countenance and we shall be saved.' We ask the hide-and-seek God to reveal himself to us. Let us learn to look for God in our everyday life.

God has shown himself to us in the face of Jesus Christ. In Jesus we have a new hope, for God's grace – that is the free gift of himself – has been given to us in Christ Jesus. This is a gift to each of us. Will we unwrap this gift and make it ours, that he may enrich us?

The Gospel tells us not to put off, or be put off, for the Son of Man comes. The times may be full of trouble and distress, yet he still comes to us. We should look for signs of his coming and of his presence in our lives.

We have been left in charge of this world, each with our own responsibility, each with our own work. We are accountable to God. He comes to see how we are dealing with his world. We need to keep alert, that we may be aware of his coming: to be awake and not go around with our eyes closed.

Illustration

It was near Christmas and in the Advent season, and Peter waited for God to come. He prayed every day, 'God, show me your face and I shall be saved.' Peter had tried to live a good life; he was now old and looked forward to the coming of God. He continued to work in his paper shop, where he had worked most of his life. Here he heard all sorts of conversations and met many people. A single mum was telling a friend how she did not have enough money to buy presents for her child. When everyone else had gone, Peter said to her, 'I heard what you said. I have a few toys on the shelves; they are not selling very well, go and pick anything you would like.' She could hardly believe it for there were some wonderful things on the shelves. As she went away with her arms full, Peter was delighted. His reward was her smile.

Later that day, he caught a young lad stealing a magazine from the shelves. He was on the way out with the magazine up his jumper when Peter stopped him. He could have called the police or told the boy's parents. He saw the boy was poor and afraid, and he felt sorry for him. 'If you want a magazine, and have no money, talk with me,' he said. 'Magazines are soon out of date; I can always find one to give you. You must not just help yourself. Take the magazine for free and ask me another time.' The boy's face changed from a look of fear to a beaming smile. He thanked Peter and ran from the shop.

An old man came into the shop and was saying how lonely he was since his wife died. This would be his first Christmas on his own – he was not looking forward to it. Peter said, 'We were expecting a friend to come for Christmas, and he has said he cannot make it. We have prepared for his coming. Would you come to us instead? We would love to share Christmas with you.' The old man's face lit up in a beautiful smile and he said, 'You have made me feel so wanted, and I would love to come.'

That night Peter prayed his Advent prayer, 'Show me your face and I shall be saved.' In a dream God spoke to him and said, 'Peter, today I came to you, and three times you made me smile. Grace and peace be upon you.'

(Apologies to Tolstoy!)

Second Sunday of Advent

Aim

To show we need to prepare for the coming of our Lord.

Readings

Isaiah 40:1-11
Psalm 85:1-2, 8-13.
2 Peter 3:8-15a
Mark 1:1-8

Thought for the day

Isaiah is sure that our God is coming to us and that we need to prepare. He tells us of the messenger that will go before his coming to see all is ready. In the olden days, when travel was difficult and dangerous, if a king was on a journey someone was sent ahead to see if the road was fit for a king. The aim was to remove obstacles in the road, to fill in holes and to level off bumps: rough places were made smooth. Then they had to make sure the king would get a good reception, that accommodation was prepared, making sure there was room for the king and he would be welcome. Once everything was ready the king would come in all his glory.

Today's psalm asks, 'Show us your steadfast love, O Lord, and grant us your salvation . . . that his glory may dwell in our land.'

St Peter is also sure that the Lord will come, and asks what sort of person you will be when he comes. Will you be a holy and a godly person? Do not put things off, for you do not know when the Lord will come. Strive to be found at peace.

St Mark is sure that Jesus is the Promised One and that John the Baptist is the messenger to prepare his way. John says to the people, 'Turn around; you are going the wrong way. You will not be ready for God if you go on like this. Repent and be cleansed. Say sorry for the wrong you have done and turn to God.'

Illustration

The Sunday before the beginning of Advent used to be called 'Stir-up Sunday' for two reasons. The prayer for the Sunday begins, 'Stir up, O Lord, the wills of your faithful people'; a wonderful prayer that wants us to 'bring forth the fruits of good works'. It is by what we do that we will be known, so it is important that our works are good, important that we do something.

Traditionally 'Stir-up Sunday' was also the time when the Christmas cake was made. Mother would get all the ingredients – the flour, the fruit, the eggs – and mix them together. Everyone in the house had a stir of the cake before it went into the oven. All this was part of the preparations before Christmas.

We now often spend weeks preparing for this one day. How much time do we spend preparing for the coming of God to us?

If someone is coming to stay, we will make sure there is room for them, that we have time for them, that we will give them some attention. Our God comes and seeks room in our lives; he wants us to be aware of him, for us to give him some of our time and attention.

Are you prepared for this?

Third Sunday of Advent

Aim

To encourage people to see that Jesus comes in acts of kindness and righteousness.

Readings

Isaiah 61:1-4, 8-11
Psalm 126 or the Magnificat
1 Thessalonians 5:16-24
John 1:6-8, 19-28

Thought for the day

Jesus chose to speak on this passage from Isaiah and relate it to his ministry. He was the 'anointed one', the Messiah. In his baptism the Spirit of the Lord was seen to descend upon him.

The Lord wants us to share in his mission. We are asked to bring the Good News to the poor – surely everyone who has not heard and received the Good News is poor! We are called to bind up the broken-hearted, to proclaim liberty for captives, and to comfort all who mourn. We must remember the Lord loves justice and hates wrongdoing.

In both the psalm and the Magnificat there is a feeling of the new order beginning, when God's people are freed to do righteous acts.

The writer to the Thessalonians asks us to 'hold fast to that which is good: abstain from every evil'.

Illustration

Once upon a time there was a man who went out to sea in a little boat. It was a lovely day and he was enjoying himself. Then the mist suddenly came down. Now he did not know which direction he was going in. He rowed around until he was very tired, then he let himself drift. He did not know that he was drifting towards the rocks. Suddenly he heard a crunch and a scraping. His boat was torn on the rocks and it began to sink. Fortunately he managed to escape on to the rocks. He was now very cold and hungry and he prayed to God to come and rescue him.

Soon a motorboat came by and invited him aboard – but he refused, saying, 'I have help coming.' A little later a fishing boat saw him and tried to persuade him to come off the rock but again he said, 'There is no need to worry I have help on the way.'

That night the man died alone in the cold. He went to heaven and complained to God that he had not come to help. God said, 'I came in a motorboat and you refused my help. I came again in a fishing boat and you still refused my help. You are here today because you did not recognise my help when it came – yet still you are loved.'

Fourth Sunday of Advent

Aim

To show God's kingdom comes when his will is done.

Readings

2 Samuel 7:1-11, 16
Magnificat or Psalm 89:1-4, 19-26
Romans 16:25-27
Luke 1:26-38

Thought for the day

David is aware that he lives in a good house and that God's dwelling is only a tent. He wants to build a splendid house for God. It is a wonderful idea but the danger is that we may feel we can only find God in his house. At least with a tent God was travelling with the Israelites: when they moved, God moved with them. God also says to David, 'I have been with you wherever you went.'

God promises David that he will make him a house and a kingdom that will last for ever. God will be ever-present within it.

The love that God showed to David is celebrated in Psalm 89. In the same way Mary praises God for the great things he has done and shall do for ever.

St Paul tells us that this same God is able to strengthen us through Jesus Christ, to whom all glory belongs.

God will not force himself upon us. If we lock him out, he will not break down the doors. If we ignore him, he will still care for us and love us. If we do not obey him, his kingdom cannot come in us. But once we say, 'Here am I; let it be to me according to your word', then the kingdom is come in us. Notice how God and the angel wait upon Mary's response. Without Mary, or someone like her, the Son of God cannot come into the world. When Mary says 'Yes' a new age begins. Let us learn to pray, 'Your kingdom come in us. Your will be done in us.' When we obey the King, his kingdom comes in us.

Illustration

Are you ready for Christmas? Have you sent all your cards? Bought presents? Got the food ready? What will you do on Christmas Day? Will you make room for Jesus: make sure Christ is in Christ-mas?

It was Jessie's birthday and she looked forward to it. She lived in an old people's home and had friends around her – but she was invited to her daughter's for her birthday. She would be with the family, including the three children. They made sure there was a nice room ready for her and the house was warm. Her daughter had bought the food she liked. All was ready.

On the first night her daughter had an evening class, the children were out with friends, and her son-in-law decided to go to the pub. On her birthday the children had other things to do and so would be out all day – football, swimming and netball are important. Jessie's son-in-law spent the day in the garage tinkering with his car, and her daughter decided to do some last-minute shopping on her own. Again Jessie was left alone. They had a meal together in the evening, then the children went on the computer and the others watched television. Jessie was glad to go back to the home where people had time to talk to her and give their attention to her.

Will we make time for Jesus on his birthday, or will we be too busy doing other things?

Christmas Day

Aim

To rejoice that Jesus Christ has come into the world.

Readings

Isaiah 52:7-10
Psalm 98
Hebrews 1:1-4 (5-12)
John 1:1-14

Thought for the day

God came down to us so that we might come with our love to him. He became human so that we might share in the Divine. This is a great mystery and full of riches for us to explore.

Isaiah invites us to sing for joy because our God 'reigns'. God is in control; he acts and the whole earth shall see 'the salvation of our God'. The Psalm repeats this, saying, 'All the ends of the earth have seen the victory of our God.'

The writer to the Hebrews tells us that what the prophets and the psalmists had looked forward to has happened. The hopes and promises of the Old Testament have happened in the coming of a Son.

John starts like Genesis – 'In the beginning' – for a new world has dawned for us. All the words of promise have become a reality in the Word made flesh. The Word, which was from the beginning, is made flesh: He comes as the light and the life of us all. And to all who receive him, who believe in his name, he gives the power to become children of God.

Illustration

Mother and Father had wrapped up the present in beautiful paper with tinsel and bows. The present was in a big box. For a long time it remained unopened as if their child was frightened of it. Then the paper was taken off and folded up carefully, the present was taken out of the box, and the child played the whole day with the box. The child enjoyed having the box and playing with it. Mother and Father hoped that their child would soon realise what a wonderful present had been given to her . . .

I knew an old lady who was uninterested in presents. Whenever she was given a present, she was very grateful. She always remembered to say, 'Thank you'. But she did not open the gift. In her house I saw a pile of unopened gifts and I felt it was rather strange and sad.

Today I would like to give you all a present of a cheque for one million pounds. But you can only have it on one condition: you are to frame it, to show how generous I am, but not cash it.

Let us get behind the tinsel and the wrappings today and discover God's greatest gift. He gives himself to us. Let us come and give ourselves to him.

First Sunday of Christmas

Aim

To show that the people involved in the birth of Jesus were ordinary people involved in an extraordinary event.

Readings

Isaiah 61:10–62:3
Psalm 148
Galatians 4:4-7
Luke 2:15-21

Thought for the day

Isaiah invites us to rejoice in the Lord and in his salvation. Likewise the psalm asks us to praise the name of the Lord; to join in with all creation and give him praise. This should be our aim throughout our worship.

God's promised time has come and his Son is born of the Blessed Virgin Mary. Like the shepherds, we are invited to glorify and praise God.

The shepherds were very ordinary men who worked on the hillsides tending sheep. By the nature of their job they rarely went to church – but that did not prevent God from knowing them and them from knowing God. They saw the angels, not because they were good but because God is good and comes to ordinary people in ordinary places. Shepherds on a hillside, Mary and Joseph travelling on a road, stars in the sky and a stable for a birth are all ordinary and familiar. We know these things and we can experience them, but it is only half the picture.

Show a negative and explain what it is. A negative is not a black and white photograph or a photograph without colour. If you look at a negative it is sometimes hard to see what the picture is, but it has the potential of making a picture. The negative is important but it is only half the picture. A print is necessary for us to see and understand the whole picture.

We all know about the shepherds and sheep but the other part of the picture makes the whole picture – angels and God are to be discovered. Our world is full of mystery, wonder and a presence.

Our minds cannot wholly grasp the mystery but our hearts can. Let us spend some time today thinking upon God and his love.

There are not two separate worlds: heaven and earth are one. God is with us. It is our own lack of vision that prevents us from seeing this.

Illustration

Sally was naughty at school. She did not pay attention to what was written on the board, nor was she all that keen on being out in the country because she was not really interested in the flowers or the birds. A beautiful scene did not move her with joy. Starry nights did not fill her with awe. Then it was discovered that Sally was very short-sighted and needed glasses. She had not been able to see what was around her, so her world and her life were restricted by her vision. Once she had glasses the world became a place full of wonder and beauty. She loved going out into the country to enjoy the scenery, to watch the birds and see the flowers. Once Sally saw more clearly, her whole world changed.

Second Sunday of Christmas

Aim

To encourage people to wonder at the mystery of Christmas.

Readings

Jeremiah 31:7-14 and Psalm 147:12-20
or Ecclesiasticus 24:1-12 and Wisdom 10:15-21
Ephesians 1:3-14
John 1: (1-9) 10-18

Thought for the day

It may be hard to realise from the readings that we are still giving thanks for Christmas. Yet all the readings are about God caring for his chosen people and coming to them as their Redeemer. They tell of the Word of God, or the Wisdom of God, taking flesh and dwelling among us. All of today's readings can be seen as songs of praise.

The reading from Ephesians is amazing in that it is all one sentence in the Greek. Here St Paul is pouring out his praise to God for caring for us and calling us. Notice how it starts, like many Jewish prayers of praise, saying, 'Blessed be God.'

It starts in a surprising way by telling us how God chose us before the world began. No, we did not choose God; he chose us (see John 15:16). He wants us to be part of his team! He wants us to be holy – that is, to belong to him – and he wants us to be blameless – without sin – before him in love (Ephesians 1, verses 3-4).

Out of his goodness and grace – for we do not deserve it – God wants us to be part of his family and to enjoy all the privileges of belonging with him as our Father, through Jesus Christ (verses 5-6).

In Jesus we have redemption; he has bought our freedom through his own death. He has ransomed us from death. Through him our sins are forgiven – not because we deserve this but through the riches of his grace that he has lavished upon us (verses 7-8).

God has made known to us the mystery of his will, to gather up all things in Christ. Divisions disappear and all are one in him, not absorbed but fulfilled in him (verses 9-10).

In Christ, because we are made part of God's family, we obtain an inheritance. In him we have heard the word, the Good News of salvation, and as an assurance of this we have received the Holy Spirit. As God's people let us live to praise his glory.

Wow! What a lot Paul packs into a sentence!

You could say John summarises this and says, 'And the Word became flesh and lived among us, and we have seen his glory, the glory as of a Father's only Son, full of grace and truth' (John 1:14).

Illustration

I get tired of letters through the door that say you have been especially chosen – I know that everyone is getting such a letter. Then it tells me I have won £10,000 – whoopee! But the small print says, 'if my number comes up', and the real chances of that are more than a million to one.

God is not like that. God's offer is not gifts (though he does offer us them); he offers himself to us in Jesus Christ our Lord. We do not deserve this; we cannot win it. God has chosen to give himself to us. All we have to do is accept his presence and his love.

The Epiphany

Aim

To show how the Christ was revealed to all nations.

Readings

Isaiah 60:1-6
Psalm 72:(1-9) 10-15
Ephesians 3:1-12
Matthew 2:1-12

Thought for the day

Many of the Jews believed that the Christ would only be for their own nation: they were the chosen people and no other. Yet throughout the Scriptures there are suggestions that the Christ was for all peoples. Today's readings are chosen to show this. Isaiah asks the Jews to arise and shine because their light has come and the glory of the Lord is risen upon them. Isaiah goes on to say that nations and kings will come to that light. He even says they will bring gifts of gold and frankincense (Isaiah 60:1, 3, 6). Psalm 72 also declares, 'All kings shall bow before him and all nations do him service' (verse 11).

St Paul declares how he was given a revelation to perceive that the Gentiles had become sharers in the promise of Christ through the Gospel (Ephesians 3:4). So, we, who are among the Gentiles, have access to God in boldness and confidence through Christ.

The fulfilment of the prophecy is seen in the coming of the wise men, who are Gentiles, to the Christ – they are the first of the rest of the world.

Illustration

The wise men were not all that wise because they went to the wrong place and the wrong person. They went to the capital, Jerusalem, and to King Herod. Fancy asking him, 'Where is he who is to be born King of the Jews?' Herod hadn't a clue but he knew who would know about the Messiah, about the Christ. He asked the chief priests and scribes. They told him, 'In Bethlehem in the land of Judah.' Lucky for the wise men it was only about seven miles away. Herod sent them off and told them to search diligently for the child and to tell him when they had found him. Fortunately, the wise men did not trust Herod or his interest in the Christ child.

We assume there were three because we are told of three gifts. We know that they were rich, foreign and wise, but we do not know that they were kings. The shepherds were ordinary Jews smelling of sheep and probably not able to read or write. These men were different indeed, almost in total contrast. It helps us to see God calls all peoples to come to him – rich and poor, the known and the stranger, simple and wise; all are invited to come to God.

First Sunday of Epiphany
The Baptism of Christ

Aim

To encourage people to think about the Holy Trinity.

Readings

Genesis 1:1-5
Psalm 29
Acts 19:1-7
Mark 1:4-11

Thought for the day

At the beginning of Creation we hear of the Creator, the word of God and the wind (Spirit) of God.

St Paul asked the disciples at Ephesus if they had received the Holy Spirit. They replied they were baptised by John the Baptist and had not heard of the Holy Spirit. Water baptism and repentance was not enough; they needed to be baptised in the name of the Lord Jesus and to receive the gift of the Holy Spirit.

Today many people are baptised in water but they are hardly aware that they are immersed in the presence of Father, Son and Holy Spirit. Such people are like the people Paul met at Ephesus. We need to see that our baptism in water is an outward, visible sign of our immersion in the presence of Father, Son and Holy Spirit. Each day we should rejoice that we are in the presence and power of Father, Son and Holy Spirit.

Jesus came to John to be baptised. He did not need to come to repent; he came to commit himself to the next stage of his life and mission. Jesus shared in our humanity and his baptism was part of his identification with us. Furthermore, it was a sign of approval and his anointing; he was now equipped for the task for which he came. The Spirit comes upon him and the voice of the Father is heard. Here we have a brief glimpse of the Holy Trinity. There is also a feeling that it is like the beginning of creation – a new world is about to begin. In the same way, the dove comes as it came to Noah after the flood destroyed the old world. Something new is about to happen.

Illustration

Have a nice mug, which is empty. Get people to admire it, tell them how beautiful it is – but it is useless unless it has something in it – it is no use empty! Only when it has something in it does it fulfil its purpose. People and their minds are the same: we are no use if we are empty.

Borrow a jacket or a fleece, lay it before you and admire it. How good it is for keeping out the cold. Now command it to raise an arm or to sit up straight. When it fails to act, say you know a secret way of getting it to do things. Now get the owner to put it on and raise an arm. The jacket is of no use unless it is occupied.

Nature abhors a vacuum – something will always fill an empty space. Let us be filled and immersed in Father, Son and Holy Spirit.

Second Sunday of Epiphany

Aim

To learn the value of listening.

Readings

1 Samuel 3:1-10 (11-20)
Psalm 139:1-6, 13-18
Revelation 5:1-10
John 1:43-51

Thought for the day

The story of Samuel at Shiloh illustrates how the Church must often appear. Eli represents the Church; he is old and losing his vision. The light in the church has almost gone out. The sons of the 'vicarage', Hophni and Phineas, are not interested in following in their father's footsteps. Into this situation is introduced a youngster and, as ever, he disturbs the church. Eli is trying to sleep. Samuel lies on his mattress listening to the sounds of the night. A voice calls. Samuel, who is about 12 years old, jumps up and wakes the old man Eli and says, 'You called.' Tired, Eli says, 'I did not call. Go back to bed, my son.' The Lord calls again, 'Samuel!' Once more Samuel jumps up and runs to Eli because he doesn't know it was the Lord who was calling. Again Eli says, 'I did not call. Go back to bed, my son.' It is not long before the Lord calls a third time. For a third time Samuel disturbs Eli. This old priest, his vision fading, is able to guide the young man and send him back to his room, saying, 'If he calls, you shall say, "Speak, Lord, for your servant is listening."'

The Church might be very old and find the young disturbing, but God speaks through new voices. At the same time the young will be lost without the guidance of the old.

Samuel heard the voice and said, 'Speak, Lord, for your servant is listening.' In this way God was able to speak to Samuel and *through* Samuel.

The reading from Revelation suggests that through Christ we will learn of the deep secrets of God.

In the Gospel, Philip heard Jesus say, 'Follow me.' He responded immediately by going and telling Nathaniel that he had found the one who fulfilled the law and the prophets – that is, the Christ. Nathaniel nearly did not listen to Philip because of prejudice, saying, 'Nothing good can come out of Nazareth!' Philip invited him to come and see.

Illustration

Hello!
Are you receiving me?
Hello!
Are you receiving me?
Hello!
Are you receiving me?

This was a conversation, if you can call it that, on a mobile phone. The person was in a bad reception area. There was too much interference from hills and trees. They would have to go to a better reception area.

It is amazing how many people and nations are good at speaking but find it very hard to hear anyone. Our speakers (mouths) seem to be far more active than our receivers (ears). A proverb from the East says, 'God gave us two ears and one mouth so that we should listen twice as much as we speak.'

Third Sunday of Epiphany

Aim

To show that miracles are mysteries and signs of the kingdom.

Readings

Genesis 14:17-20
Psalm 128
Revelation 19:6-10
John 2:1-11

Thought for the day

All of today's readings are full of mystery. There is King Melchizedek who meets Abram and brings him bread and wine; Revelation invites us to the marriage supper of the Lamb.

We will concentrate on the Gospel and, according to St John, the first miracle of Jesus.

Miracles are wonderful events that we cannot fully explain – if we could, they would not be miracles. We are to see each miracle as a sign of the kingdom of heaven and the kingship of Christ.

The first miracle is a joyful occasion for it is a wedding. For the people who lived in Cana, weddings were usually held on a Wednesday evening. The couple would wear wedding robes and crowns on their heads. They would be treated like a king and a queen. This might be the greatest celebration of their life. They would be led home by torchbearers filling the street with light. A canopy would be carried over their heads, just like royalty. They would not go away for a honeymoon but would have 'open house' and a party, which would last for a week! That would take a lot of planning. There would be lots of guests and they would all wash their hands and their feet when they came to the house. There were large water jars outside for this purpose.

Jesus, his mother and disciples were at the party. It is thought that the bride or groom might have been a relative of Jesus. Cana was near Nazareth where Jesus lived.

There was singing and dancing and all were enjoying themselves. Suddenly Mary said to Jesus, 'They have no wine.' The party was not meant to end but soon it would be over. The wine had run out. The bride and groom would be embarrassed for they had run out of resources.

Jesus looked at the six big water jars that had been used for washing. Each jar held between 20 and 30 gallons. Jesus said to the servants, 'Fill the water pots.' They filled them right to the top. 'Now,' said Jesus, 'take some to the steward who is in charge.' They obeyed Jesus again. When the steward tasted the water it had become wine. He called the bridegroom and said, 'Everyone serves good wine first. But you have kept the best until now.' He did not know of the miracle; only the servants knew. You can imagine the surprise of the groom. The party could go on and people could enjoy themselves.

Illustration

Have you ever heard of Dracula? Dracula is supposed to come when you are asleep and drain away your life. When you wake up in the morning you are at least half dead. It is not a true story but sometimes we can wake exhausted; we can feel we have no energy. Human resources do run out. Our batteries need recharging; we need to be refreshed and renewed.

When we feel we have reached the bottom of the barrel we need outside help. There are times when we are unable to help ourselves but Jesus is able to help us. In John 10:10, Jesus says, 'I came that they may have life, and have it abundantly.' You can trace this giving of abundant life, and how Jesus meets various needs and losses of well-being, in John's Gospel:

Need more wine – 2:1-11
Loss of well-being – 4:46-54
Lack strength – 5:2-9
Lack energy (food) – 6:1-14
Lack of security and safety – 6:16-21
Lack of vision and light – 9:1-7
Loss of life – 11:1-44

Jesus meets our drained resources with his generosity and power.

Fourth Sunday of Epiphany

Aim

To continue to show signs of the Christ.

Readings

Deuteronomy 18:15-20
Psalm 111
Revelation 12:1-5a
Mark 1:21-28

Thought for the day

The people of Israel recognised the dangers of approaching such a powerful person as God. Being too close made them aware of their sinfulness and their mortality. They feared both the voice of God and the fire. They asked that someone stood between them and God. As light reveals darkness, so the presence of God can reveal our weakness and sinfulness.

If there is any evil in the world, and I am sure there is, we should expect it to cry out against or oppose goodness. Evil and God cannot exist side by side.

In Mark's Gospel we are shown Jesus at the beginning of his campaign. Jesus has received the Father's approval at his baptism. He has been tested by the devil and chosen the way he will take. Disciples have been selected. Now he must begin his campaign. As you might expect, we hear of his beginning in a church. People recognised a personal authority. But there was also opposition. The Church is made up of humans; it is not perfect, and it needs salvation. The man with the unclean spirit shouts out, 'What have you to do with us, Jesus of Nazareth? Have you come to destroy us? I know who you are, the Holy One of God.' Whatever you make of 'unclean spirits', for Jesus here is opposition. It is worth noting that the unclean spirits recognise Jesus; they know him. Knowing of Jesus is not enough. We are called to love him and obey him.

Here was confrontation, a testing time for Jesus. Talk is all right, but can Jesus produce the action to go with his words? There was even more at stake, for most believed that demons were so powerful that only God could cast them out. Did Jesus have the power? Jesus showed that even his words were powerful enough. It was not the man but the evil spirit Jesus addressed: 'Be silent and come out of him.' This was not a request but a command, and the spirit came howling out of the man.

The people were amazed. This was a new teaching with authority ('Whose authority?' we must ask). He commands even evil spirits and they obey him. (Surely only God can do that!)

We may find it hard to believe in evil spirits, yet there are many people who struggle against evil and disease, and have the feeling they are not dealing with something passive but with a cunning and resourceful enemy.

Jesus began his ministry in the synagogue at Capernaum and immediately his fame spread throughout all Galilee. But only some will see the signs pointing to Jesus as the Son of God.

Illustration

Show an array of lights.

An ordinary lamp is useful when the sun goes down for it helps us to see around the house in the dark. A torch is useful for it is the sort of light you can carry around with you and use whenever you need it. Laser light is used in hospitals for surgery and it is also used as a military weapon – laser always has to be used with great care. A security light is good to welcome you home and also to show up any intruders. People who like to sneak about in the dark do not like security lights – especially if linked with a burglar alarm.

The greatest light we have is the sun. Without the sun all life on earth would perish. We need the sun to survive. We also need it to see where we are going. Yet we cannot look directly at the sun and sometimes we cannot even stay in the sunshine without some protection.

In the same way, we cannot behold the full glory of God but Jesus reveals God to us.

The Presentation of Christ

Aim

To rejoice in the Light of Christ.

Readings

Malachi 3:1-5
Psalm 24:(1-6) 7-10
Hebrews 2:14-18
Luke 2:22-40

Thought for the day

Forty days after the birth of Jesus, Joseph and Mary went to Jerusalem to give thanks in the Temple for the birth of Jesus. By Jewish law, Mary could not enter a holy place or touch anything holy until she had given thanks to God for her child. They brought the traditional offering of a pair of doves.

In the Temple there was a man called Simeon. He was a righteous and devout man. It had been revealed to him by the Holy Spirit that he would not die before he had seen the Lord's Messiah – that is, the Christ. It was no coincidence that he was in the Temple. The Holy Spirit guided him. He came into the Temple exactly when Mary and Joseph brought in Jesus.

Archbishop William Temple said, 'When I pray coincidences happen; when I do not pray they do not happen.' Obviously prayer opened his eyes and enlightened him.

Simeon took Jesus in his arms and said the words we call the 'Nunc Dimittis', which is the beginning of his prayer in Latin. Simeon would now be happy to die, for he had seen the salvation of God in the child Jesus. He saw Jesus as a light that would lighten the nations of the world and someone who would bring glory to Israel. It is this image of Jesus as the Light of the World that we celebrate today with lighted candles. By tradition this is the fortieth and last day of the Christmas season, as we turn towards Lent. Some churches have lit a Christmas candle at every service until today. As this is the last day, everyone has been given a candle to light from the Christmas candle and processes around the church. This is to rejoice in Christ as the Light of the World.

Simeon blessed the family and warned them that there would be opposition to Jesus. They had hardly time to be amazed at all of this when Anna, an 84-year-old widow, came and gave thanks to God for Jesus. She was a prophet and told how Jesus was the Redeemer. Here, in the holiest place of Israel, Jesus was welcomed as the Light and the Redeemer by these two people.

Illustration

The illustration today is one of action. We will look to the candle that represents Christ in our midst and we will ask the light of Christ to shine in our lives. Then we will come forward during the singing of a hymn and receive a light. (If this is difficult, photocopy templates of candles and people can come forward and receive one of these candles.)

Have a short silence, then pray:

> Blessed are you, Lord our God,
> for you have called us out of darkness
> into your bright light.
> You have called us to be children of light.
> May the brightness of your presence
> scatter all the darkness that is within us and about us.
> Grant that the lights that we receive
> may remind us of your light
> and of your love towards us,
> Jesus Christ our Lord.
> Amen.

Let everyone come the shortest way to the Christ candle and walk back by going right around the inside of the church.

Sing the hymn 'Walk in the light'.

Let the leader say, 'Receive this light and shine as lights in the world.'

Let the candles remain lit as long as is practical. You can say, 'The Christmas season is ended. We now turn towards Lent and Easter.'

Proper 1

Sunday between 3 and 9 February inclusive
(if earlier than the Second Sunday before Lent)

Aim

To show the need for prayer.

Readings

Isaiah 40:21-31
Psalm 147:1-12, 20c
1 Corinthians 9:16-23
Mark 1:29-39

Thought for the day

Isaiah tells us that God is Almighty; that he gives power to the faint and strengthens the weary. There is no doubt of God's power and that he knows all that he has made. Then we are told 'those who wait for the Lord shall renew their strength'. We should all take these words to heart.

The psalm tells us though the Lord knows all the stars he is still concerned for us and heals the broken-hearted, and has pleasure in those who await his gracious favour. It would be good if we knew this in our lives.

In Mark's first chapter we get a glimpse of how busy Jesus was. On the day of rest he went to the synagogue. He taught with authority and healed the man who had an unclean spirit. At mid-day he went home with Simon Peter. Here Simon's mother-in-law had taken ill and was lying down with a burning fever. Jesus went to her and took her by the hand and raised her up. How many people does Jesus, the risen Lord, still take by the hand and help them to rise? Peter's mother-in-law immediately feels well and looks after her guests. There are two things to notice here. First, Peter is obviously married. The second is that the ministry of Jesus often depended on the care of such noble women as Peter's mother-in-law.

As it was the Sabbath, movement was restricted. When the sun went down a new day began. Because there were no clocks, it was said to be evening when three stars could be seen in the sky or when the last rays of sunlight had gone. The people waited patiently but were anxious not to miss Jesus. As soon as it was dark the streets were full of people coming to see Jesus and bringing the sick and indisposed with them. Often, in history, people come out of the darkness to him who is the Light of the World. It looked as if the whole of Capernaum had come out. Jesus must have looked after people well into the night and was probably exhausted.

Like any sensible person, Jesus knew he could not go on pouring out his energies without being renewed and refreshed. He needed new power. So, we are told, 'while it was still dark he got up and went out to a deserted place and prayed'. His ministry could only continue if he maintained a constant link with the Father. We often lack power and energy because we seek to go in our own strength. Remember the words of Isaiah: 'Those who wait for the Lord shall renew their strength.'

Jesus put himself out to get up extra early. Then he sought a place where he would have a time of quiet, and there he prayed. If Jesus felt the need to do this, there must be something wrong in our lives if we do not make time to pray.

Illustration

It is not often you see one of these in church – a battery charger. Sometimes, even when there is fuel in the tank, the engine will not start. This is because there is no spark, no electricity to fire the engine. Then you need the battery charger. It will slowly revive the flat battery and give it new life. Then we will be able to get going again. Also a car cannot run for long without being refuelled. You need to fill it up regularly with petrol. The more miles you do, the more petrol you need.

Some of you may have battery chargers at home to charge up batteries for CD players or other things that need electricity to keep them going. Many modern torches come with a charger so that the battery can produce a bright light.

Sometimes people are a bit like a beautiful car with a full tank of petrol but a flat battery. They should be able to do all sorts but they are flat and dull or feeling run down. So many seem to lack a bright spark in their lives. When this is so, we need power from outside ourselves. Listen again to Isaiah: 'Those who wait for the Lord shall renew their strength.'

Proper 2

Sunday between 10 and 16 February inclusive
(if earlier than the Second Sunday before Lent)

Aim

To show that Jesus cares for the lonely, rejected and outcast.

Readings

2 Kings 5:1-14
Psalm 30
1 Corinthians 9:24-27
Mark 1:40-45

Thought for the day

Leprosy was the most terrible of diseases and still can be. It was often wrongly diagnosed and people were sent into exile when they could have stayed at home. At its worst, parts of the body would drop off. You could lose fingers or toes, even whole hands and feet.

Almost as bad as the illness was the isolation. If you became a leper you were forced to leave your home and loved ones. You had to go and live in wild and lonely places. Lepers were not allowed into towns or cities. If a leper popped his head through a door, the house became unclean. No one was allowed to touch a leper. The leper had to keep at least two metres away and shout, 'Unclean'. If the wind was blowing towards you, the leper had to keep over 50 metres away. If a leper disobeyed this rule, the leper could be put to death. Being a leper was a lonely and sad life. The only people you could meet up with were other lepers.

The leper in today's Gospel was desperate. He came close to Jesus. It would seem he trusted Jesus and was confident that Jesus could heal him. The disciples probably held their noses and pulled away. In faith, the leper said to Jesus, 'If you choose, you can make me clean.' Jesus had the power of life or death over this man. As ever, Jesus came to give life. Jesus touched him and said, 'I do choose. Be made clean.' No doubt the touch was as important as the words; Jesus often made actual physical contact with people. Jesus was more concerned for the man than the law. He wanted the man to know he was touchable and lovable.

Illustration

There was a lady who lived off the west coast of Scotland on one of the islands, the island of Harris, and she had leprosy. She was forced to live alone on the seashore, where she lived off plants and shellfish. She bathed in the liquid off the shellfish and plants. All her flesh became healed and without leprosy. She praised Jesus in these words:

There is no plant in the ground
but is full of his virtue.
There is no form in the strand
but is full of his blessing.
Jesu! Jesu! Jesu!
Jesu! meet it were to praise him.

There is no life in the sea,
there is no creature in the river,
there is naught in the firmament,
but proclaims his goodness.
Jesu! Jesu! Jesu!
Jesu! meet it were to praise him.

There is no bird on the wing,
there is no star in the sky,
there is nothing beneath the sun,
but proclaims his goodness.
Jesu! Jesu! Jesu!
Jesu! meet it were to praise him.

Proper 3

Sunday between 17 and 23 February inclusive (if earlier than the Second Sunday before Lent)

Aim

To show our God is a healing and forgiving God.

Readings

Isaiah 43:18-25
Psalm 41
2 Corinthians 1:18-22
Mark 2:1-12

Thought for the day

In the mind of the Jews at the time of Jesus there was a definite link between illness and sinfulness. If you were ill it was because God was punishing you for your sins. God was a stern God who often punished his people. Jesus came to show that God has always been a loving and forgiving God. A parent may not like what a child is doing but the parent will still love the child. God hates sin but it does not stop him loving the sinner. This love is a free gift; it is the grace and goodness of God towards us. We cannot earn this gift but we need to learn to accept it.

In the reading from Isaiah, God tells the people to realise he is active now and is doing new things. There will be rivers flowing in what was a desert. Though his people had forgotten him and sinned against him, God will forgive them and not hold their past sins against them.

The Psalmist asks God for forgiveness and healing; the two go together.

We are told Jesus was 'at home' in Capernaum, but at whose home? Was it Peter's or even the home of the writer of this Gospel? We are not told, but Jesus is at home. Are you sure Jesus is at home in your house?

Here in Capernaum Jesus healed the man in the synagogue, Simon's mother-in-law, and all those who came to him once the Sabbath was over. It is not surprising that crowds came again for teaching and healing. This time there were some scribes keeping an eye on Jesus and making sure he did the right thing.

Four men brought a paralysed friend to Jesus. When their way was barred by the crowds, they struggled on to the roof and broke through the plaster and brush wood. (Remember, the houses had flat roofs and outside stairs up to them.) Then they lowered the man. It is a wonderful action to bring people to Jesus.

Jesus looked at the man and said, 'Son, your sins are forgiven.' I am sure the man hoped for more but perhaps this had to be said first. The Scribes were annoyed because only God can forgive sins. Who did this Jesus think he was? Jesus could see what they were thinking and turned to the paralysed man and said, 'I say to you, stand up, take your mat and go to your home.' With those few words Jesus healed the paralysed man. If sin is portrayed as illness, surely if the man was healed he was also forgiven. This is another sign, a pointer to who Jesus really is. The people glorified God and said, 'We have never seen anything like this.' Let us be sure we have come before Jesus and found forgiveness and healing.

Illustration

Everybody sing 'Now, every morning is the love'; we need to take it to heart. Read verse 1. We are here awake and alive due to the love of God. During the night we have been refreshed and restored in our powers.

Read verse 2. This verse can change our lives if we take it to heart. 'New perils past': some of the things we feared yesterday did not happen or were not half as bad as we thought. 'New sins forgiven': you need to accept this. What wrongs you did before today are forgiven as long as you intend to lead a new life. You need not carry a great load of guilt around with you; guilt does not change the past but forgiveness changes the future. In the grace and goodness of God you are given a new day – learn to live it. Do not drag old sins and guilt around with you, for they will hamper your life. Start the day anew. Give thanks for the love and the healing power of God in your life. Know you are 'ransomed, healed, forgiven'. Start each day in the presence of God and with new hope in your heart: 'new thoughts of God, new hopes of heaven'.

Second Sunday before Lent

Aim

To show that Jesus Christ was with the Father before the foundation of the world.

Readings

Proverbs 8:1, 22-31
Psalm 104:25-35
Colossians 1:15-20
John 1:1-14

Thought for the day

Today's readings are telling us that Jesus was there before the creation of the world and working with the Father. John's Gospel starts with the same words as Genesis: 'In the beginning'. Genesis says, 'In the beginning God . . .' and John says, 'In the beginning was the Word, and the Word was with God, and the Word was God.' Not only was Jesus present but Jesus shared in the creation: 'all things came into being through him . . . in him was life and the life was the light of men' (John 1:3-4).

Not only was Christ there, but we are actually in him. All creation is in him, as it is in the Father and the Holy Spirit. Paul in Colossians says of Christ, 'In him all things in heaven and on earth were created.' This is a great mystery, which we will never fully understand with our minds, but we can know it with our hearts. We need to rejoice in God and need to know in our hearts that we are never outside of him.

Illustration

There is a fountain in India with fish around it. On the fountain are words by the Indian poet Kabir: 'I laugh if I hear the fish in the sea are thirsty. I laugh if I hear man goes in search of God.'

Just think of a little fish living in a mighty ocean being told its whole life depends on water. One morning it sets out to find water. It leaves its home and travels to cold seas but it cannot find water there. It then travels south to warmer climes, still seeking, but it cannot see water there. It searches all of the seas and all this time it is restless and weary, spending much of its energy. At last it meets an old fish on the seabed and asks, 'Where is the water for I would like some?' 'Do you not know you live in the water, you move in the water, you only exist because of the water? There is no need to look for it, you are in it. If you did not have it you would die. Enjoy being in it; know that it is all around you.' This was wonderful news; there was no need to seek but there was a chance to enjoy the element in which it lived.

St Paul, when he was speaking about God to the Greeks on the Areopagus, says, 'In him we live and move and have our being' (Acts 17:28). This is a wonderful reality to discover: we need not seek God for we are in God, in his presence and in his love. Let us enjoy this reality.

Sunday before Lent

Aim

To show that Jesus is the Son of God and fulfils the longings of the law and the prophets.

Readings

2 Kings 2:1-12
Psalm 50:1-6
2 Corinthians 4:3-6
Mark 9:2-9

Thought for the day

A week before the events in today's Gospel the disciples were at Caesarea Philippi. It was there that Peter had confessed Jesus as the 'Christ' and there that Jesus told them of the suffering ahead. Perhaps there was a need for some of the disciples at least to see some brightness behind the dark clouds that threatened.

Jesus took Peter, James and John up a mountainside for them to be alone. Tradition says this was Mount Tabor but this is a good way from Caesarea Philippi and it has a fortress on the top. It is more likely to have been Mount Hermon. Maybe they even went up to the snow line.

What happened on the mountain was an experience the disciples could not put into words. They became aware of the radiance of Jesus and of the presence of Moses and Elijah. In Jesus they were aware that all that Moses and Elijah had hoped for was fulfilled. Like Moses, Jesus would bring his people to the freedom of the Promised Land. He would give them a new way of life and free them from slavery. Elijah was said to be the greatest of the prophets. Now, in Jesus, all the hopes of the prophets were to be fulfilled. In the Christ is the second Moses and the second Elijah whom the people of God longed for. Such a vision would carry the disciples a long way, but there was more: the cloud that overshadowed them was hiding the presence of the Father. God was there in his fullness but for their sake his glory had to be hidden. As God had appeared to Moses in the cloud, now he was present on this mountain. Then there was the voice from the cloud saying, 'This is my Son, the Beloved, listen to him!'

Then the vision faded and they descended the mountain and made their way to Jerusalem. But they had been there; they had a glimpse of the glory of God as revealed in Jesus Christ.

We are offered a glimpse of this glory as we turn towards Lent and the events of Holy Week. We are also asked to 'Listen to him!' Listening also means obeying.

Listen again to the words of St Paul:

> For it is the God who said,
> 'Let light shine out of darkness',
> who has shone in our hearts
> to give the light of the knowledge of the glory of God
> in the face of Jesus Christ.
> *2 Corinthians 4:6*

Even when the vision faded the disciples had their eyes fixed on looking at Jesus. We seek in the days ahead to look at Jesus and to get a glimpse of the glory of God.

Illustration

The day before the civil rights campaigner Martin Luther King was killed by a sniper's bullet he said words of encouragement to a large crowd:

> We've got difficult days ahead. But it does not matter to me now. Because I have been to the mountain top, I won't mind. Like anyone else I would like to live a long life . . . but I am not concerned about that now. I just want to do God's will. And he's allowed me to go up the mountain. And I have looked over and seen the Promised Land. So I am happy tonight, I am not fearing any man. Mine eyes have seen the glory of the coming of the Lord.

Like Martin Luther King, if we are to survive dark days, we need to have a vision of the glory of our God.

First Sunday of Lent

Aim

To encourage a positive approach to Lent.

Readings

Genesis 9:8-17
Psalm 25:1-10
1 Peter 3:18-22
Mark 1:9-15

Thought for the day

You may have noticed a colour change in some of the things in church. We have changed to purple or Lent array for this new season, which began on Ash Wednesday. There are forty days in Lent to remind us of the forty days Jesus spend in the wilderness. Lent is a time when we look at our priorities and make sure we are on the right track: it is about trying to truly be the people of God. Lent is not so much a negative time as a positive time when we check that we are not going astray. It can partly be summed up in today's Psalm: 'Show me your ways, O Lord, and teach me your paths'(Psalm 25:4).

In the Gospel we hear of the baptism of Jesus, the descent of the Spirit and the voice of God. It would seem all is wonderful but immediately the same Spirit drives him into the wilderness. It is his own abilities and talents that will tempt Jesus. Remember temptation is not wicked: temptation is about choice and decision. Wickedness only gets the upper hand if we take the lower road and miss our target. Being lazy or a couch potato when we have so much ability is wicked.

Temptation helps us to strengthen in our purpose and choose a better way of living. Sin is when we lower our aims, choose a way without God and when we live below our potential.

In the wilderness Satan tempted Jesus. Satan means the adversary, the one who is against us. At this stage the temptations of Jesus come from within. Another word for Satan is 'Diabolos' which means 'that which throws apart' or 'that which is divisive'. Quite often it is when we do not make up our mind or commit our heart that we are defeated. For Jesus the time for decision and commitment had come. In the wilderness Jesus would ask of himself, 'Who am I? What am I called to do? How will I do it?'

Mark tells us that Jesus was with wild beasts: this could be leopards, lions, bears, jackals or snakes. All these creatures are signs of danger but perhaps Mark was thinking of the prophecy of Isaiah 11:6-9, which said that in the times of the Messiah all animals will live in harmony and peace.

Mark also mentions the ministration of angels. Whenever we are tempted, troubled or distressed we are not alone, divine help is at hand: our God is with us.

Illustration

Some people say they like doing what comes naturally. A man let his garden grow naturally and when asked why it was a mess he said, 'I was leaving it to God.' God will not do for us what he has given us the ability to do. If you want a good garden or a good life, you have to work at it. With the garden, if you want flowers it is no use filling the beds with vegetables. You will get out what you put in. You will get more, for you will also get weeds. If you leave your life to run itself, it will also produce weeds. Gardens and life need regular tender loving care.

Lent is a time for looking at what you have and making improvements.

In the garden some plants need splitting to give them more room to grow. You can often give away the extra to someone else. If you do not divide some plants, they will choke themselves. If we do not learn to give, we will do the same. Make room for the new in your life.

There is a constant need to weed and also to prune. Get rid of what hampers growth. Cut back on what has become rank and is taking over.

Learn to work in relationship with the soil and the climate. Learn to work in relationship with God.

Nothing is achieved without effort, without practice, without learning. If you want a good garden you have to give it priority over other things and the same is true of life.

Second Sunday of Lent

Aim

To encourage people to be faithful to their Lord.

Readings

Genesis 17:1-7, 15-16
Psalm 22:23-31
Romans 4:13-25
Mark 8:31-38

Thought for the day

Have you ever played 'Follow the leader'? It is fun when the leader is doing nice things and safe things, but you have to think twice if the leader starts to do things that are dangerous.

Jesus called the disciples to follow him. They left their homes and their work and went around the country with Jesus. It was a wonderful time of miracles and crowds following him. Life was a great adventure. When they were sitting around a campfire one evening, Jesus asked them if they knew who he really was. After a while Peter said, 'We know that you are the Anointed One of God. You are the Christ.' Peter was very excited about this because he believed Jesus was very popular and powerful. But Jesus warned them of the troubles ahead. He told them the elders, the chief priests and the scribes would reject him and that he would be killed. Jesus did not want to be killed but he knew if he did God's work he would face opposition. He knew that evil is always against goodness. Peter would not believe it. He took Jesus aside and told him it could not be so. Jesus wished it was not so but he knew trouble lay ahead. Peter was trying to persuade him to run away or hide or go somewhere else. Peter did this because he loved Jesus. Jesus saw that Satan was using Peter's love to tempt him. He spoke very strongly to his friend and said, 'Get behind me, Satan! For you are setting your mind not on divine things but on human.' We have to be careful that our friends do not lead us astray from what God wants us to do. Sometimes they cannot understand that we need to be willing to give up all to follow our Lord.

Jesus did not promise that following him would be easy. He said there would be times when we would have to deny even our own desires. If we are following the crucified one, we too have to take up our cross. Jesus knew that some things are lost by being kept to ourselves. We lose the ability to play the piano or to do well at sport if we do not practise. Practice means denying ourselves the time to go out whenever we feel like it. To follow Jesus means discipline. There can be no discipling without discipline.

Illustration

When Columbanus wanted to go and serve God as a monk his mother was not pleased. She loved him dearly and was afraid that he was wasting his life. He had lots of talent and ability. He could be someone very important in Ireland. She talked to him and tried to dissuade him, but he knew God was calling him to leave home and serve him in a monastery. His mother tried all sorts of ways to stop him. Though she loved him dearly, she was acting for Satan. Columbanus got ready to go. His mother went to the door of the house and lay down in the doorway to stop him. Columbanus was very sorry to see his mother do this, but he carefully stepped over her and went to serve God wherever God called him. In time, Columbanus did wonderful work for God in France and Italy. For a moment it would have been easy to give in and stay at home.

Third Sunday of Lent

Aim

To show we are accountable for our actions.

Readings

Exodus 20:1-17
Psalm 19
1 Corinthians 1:18-25
John 2:13-22

Thought for the day

It was about mid-April. Jesus went to the holiest place in the Holy City: the Temple in Jerusalem. It was a very special place where God promised to be present. It was the time of the Passover when the people celebrated God delivering them from slavery and the beginning of the journey to the Promised Land. Every Jewish male who lived within 15 miles of Jerusalem was obliged to attend the feast. The aim of every Jew is to spend at least one Passover in Jerusalem. It is thought there could be anything from a quarter of a million to two million Jews attending the Temple over eight days.

Every Jew over the age of 19, including Jesus, would have to pay the Temple tax, so that the services and the sacrifices could continue. Each had to pay half a shekel, which was about two days' pay. This had to be paid in Temple shekels or Jewish shekels; other currencies were seen as unclean. As pilgrims came from all over the known world, in the Temple Courts there were moneychangers. If trade had been straightforward, there would have been no objection. But this is what Jesus saw: the exchange rate was extortionate. For the exchange to the shekel people were being charged a whole day's wage or 50 per cent profit. Outside, doves could be bought for about a day's wage; inside they were being sold for almost twenty times as much. In the name of religion people were being cheated; this was extortion. It seemed no one spoke against this injustice. It made Jesus really angry that the Church was being used like a robbers' den. Jesus made a whip and drove the sheep and the oxen out of the Temple, overthrew the tables and poured the money out.

There are times when it is right and necessary to be angry. Jesus was angry against the evil being done in the name of the Church. Evil often triumphs because good people are afraid to speak out. When we hear of people being driven out of their homes, or the great rain forests being destroyed, we should be angry and we should act. When we hear of the loss of animal species through greed and carelessness, we should act. It was because he was angry with the slave trade that William Wilberforce acted and brought about its abolition.

Illustration

There was a farmer who planned to go to France for his holidays. As he would be driving on the Continent he decided to get some practice in. He started to drive on the right-hand side of the road and to go around roundabouts anticlockwise. To say the least, he caused all sorts of trouble and had one or two close accidents. He was finally stopped by the police and charged with dangerous driving. He had broken dozens of rules in the Highway Code, and that mattered because it is written for the well-being and safety of us all. We need rules to protect us and to help us to get the best out of life. Rules are not to restrict us as much as to give us the greatest freedom within certain parameters.

What if there were no rules in a game of football? You could have as many people as you like on your team. You could pick up the ball and run or even take it home! You could make the goal-posts narrower than the football so that no one could score. But you would not have a game; you would have chaos. We need rules and standards to enjoy living together in community.

Jesus was angry with the moneychangers because they were being unjust. They were using their privileged position to make unfair demands. They were robbing people in the name of God. Jesus could not turn a blind eye. He had to act. He had to show that what was being done was not right and needed to be changed. Perhaps on a larger scene Jesus was already hinting that the time for animal sacrifices had come to an end and that a great sacrifice was about to be made in his own crucifixion.

Fourth Sunday of Lent
Mothering Sunday

Aim

To help us to appreciate the love that is given to us through our mother.

Readings

Exodus 2:1-10 or 1 Samuel 1:20-28
Psalm 34:11-20 or Psalm 127:1-4
2 Corinthians 1:3-7 or Colossians 3:12-17
Luke 2:33-35 or John 19:25b-27

Thought for the day

Whichever set of readings you use today, they have something in common. What do Moses, Samuel and Jesus have in common? The clue is in the readings. Like us, they all have a mother. Each has a mother who loves them and wants to care for them. The mother of Moses had to hide him from the cruelty of Pharaoh. If she had not done this, Moses would not have survived and all of history would be changed. For three months the mother of Moses fed him, cared for him and hid him from the soldiers, all at a risk to her own life, because she loved him. This brave woman changed the pattern of history and yet hardly anyone knows her name. Does anyone here know the name of the mother of Moses? She was called Jochebed (see Exodus 6:20, Numbers 26:59). She saved another son from Pharaoh and his name was Aaron. Jochebed and her daughter Miriam were brave women who risked their lives because of their love.

Who knows the name of Samuel's mother? She was called Hannah. For a long time Hannah thought she could not have children and it made her sad. One year when she was praying at the Temple church at Shiloh, she told the priest Eli of her troubles. He told her that she would have a child. When her baby was born Hannah called him Samuel, which means 'asked of the Lord'. Samuel was an answer to her prayers. As God gave her a child, she promised when he was old enough she would give him to the Lord. So she took him to the old priest Eli and let Samuel work for him and for God.

Without Mary saying 'Yes' to God, Jesus could not have been born. Because of Mary and her obedience to God, the Saviour was able to come into the world. Mary was amazed at the things that were said about Jesus when he was still a baby. She was warned that she would suffer because he would suffer. We learn in a family when one person suffers all share in the pain: mothers often suffer deeply for their children. It is not just sleepless nights and giving time and attention; it is the pain in a mother's heart at the suffering of her child. When Mary stood by the cross and saw the suffering of her son it must have caused her tremendous pain.

Today we rejoice in the love of our mother. We give thanks for her constant care and grace. Let us make sure that today our mother knows that we appreciate what she has done and is doing for us.

Illustration

By tradition this middle Sunday in Lent was a time when young children who had left home to work in a big house or on a farm were allowed home for the first time in the year. Lots of children had to work for very low wages, sometimes only their keep, and it was very hard. They missed their homes and the care of their mother. At home much had been done for them. Now they had to look after themselves. It was lovely to come home and be looked after and loved. Usually the children had little they could bring as they had little. They may have been allowed to make a cake. More often they would bring a posy of flowers they picked on the way. Perhaps the first time they had thought of giving their mother flowers and saying 'Thank you' for all that their mother had done for them. It is very easy to take our mother for granted and not notice all the work she does for us. She does this work freely, gratis, out of her own grace and goodness. What most of us learn about love, grace and goodness has its foundation in our own homes.

Do you know how much a cup of tea or coffee costs in a café? How much is a meal? What would it cost you to hire a servant to clean for you? Our mother does all this out of love. We should show we appreciate all she does and that we are truly grateful. We should never take our mother for granted or make her work more difficult. As we grow we should know we have a share in that work, because as she loves us, we love her.

Fifth Sunday of Lent

Aim

To look at the Passion of Christ and beyond to the resurrection.

Readings

Jeremiah 31:31-34
Psalm 51:1-12 or Psalm 119:9-16
Hebrews 5:5-10
John 12:20-33

Thought for the day

Philip told Andrew about some Greeks wanting to see Jesus. Andrew in his usual fashion brings them to Jesus. Here were seekers who were not Jews coming to meet the Saviour. It was an exciting moment. Jesus increases the excitement by saying, 'The hour has come for the Son of Man to be glorified.' The disciples would see this as the coming of the promised kingdom of God. This was exciting indeed. So the next words came as a shock as Jesus started to talk of death. He told them how troubled his soul was. Like any human being he did not want to die. He was only 33 years old; he did not seek out death. But he came to do whatever was the will of the Father.

On this Sunday we turn to look at the Passion of Christ in more detail and this will continue until his death on Good Friday. For grains of wheat to grow, their burial is necessary. Only by death comes new life. If we hide the grain in a box to keep it safe and secure, it will be useless. Only when it is put in the cold earth can it rise to new life. Only by giving it away to the earth can we receive a good return.

Often we seek comfort and safety. We avoid conflict or having to put ourselves out. We look after ourselves. Jesus tells us that anyone who hoards their life or their talent will lose it. It is no use just surviving; we need to live life to the full. This will involve risk and danger. But of life it can be said: 'Use it or lose it.'

Bearing in mind what the world did to Jesus, whoever wants to serve him must realise they will not escape from similar troubles.

Today we end with a vision of the future. When Jesus has triumphed over the rulers of this world. 'When I am lifted up from the earth, I will draw all people to myself.' Looking back through two millennia, we can see how the cross has drawn all nations to come before him. We come to him who understands our suffering, who has borne our grief and our sins. We come to him who has triumphed over evil and through death opened to us the way to eternal life.

Illustration

Lazy Jack was given a sack of grain. His task was to sow the seed for the village so that they would have a harvest in the autumn. Jack looked at the seed. It was golden and beautiful. He thought it would be a shame to bury it in the ground. So he took it home and put it in a cupboard. No one knew that he had not sown the seed. Jack took it easy. It was only later in the year when there were no shoots, no signs of new wheat growing, that the village realised there was something wrong. Obviously the seed was not in the ground. After a search they found it in Lazy Jack's cupboard. The mice had eaten some, but most of it was still intact. Jack had almost allowed a community to starve by not sowing the seed. Like much in our lives, it was a case of use it or lose it. The villagers put the seed in the ground – it was late for sowing but they trusted in the power within the seed to grow and it did. In the end nothing was lost and the harvest was good.

Palm Sunday

Aim

To share in the joy of the triumphal entry into Jerusalem, and in the sorrow for the events that followed.

Readings

Liturgy of the Palms
Mark 11:1-11 or John 12:12-16
Psalm 118: 1, 2, 19-29

Liturgy of the Passion
Isaiah 50:4-9a
Psalm 31:9-16
Philippians 2:5-11
Mark 14:1–15:47 or Mark 15:1-39 (40-47)

Let the dramatic readings of the Passion narratives replace the sermon today. Allow the Scriptures to speak for themselves. Use as many people as possible to share in the readings. I have provided ideas for the Liturgy of the Palms rather than comment on the Passion: I hope Holy Week will be used to do that.

Thought for the day

It would seem that Jesus had planned ahead for this visit to Jerusalem. The donkey was where Jesus said and the password 'The Lord needs it' would allow the disciples to take it. The fact that the colt had never been ridden made it especially suitable for religious purposes. The cart on which the ark of the Lord was carried had never been used for any other purpose (1 Samuel 6:7).

Jesus was received like a king as he approached Jerusalem. People spread their cloaks in front of him. This is what the friends of Jehu had done when he was proclaimed king (2 Kings 9:13). People waved palm branches as they did when Simon Maccabaeus came to Jerusalem after a great victory (1 Maccabees 13:51). The words of welcome came from today's Psalm 118, which was used to welcome pilgrims to the feast. The word 'Hosanna' means 'Save us now': people used it when addressing their king or their God.

The prophet Zechariah talked of the king to come entering Jerusalem upon an ass. Jesus is fulfilling a Messianic prophecy. The ass was seen as a noble animal but not an animal to ride to war with. Jesus was coming to conquer but with love and not by force. The ass was seen as an animal of peace and Jesus enters in peace. He comes not to destroy or condemn but to set free and to encourage. He will not force himself upon the people: love will be his restraint. In the days ahead we will see how people edge him out of their lives, out of their city and out of their world. We need to welcome him into our lives and into the world in which we move.

(The readings replace the sermon and illustration.)

Easter Day

Aim

To rejoice in the resurrection and in the presence of the risen Lord.

Readings

Acts 10:34-43 or Isaiah 25:6-9
Psalm 118:1, 2, 14-24
1 Corinthians 15:1-11 or Acts 10:34-43
John 20:1-18 or Mark 16:1-8

Thought for the day

Regularly someone will say, 'I would believe in the resurrection if someone came back from the dead.' Well, today we rejoice because someone has. Christ is risen. Alleluia!

Let Mary Magdalene and Peter tell their story. (Have three voices – Mary, Peter and Jesus.)

Mary starts.
I had another sleepless night. My eyes are red with crying. One of those nights when the darkness seems to last for ever. When Jesus died something in me died also; it was all so cruel. He forgave me my many sins, he loved me dearly and now he is dead. There is a weight on my heart like a heavy stone; like the stone rolled on to the tomb. Such a weight, for I saw him die, I saw his agony, I saw him deserted by his friends. It turned my heart to stone. Who can lift the stone from my heart? Jesus could but he is dead and a stone is rolled against his tomb.

I will go and be beside him. It is still dark – it is about 5am – but I will go. If only someone would roll the stone away.

Please, God, lift the stone from my heart and from the tomb.

O Lord! Somebody has been here, somebody with great strength. The stone has been moved. I will go and see my Lord. Oh no! They have taken away my Lord. They have stolen his body. O Lord, what have they done? I will go and tell Peter.

Let Peter take up the story.
I haven't cried in years. I do not like to see grown men cry. I am so

ashamed of myself. How can I forgive myself? I said that I did not know Jesus; I denied him . . . At about 5.30 there was a banging on the door . . .

I was afraid. Then I realised it was Mary Magdalene, shouting and weeping. I could hardly get any sense out of her. She kept saying, 'They have taken away my Lord.' Young John and I were quickly on the road, running to the tomb. I am not as young as I used to be and John got there first. But he did not go in. I went in and saw the grave clothes discarded but there was no body. It was the way the clothes were wrapped that was odd; it looked as if he had just vanished from them or come through them. John came in and later he said, 'The empty grave clothes convinced me he had risen.' But at that moment we went back home. We passed Mary on the way.

Mary continues the story.
I went back hoping to find someone who had moved him. But I could not see for tears. I cried and asked aloud, 'Where is he?' . . .

But I must get a grip of myself. My vision is blurred. My heart aches. (*Jesus joins Mary*) Who is this? Is it the gardener? He seems to be looking at the spring flowers that have burst into life. Sir, they have taken away my Lord. Do you know . . .

'Mary.'

No, it can't be! Is it really you? This is madness.

'Mary.'

It is you! Jesus, it really is you!

'Mary.'

Master, Master. Let me stay here close to you. Let me hug you and be with you for ever.

'Mary, do not cling to me. You cannot keep me to yourself. You will have to let me go. You will have to go, Mary. Go and tell the disciples that I am alive, I am risen. Tell them you have seen me.'

I did not want to go but he asked me. I ran again to the house and told the disciples, 'I have seen the Lord! Alleluia!'

Illustration

Napoleon escaped from his island prison. His armies regathered under the French flag and Europe was plunged into war. The British army under Wellington landed in Belgium and prepared to fight near a small village called Waterloo. There was no way of communicating to England the news except by semaphore. Day after day a man watched from the tower of Winchester Cathedral, peering towards the south coast. On a misty day the watcher received a message: 'Wellington defeated.' The mist came down and a sadness filled Winchester and spread over England. The watcher stayed at his post. After a long while the mist lifted and the message was repeated: 'Wellington defeated.' But now two more words were added and they made a great difference: 'Wellington defeated the French.' The assumed defeat was a victory. A new message sped to London. Bells rang out and flags flew. The message, which seemed one of defeat, was in fact the start of the news of victory. Likewise we must move from the crucifixion to the joy of the resurrection. We are able to proclaim, 'Death is conquered. We are free. Christ has won the victory.'

COMPLETE COMMON WORSHIP

Sermon Illustrations

Second Sunday of Easter

Aim

To share in the wonder of the resurrection.

Readings

Acts 4:32-35
Psalm 133
1 John 1:1–2:2
John 20:19-31

Thought for the day

The disciples were locked in through fear. The room they were in was like the tomb; they were sealed in and afraid to venture out. They had lost their Lord and leader. They felt powerless, lifeless. How often do we feel like this, locked in and unable to do what we ought to do? Then Jesus came. There was no fuss. Suddenly he was there, alive and well. He greeted them as normal: 'Shalom. Peace be with you.' But this was a new peace, for the risen Lord offered it to them. He showed them his hands and his side (interesting to note not his feet; feet were usually bound to the cross and not nailed). 'Then were the disciples glad when they saw the Lord' must be one of the great understatements of the Scriptures. What joy, what wonder must have been theirs. Then Jesus again said, 'Peace be with you.' Jesus said that as God sent him out, he would send them out.

Jesus needs disciples to continue his work. He will work in them and through them but he needs disciples. Think on these words concerning the risen Lord by St Teresa of Avila:

> Christ has no hands, but your hands
> to do his work today.
> Christ has no feet but your feet
> to speed men on his way.
> Christ has no lips but your lips
> to tell men why he died.
> Christ has no love but your love
> to win men to his side.

We are called to be Christ to others and to see Christ in others. This is only possible if we are filled with his Spirit. Jesus breathed on his disciples. There can be little doubt the Gospel writer saw this as a new creation. With the resurrection, a new world was dawning for us all. It is his Spirit that equips us for the work we need do. It is not in book learning but in the power of his Spirit that we are able to go out in mission.

This happened to ten disciples; Judas was already dead and Thomas was away from the company. When Thomas was told, he refused to believe. Faith can be handed down but it must become first-hand for us. We need a relationship with the risen Lord. Thomas wanted to experience this wonderful event for himself. But to do it he stayed with the fellowship of the faithful. Jesus came again. Again we hear the words, 'Peace be with you.' Thomas is invited to touch and feel; this is no ghost – Jesus bears the marks of the crucifixion. Then Jesus says, 'Blessed are those who have not seen and yet have come to believe.'

Illustration

Suddenly a man fell to the ground. He had stopped breathing and it would not be long before he was totally dead. But help was at hand. Someone was willing to give him mouth-to-mouth resuscitation. They breathed their breath into him, filling his lungs, and then helped his lungs to expel the air and then receive some more breath. This process went on for a while at ten breaths a minute; without it the man would have died. By the time the ambulance came the man was breathing freely on his own. The person had saved his life. Jesus breathes new life into us and gives us eternal life. Jesus defeats death and brings us to eternal life.

(You may be able to get a St John Ambulance person or a paramedic to offer to demonstrate 'Breath of Life' – they also provide a useful card with this title.)

Third Sunday of Easter

Aim

To rejoice in the presence of the risen Lord.

Readings

Acts 3:12-19
Psalm 4
1 John 3:1-7
Luke 24:36-48

Thought for the day

Two of our readings today come from the writings of St Luke. He wrote the Acts of the Apostles as well as the Gospel according to St Luke. In Acts we hear of Peter telling his fellow Jews that the power he has comes from Jesus, whom they killed and God raised from the dead. Peter tells how the disciples are witnesses to the risen Lord. He invites the people to repent and to turn to God, just as Jesus asked him to do. The change in the disciples, from locked in and fearful men to being men willing to die for the Gospel, is the great proof of the resurrection. Peter points out that it is not in their power but in the power of the Lord that they are able to heal the lame man.

Luke's account of Easter Day differs slightly from the account of Mark and Matthew. Interestingly, Luke has the eleven disciples together (did he not know the Thomas story?). He also tells us of 'companions' being present: here is a brief insight into the fact that there were others and not all male. Suddenly Jesus is there among them, saying, 'Peace be with you.' This was the group that knew all about the crucifixion and burial – they had seen him die. They had watched his burial. Now they were startled and terrified for they thought it must be a ghost. Jesus tells them not to be afraid or doubting. It is Luke who mentions the feet of Jesus when Jesus invites the people to touch him and to look at his hands and feet. He wants them to know he is solid. Yet they still found it hard to believe. Jesus had to deal with them quite gently. He asked for something to eat and they gave him some fish. Ghosts do not eat. Jesus ate the fish in their presence.

Only when they are more relaxed does Jesus talk to them of the prophecies in the Scriptures, of how the Messiah would suffer and rise from the dead. They are to proclaim repentance and forgiveness of sins. They are to be his witnesses. St John, in today's second reading, witnesses and calls for awareness that we are children of God and so we should turn away from evil and turn to God.

Illustration

Have you ever been caught in the fog? The whole world becomes cold and grey. Vision is greatly restricted. Everything around appears to be dull and damp. Then suddenly there is a shining, an extra amount of light; there is a radiance that begins to appear all around. The sun breaks through and the fog lifts and disappears. The day seems so glorious and bright. This was the experience of the disciples with the resurrection. They shut themselves in and shut the fullness of life out. They were locked in by sorrow and fear. They just wanted to hide. It was then he came. He came because he was needed. He came back from the dead. He came to be with them. He came to guide them. He came to help them. He came to be friends. He came to transform their world. He comes now and he comes to us. He comes to chase away our darkness and fear and to make our world bright.

Fourth Sunday of Easter

Aim

To show how much the Good Shepherd cares for us and will do for us.

Readings

Acts 4:5-12
Psalm 23
1 John 3:16-24
John 10:11-18

Thought for the day

In most jobs there are those who work because they love what they are doing and those who only do it for the money. The people who only work for money rarely get as much pleasure out of their work. Those who are in it just for the money rarely choose dangerous work or work that demands some personal sacrifice.

In the time of Jesus, being a shepherd was recognised as a dangerous occupation. When he was a shepherd, David had to battle with a lion and a bear (1 Samuel 17:34-36). Isaiah tells of a group of shepherds coming together to chase a lion (Isaiah 31:4). Added to the risk from wild animals was the risk from thieves and robbers. A shepherd was called to risk his life for the sheep.

The false shepherd, when he saw trouble coming, would run away. He did not really care for the sheep; he certainly would not risk his life for them. It is not sensible to die for a few sheep. They were not worth it.

The good shepherd loved his sheep. He knew them by name and they knew him. Because of his love he would risk his life for the sheep; he would lay down his life for them. The false shepherd would say that was stupid. Is not a human worth more than the sheep? You will not be able to answer that question unless you understand about love.

Jesus died on the cross for us before we ever turned to him or loved him. You could argue it was not worth the Son of God suffering for us. He did it because of his love for us. Not even because we loved him but because he loved us. He could have avoided the crucifixion; he could have called down help from heaven. Then he would not have died for us and we would not have been saved from death. Out of love and obedience to the will of the Father, Jesus gave himself willingly for us and rose again for us.

Jesus reminds the Pharisees that his love was not exclusive: 'There are other sheep not of this fold.' Because of the outreach and love of Jesus, the Church can never be exclusive. We need to reach out and share in his rescuing and redeeming work.

Illustration

There was a group of shepherds who often talked about caring for their sheep. Yet, when trouble came, some did not want to bother; others said the sheep were not worth the risk; one or two took the money and left. One could be heard saying, 'You cannot believe a lamb is worth the life of a shepherd.' The reply from a hired man was, 'Of course it is not.'

Listening to all this was the good shepherd. It made him sad to think that the sheep were not truly loved. He loved his sheep dearly and would do anything to save them. Suddenly an old man came to him and said, 'I have been looking at your flock and you have a ewe lamb missing. She has wandered off and is in danger of death.' The shepherd left the comfort of home and the safety of his surroundings and began the search. Some were sure he should not have bothered. There were plenty of other sheep; why bother with a wayward one? The shepherd's life was more precious than the lamb's. The shepherd was soon travelling dark valleys. More than once he was at risk himself. Briars tore at his hands and his feet. There was a gaping hole in his side. Thorns had pierced his head. He was calling the lamb by name. At last there was a weak response. It was down a steep slope and in danger of falling further. The shepherd did not fear but descended into the depths. The darkness was trying to hold on to the lamb. The shepherd reached into the thorn bushes and became entangled; he was caught alongside the lamb. Even now he reached out to comfort it. There he lay, life ebbing out of him. He was trapped for more than 48 hours. But on the third day he broke free and rising up brought the lamb with him. He carried it all the way home. When they saw him they rejoiced. 'Just see how much he loves his flock and what he was willing to suffer for one little ewe lamb.'

Fifth Sunday of Easter

Aim

To show we are one with Christ and that we are called to bear fruit.

Readings

Acts 8:26-40
Psalm 22:25-31
1 John 4:7-21
John 15:1-8

Thought for the day

The vine was one of the most common plants in Israel. It would grow almost anywhere: it grew on walls, up trellises, around the doors of houses; it grew up sticks. It also grew in the wild. For the vine to grow well, it needed the ground to be prepared carefully and it needed regular attention. If you wanted good fruit, you could not just leave it to chance.

Could it be that with Jesus who says, 'I am the vine', we need to give the same attention? There is no one in whom he will not grow if only the preparation of the 'soil' is properly done. Today we expect instant results, instant responses, instant changes in people, instant conversions, and they do not happen because we ignore what is going on at ground level. We tend to ignore the weeds, the poor environment, the lack of sustenance; we want growth without having to make an effort.

Let us learn from the preparation of the vine. First it is necessary to prepare the ground, to see that the atmosphere is as good as possible for growth. We need to be sure that it will not be choked by weeds or die from lack of attention. Many who are young in the faith are lost because we do not give them the sustenance they need.

It is lovely when growth begins. For a long time it seems little is happening and then suddenly growth speeds up. The vine is so luxuriant in its growth that young slips are usually set at two metres apart: to have room to grow is important. In the first three years the vine is not allowed to fruit so that it can conserve its life and energy. We often send people out before they have grown, and so they exhaust themselves and their fruiting is lost. Too often we rush young Christians into action, and they expect it, when we have spent little time building them up in the faith. We need those who are mature in the faith and who have the resources for bearing fruit.

The vine has two kinds of branches: one is fruit-bearing and the other is not. The non-fruit-bearing branches are drastically cut off so that they will not take away energy and strength from the plant. The vine will not produce a good crop without pruning. We are all meant to bear fruit in one way or another.

Lastly, though of utmost importance, we need to note that Jesus says he is the whole vine and we are the branches. We are not separate from Jesus. Without him we cannot bear fruit. But we are not without him. In fact, we dwell in him and he is in us. Without him, our lives will wither and die. If we abide in him and he in us, his life flows in us and through us. We are one with him and one in him. Then, in turn, we are the vine and we are called to be Christ to the world.

Illustration

We hear little of the disciples after the resurrection but we know they all bore the fruit of being with Jesus. After the death of Stephen, the disciples scattered because of persecution. We know Philip went to Samaria and told the story of Jesus. He preached of the love of God. Through the disciples the Church was growing rapidly and beyond the boundaries of Jerusalem (see Acts 8:5-13). Peter and John also went to the Samaritans.

A road from Jerusalem went by Bethlehem and, just south of Gaza, joined the main road to Egypt and beyond. St Luke points out that this is the Old or Desert Gaza, not the more modern one. Along this road travelled the Chancellor of the Exchequer of the queen of Ethiopia. He had been to Jerusalem to worship. He is at least a seeker of God. He was in his chariot reading Isaiah 53. Philip simply asked if he understood what he was reading. The Ethiopian said how could he without a guide? Philip was invited into the chariot and they looked at the words: 'He was led like a lamb to the slaughter.' Philip talked of Jesus of the crucifixion and resurrection. The Ethiopian was moved and wanted to be baptised in the nearby water. After being baptised the Ethiopian went on his way rejoicing. Again we see Philip bearing fruit as he does the work of Jesus. Tradition has it that the Ethiopian went home and started to evangelise Ethiopia. And through the witness of many the Church grew in the faith and in number.

Sixth Sunday of Easter

Aim

To know that we are chosen by God.

Readings

Acts 10:44-48
Psalm 98
1 John 5:1-6
John 15:9-17

Thought for the day

Have you ever been chosen to play for a team or to represent your school or firm? You are chosen because you can do certain things. You do not choose but you are chosen. You can try to earn a place but you cannot choose to be in the team. You are chosen.

A lot of people talk about choosing to be a Christian or not as if the choice was theirs. The choice is not ours; it is Jesus who chooses us. Jesus says, 'You did not choose me but I chose you.' We are asked to respond by saying whether or not we want to be part of his ministry and have a relationship with him. Any who excuse themselves exclude themselves.

Out of his love and grace God has called us. In today's Gospel we can see what that calling implies.

(1) We are chosen for joy. No matter which way the road goes, whether life is tough or easy, we are called to rejoice in the Lord (see Philippians 4:4). The Christian is a person of joy, knowing that God calls them and knowing that the Lord is with them. This is a joy no one or nothing should be able to take from us. Amidst all the gloom a Christian is to show joy, for we are loved and have an eternal destiny.

(2) We are chosen for love. Jesus gives to us an awareness of the love of the Father. He gives us his own love. What greater love can he give us than laying down his life for us? Jesus demonstrated his deep love for us on the cross. We are called to respond to this love by loving him. Then he has chosen us to love one another as he loves us. 'This is my commandment, that you love one another as I have loved you.' Warring factions among Christians betray the love of Christ.

(3) We are chosen to be friends of Jesus: 'I do not call you servants (slaves) any longer.' It was counted a great honour to be called slaves or servants of God. Moses was called the 'slave of God' (Deuteronomy 34:5); so was Joshua (Joshua 24:29); so was David (Psalm 89:20). St Paul also was proud to call himself a slave (Titus 1:1). One of the titles of the Pope is 'Servant of the servants of God'. But Jesus has called us to a far greater privilege: we are to be his friends and friends of God. We need not stand far off; we have immediate access to the presence of our friend. We are not like someone who gets a rare glimpse of the King; we are able to enter into his presence whenever we want. He has chosen us to be his friends. Because Jesus is alive he is not a theory or an idea; he is a person. We need to talk to him and make friends with him.

As always, with privileges come responsibilities. We have been chosen to 'go': Jesus sends us (in the way some are 'sent' by their favourite pop star). We need to learn to 'go for Jesus'. We are all called to share in the outreach and mission of our Lord.

We are called to bear lasting fruit, to be ambassadors for Christ. We are to show by our way of living that it is a joy to be a friend of God and to love as he loves us. We are his witnesses and witnesses to the riches of his glory. We are advertisements to our God and his love – or we ought to be.

To be able to do all this we are asked to pray to the Father in the power of Jesus. We cannot achieve this work in our own strength but only in the power and presence of God.

Illustration

Once upon a time there was an explosion that radiated out through the world. Countless people were touched, infected: many found it contagious as someone who was already touched passed it on to them. The explosion happened on a hill called Calvary just outside Jerusalem. Here love broke out in great power, defeating darkness. In a flash of blinding love, the Christ released a new way of life for the world. The love of God radiated through the whole earth and all times. The results of that explosion are still being felt today because he who died rose again. He lives and seeks to share his love with us. He comes to us and wants to be our friend. There are always those who will protect themselves against such an event; who will ignore his presence and avoid his radiant love. But he will transform all who come to be touched and give them the power to become the true children of God. They will shine with his presence and his love.

Ascension Day

Aim

To rejoice in the presence of the ascended Lord.

Readings

Acts 1:1-11 or Daniel 7:9-14
Psalm 147 or Psalm 93
Ephesians 1:15-23 or Acts 1:1-11
Luke 24:44-53
(*The reading from Acts must be one of the readings for the day*)

Thought for the day

The Ascension is of the utmost importance: it marks a new stage in the ministry of Jesus and a new stage in the history of humankind. Jesus did not come down just to walk the earth and be friendly; he came down to lift us up that we might share with him in his kingdom. At Christmas we celebrate 'God made flesh'; at Ascension we celebrate our humanity being raised to God. Jesus became human that we might share in the divine!

When on earth, Jesus, like all humans, was restricted by space and time. There was no way that Jesus could be in two places at once: if he was in Jerusalem he could not be in Nazareth; while he was in Galilee he could not be at Bethany. He was late in coming to his friend Lazarus because he was not nearby when his friend took ill. After the resurrection it seems to be a little different as he suddenly appears in the room with the disciples or in the garden to Mary. But he still seems to be in one place at a time. A new stage is marked by the Ascension: it is summarised in the words, 'Remember, I am with you always' (Matthew 28:20).

Mark, at the end of his Gospel, tells of Jesus being taken up into heaven and then say how Jesus continued to work with the disciples (Mark16:20). Jesus is freed from the restrictions of space and time; he is now available to us wherever we are. He is here and with us now. We begin many of our services by saying, 'The Lord is here. His Spirit is with us.' It is sad that we do not acknowledge the wonder and the full meaning of this great truth: The Lord is here.

Jesus returns to the Father. Luke in his Gospel says, 'He was carried up to heaven' (Luke 24:51). In Acts, Luke says, 'He was lifted up and a cloud took him out of their sight' (Acts 1:9). This is no ordinary cloud; it is to be seen like the cloud that hid the presence of God from Moses and the people of Israel. The cloud is about the hidden glory of God ever present in our midst. In returning to God, Jesus has taken our human flesh into the fullness of God's kingdom. Jesus remains our friend and in him heaven and earth are one.

Illustration

At first there was a silence, as if we had been left to our own devices. Through our foolishness we had been caught by a rising tide. We had sent up a plea, by means of a telephone in the refuge box that was placed on stilts above the waves. Some caring people had built this place of comparative safety on the sands to accommodate fools who disobeyed the guidelines of safe crossings.

Suddenly there was a whirring sound from on high. It was no vision. It was a Sea King helicopter. A man was coming down from the safety of the helicopter and being lowered to where we were. He was very friendly. He did not tell us off. He did not say he came to admire the scenery! He said to each of us in turn, 'Do not worry. You will be all right. Fasten yourself to me.' Once one of us was fastened to him he signalled to the helicopter above and we were raised to safety. He came down four times altogether. He told us sometimes he was actually dropped into a raging sea to pick someone up. His purpose was always the same: he came down that we might be lifted up; he descended that we might ascend with him. Then we were taken to dry land. I looked back on my poor old car with water flowing almost over its roof. It would be a write-off. But we were safe. A little like the resurrection of the body and our being lifted to heaven. Words of Psalm 18:16-19 came to mind: 'He reached down from on high, he took me; he drew me out of mighty waters . . . He brought me out into a broad place: he delivered me because he delighted in me.'

Jesus came down that we might be raised up on high.

Seventh Sunday of Easter

Aim

To show the importance of knowing Jesus personally.

Readings

Acts 1:15-17, 21-26
Psalm 1
1 John 5:9-13
John 17:6-19

Thought for the day

If you had to help to choose your next priest or minister, what qualifications would you look for? In some parishes it is easy: they look for an Oxford or Cambridge graduate only. That would weed out an awful lot. We want a learned man, but is intellect of the prime importance? A degree in theology may impress but it does not guarantee that the owner is a committed Christian! There is a big distinction between knowing about Jesus and knowing Jesus.

The disciples had to face this problem with the death of Judas. They were used to working as a team. They went in twos: rarely did they work alone. So eleven was definitely an odd number. Twelve is a special number, like the twelve prophets or the twelve tribes of Israel. If the apostles were like the new Israel they would need to make up their team to twelve. If we play with a team member short, it will affect our overall performance. They needed to find a replacement, so they got together and asked what was required. It is worth noting that at this stage there were about 120 gathered together – that could be ten for every apostle.

They decided together it should be someone who had been with Jesus from the beginning, from the baptism of John until Jesus was taken up from them. (Here we discover there were more than just the twelve going around with Jesus, but nevertheless twelve is a special number.) Then they would require that person to witness with them to the resurrection. Definitely called as a team member and definitely called to witness to the resurrection.

If they were able to put an advert in Situations Vacant it might sound like this:

> Due to the untimely death of an apostle,
> one person needed to join a team of twelve.
> Will normally be required to work with others.
> Needs to know Jesus personally
> and to be ready to witness to the resurrection.

The important things became obvious. They wanted someone who knew Jesus, not someone who had just heard of him. The person had to have followed and loved Jesus. What mattered was their personal experience of the Lord.

What would such a man see as his work?

Take services, look after churches, do social work? Above all he would have to witness to the resurrection. He would have to show others that Jesus is alive. Jesus is not a figure of history or just a holy man of the past: he *is* the *Living Lord*. We need to know him in the present tense, to know him now.

There seemed two obvious candidates, Joseph and Matthias. Now the followers of Jesus wanted to show that it was God's choice, not theirs. They prayed, 'Lord, you know everyone's heart. Show us which one of these two you have chosen.' Then they cast lots. We may find this a little strange but they wanted the choice to be God's and in those days this was a natural way of seeking that choice. The names of the candidates were written on stones. They were then placed in a vessel and shaken until one stone fell out. He whose name fell out was the chosen one. In this case Matthias' name came out and he became apostle number 12.

Illustration

In the film *Oliver!*, Oliver Twist is in the poorhouse with many other young people. They want someone to complain that they are hungry and want more food. In this case no one wants to do it for they know they are likely to be punished. They decided to pick straws and whoever draws the shortest straw has to do it. If you draw the shortest straw, it means you are chosen. Oliver draws the shortest straw. The others have elected him. So though he is frightened, he goes to the front and asks for more. 'Please Sir, I would like some more.' In the poorhouse this is unthinkable and, as the young people expected, Oliver is punished for asking.

Pentecost

Aim

To rejoice in the presence and power of the Spirit.

Readings

Acts 2:1-21 or Ezekiel 37:1-14
Psalm 104:24-34, 35b
Romans 8:22-27 or Acts 2:1-21
John 15:26-27; 16:4b-15

Thought for the day

Today we hear in the Acts of the Apostles how there was a great wind that rushed through the house where the disciples were, and that on each of the disciples there appeared to be tongues of fire.

Now here is something else to look at: it is a drill but it is useless (you could use anything that needs a power pack). It should be able to work but it does not. Who can tell me why it does not work? It could be that its batteries are flat or, like this one, it needs a power pack. Now if I snap this power into place, away it goes (demonstrate).

Pentecost was a time when all the Jews who lived near Jerusalem came to give thanks for the giving of the Law to Moses on Mount Sinai. It was also time to give thanks for the barley harvest. Pentecost was 50 days after the Passover, so for us it is 50 days after Easter. If you do not count Easter Day itself, it is only 49 days, 7 x 7, a week of weeks. Sometimes this was called the Festival of weeks.

The disciples were all together in a room. Perhaps they were still afraid to venture out. They did not show any signs of going out and talking about Jesus. In fact, they were waiting to be given the power. They had known Jesus; they had seen the risen Lord and they knew his presence in their lives. They had been commissioned by him to go out and preach the Gospel. But they were waiting for the power to go out. Jesus had foreseen this and had asked them to wait: 'Stay here in the city until you have been clothed with power from on high'(Luke 24:49). It was there, in the room where the disciples were, that the Spirit came with the sound of wind and tongues of fire. Wind and fire were symbols of great power in the ancient world and both were associated with the presence of God. Wind, breath and spirit were all linked together in the ancient world and all were signs of the Spirit of God.

Whatever happened, we know that on this day the disciples were empowered. They were given courage and the ability to go out and proclaim the Gospel. These 12 ordinary men were given the power that would transform the world. If we look at what they were like before the coming of the Spirit and what they were like after, we have proof that something great happened. They would all tell you the Spirit came. He comes to us too.

The Lord is here.
His Spirit is with us.

Illustration

One of Europe's leading ecologists has said the energy crisis we face is not so much in energy supplies but in our own thinking. There is enough energy in the ebb and flow of the tides, in the running of rivers, in the winds and in the rays of the sun to supply our needs if we would give time and attention to these. Three things are obvious:

(1) Many energy supplies are limited and will run out.

(2) Wrong thinking or lack of proper attention makes us do nothing.

(3) All around there is power that we do not realise.

Too often the Church tries to go along in its own resources and strength, and it can be seen to be running out of supplies. We spend too much of our attention looking in the wrong direction.

The power of God is here, for the Lord is here: His Spirit is with us.

We need to learn to wait upon the Lord and the power of his might.

Trinity Sunday

Aim

To encourage a greater awareness of the Trinity.

Readings

Isaiah 6:1-8
Psalm 29
Romans 8:12-17
John 3:1-17

Thought for the day

Do you have a proper diet? We do not all need to eat the same things but we do need a balanced diet. The body cannot live for long without the proper sustenance – fasting can be useful but starving yourself is useless. Many starving people get weak and disorientated. While most of us are not likely to starve, even a slight deficiency can reduce our well-being. A lack of calcium or iron or even zinc in their minute quantities can affect our health.

There was a farm that was not prospering. The cows were losing weight and dying. The family was being reduced to poverty. It seemed disaster was inevitable. Then the vet discovered a chemical deficiency in the cows' feed. The necessary chemical was added and, almost immediately, cows, farm and family improved.

Why are we talking about deficiency? It is because so many people are deficient in their Christian life; there is an element lacking and that leaves them poor when they should be rejoicing in the great riches that are offered to them. They have not experienced the Trinity: they have latched on to one of the persons of the Trinity and missed out on the other two. Quite often if you look at your prayers, you will discover you neglect to have a relationship with one of the three, either Father, Son or Holy Spirit. In the words of Saint Paul: 'The grace of the Lord Jesus Christ, the love of God, and the communion of the Holy Spirit be with you all' (2 Corinthians 13:13).

Check your own experience. Are you aware of a loving Creator who cares for his creation? Do you know he made you out of his love and for his love? He surrounds you with love and wants you to respond to him with love. Do you rejoice to know that nothing in this world can separate you from the love of God? He is with you, the Almighty, the Creator and seeks your love.

Have you discovered the grace – that is, the free gift and the beauty – of our Lord Jesus Christ? Know that he came to earth for you. He lived and died and rose again for you. You do not have to earn his love; it is a free gift (gratis). When you cannot help yourself, he comes to your aid. He is your Saviour and Redeemer. He loves you and he seeks your love.

Are you in common union – communion – with the Holy Spirit? He is with you at every encounter; he shares in every bond of fellowship. The Spirit brings gifts and talents for you to use. As last week, all need learn to wait upon the Spirit.

Father in heaven, you are our Creator.
Jesus, you are our Saviour.
Spirit, you are our Guide and Strengthener.

Make sure you know this and rejoice in Father, Son and Holy Spirit, in the Holy Trinity.

Illustration

A child went down to the beach and dug a hole in the sand. She then went down to the sea and brought some water to fill the hole. In a moment the water disappeared. She went back for more water, and then more. But the same thing happened each time. The little girl became exhausted and began to cry. Meanwhile the tide had been coming in. Her father showed her how to make a channel for the sea, so that it would flow naturally into the hole and fill it. We are like the little girl: we try to fill our minds with ideas about God and often exhaust ourselves. We talk too much. We need learn to wait upon God, knowing he will come to us. Trying to understand the Trinity is like trying to pour the whole sea into a small hole. Yet we can rest in the Trinity and enjoy the love of Father, Son and Holy Spirit.

Proper 4

Sunday between 29 May and 4 June inclusive (if after Trinity Sunday)

Aim

To show that lives are richer than the keeping of rules – but that rules are necessary.

Readings

1 Samuel 3:1-10 (11-20) or Deuteronomy 5:12-15
Psalm 139:1-6, 13-18 or Psalm 81:1-10
2 Corinthians 4:5-12
Mark 2:23–3:6

Thought for the day

Self-righteous church people can be very frightening. They are usually full of negative goodness. 'I don't smoke, I don't drink, I don't chase after women (or men), I don't swear.' I want to ask, 'What do you do? What is your positive contribution to life?' It is sad when religion is portrayed as something that is life-restricting and negative. Jesus said, 'I came that they may have life and have it abundantly' (John 10:10).

In today's Gospel we meet religious people who are opposed to Jesus and his ways; in fact, they are out to kill him. We should not be surprised when we are faced with opposition as Christians: Jesus faced it throughout his ministry.

It begins in a cornfield. As the disciples were going through the field they plucked the ears of corn and ate them. It was all right to do this as long as they did not use a cutting instrument such as a sickle. Travellers were allowed to take and eat corn, but not on the Sabbath. Then it was not lawful because it was counted as work; in fact, it broke at least four rules of working on the Sabbath. The disciples could be accused of reaping, winnowing, threshing and preparing a meal! You wonder who was spying on them.

The Pharisees expected Jesus to tell his disciples not to do such things. In reality, the Pharisees were out to stop Jesus. If he gave in to this pettiness, he would hardly lead people to freedom. Jesus replied by telling them how David, when hungry, ate the sacred bread that only priests could eat (see 1 Samuel 21:1-6), citing this as a precedent for what the disciples were doing. Religion was not about rules and regulations but about a relationship with God. It is no use keeping the rules without a loving relationship. God wants our obedience but not as slaves. He wants us to do his will out of love. It would appear there was little love among these Pharisees.

The opposition continued in the synagogue. It is sad when a church reflects all too human feelings of violence and hatred. The Pharisees almost wanted Jesus to heal the ill man so that they could condemn him. Jesus does not play for safety. He could have healed the man after the Sabbath. He asks the man to come forward to let it be seen what he is doing. He faces the Pharisees and asks them, 'Is it lawful to do good or to do harm on the Sabbath, to save life or to kill?' Jesus had come to heal and to save; the Pharisees were plotting the death of Jesus. Such an attitude angered Jesus; he was saddened at their hardness of heart. Like Pharaoh dealing with Moses and the people of Israel, hardness of heart comes through regularly hardening ourselves.

Jesus heals, giving new life to the man with the withered hand. The Pharisees go out and make an unholy alliance with the Herodians. Normally, the Pharisees would have no dealings with the Herodians who were considered untouchable. Opposition mounts as members of government and church join forces to destroy Jesus. So often there are groups in our society that still seek to do this and we need be aware of it.

Illustration

Rules and regulations are there to help us and the society we live in. Occasionally you hear of some absurd application of the law, usually by someone who says something like, 'It's more than my job's worth.' A young motorcyclist was knocked off his bike in an area of parking meters. His bike was put carefully at the side of the road. Even though the traffic warden knew of the event, he placed a parking ticket on the bike. Fortunately, the city council was more understanding when a plea was made. Some people find it very hard to understand that rules are there to help us rather than hinder us.

Proper 5

Sunday between 5 and 11 June inclusive (if after Trinity Sunday)

Aim

To show how Jesus risked safety and security for us.

Readings

1 Samuel 8:4-11 (12-15) 16-20 (11:14-15) or Genesis 3:8-15
Psalm 138 or Psalm 130
2 Corinthians 4:13–5:1
Mark 3:20-35

Thought for the day

Jesus was very popular with the ordinary people: wherever he went crowds followed him. He went into a house and the crowd that followed was so large that Jesus and his disciples did not even have time to eat. It was not the first time this had happened and his family was worried for him. They loved him and wanted to protect him. They came to where he was because people were saying, 'He has gone out of his mind.'

Jesus had left the security of Nazareth for a life on the road. His work as a carpenter in Nazareth must have provided Jesus with a good way of life. He would have his family around him; there would be love and care. His family thought it was foolish to leave this to become a wandering preacher who did not have time to eat.

Not only did Jesus leave his security behind; he left the safety of a peaceful life. He was running into trouble with the religious leaders. There are some people whom it is better not to upset and Jesus was upsetting them. Very soon, if not already, Jesus' life would be in danger. He would be safer at home in Nazareth.

He wanted to lead people and show them a better way of life. But look at the people he gathered around him – they were neither learned nor great strong characters. He chose fishermen, a traitorous tax collector and a freedom fighter to be part of his team. He risked society laughing at him. Out of love, his family wanted to take him home.

Jesus could not go with them. He would risk his life for us. He would leave safety and security behind and go on the road towards the cross.

As his family loved him, another group was out to condemn him. The Scribes had followed from Jerusalem, not because they believed or loved him but because they wanted to find fault. They could not deny that Jesus healed people: they actually saw it happen. They tried to frighten people off Jesus by saying he was in league with Beelzebul. This was a pagan god and the name means 'lord of the flies'. They suggested that Jesus worked for Satan, the ruler of demons.

Jesus pointed out how wicked it was to say this. Evil would not fight evil (evil fights goodness). To call good evil is wicked and perverts life.

Jesus accepted that life is a struggle between good and evil, and there is no doubt on which side he stood. Jesus regarded healing as a defeat of evil. He wanted people to be whole and healthy. Jesus cared for the whole person – body, mind and spirit – and not just part of them.

He confronted the Scribes. This was a great risk but he was determined to stand against evil. By their attitude, the Scribes separated themselves from Jesus.

Illustration

Jesus risked his own safety and security for us. As Christians, we are often called to share in this risky adventure. The call is often like the call to the man with the withered hand: 'Come forward . . . stretch out' (Mark 3:3, 5).

Very often the Church hides behind set services and conventions. The words and the patterns are fixed so that no one is disturbed. Jesus calls, 'Come forward.' Stand where everyone can see you. Where every fault-finding eye can fall upon you. Where those who reject Jesus can vent themselves upon you. 'Safety first' is not our policy: the Church is not meant to be hidden – 'Come forward' for Jesus. Then 'stretch out', even if you feel your talent has withered. Attempt the impossible for God, trusting in his power. Take risks for God and let him work through you. The call of Jesus to the man with the withered hand is a call to the Church to let him work through us. Come forward . . . stretch out.

Proper 6

Sunday between 12 and 18 June inclusive (if after Trinity Sunday)

Aim

To show that the kingdom of God is waiting to grow in us.

Readings

1 Samuel 15:34–16:13 or Ezekiel 17:22-24
Psalm 20 or Psalm 92:1-4, 12-15
2 Corinthians 5:6-10 (11-13) 14-17
Mark 4:26-34

Thought for the day

The Church is in the growth business. We are called to sow seeds and to encourage growth. Today's Gospel has two of the parables of Jesus about the kingdom of God and growth.

'The kingdom of God is as if someone would scatter seed.' There has to be a sowing: the Church must proclaim the message. We may often feel we have failed but we need to have patience and to trust in God. The seed must be given time to germinate. Once the sowing is done, the farmer gets on with other things, including other sowings. While he sleeps and does other things the seed starts to grow – remember it can only do this if it was sown in the first place.

'The earth produces of itself'; it does this automatically for that is what the Greek word means. We do not create the kingdom. We can prepare for its growth in us and in others, but God gives the increase. Growth is often imperceptible, sometimes slow; sometimes it takes much patience. But if we sow, we should trust that God is at work. There will be a harvest – that is, if you have sown the seeds.

(Show a mustard seed.) Most of you will not be able to see this because it is so tiny. In fact, I must be careful I do not lose it. It is a mustard seed. When talking of something small, the people who lived in the Holy Land would say, 'as small as a mustard seed' because it was the smallest of things. Yet in our amazing world, packed into this tiny seed is a large shrub. In the Holy Land it grows to something that looks like a tree, nearly two and a half metres high. Often you see birds sitting in its branches picking off the little black seeds. This is a wonderful thing if you think about it. God's kingdom is also amazing in the way it grows. Again, we have to do the sowing but God will give the increase.

To the early Church which was often facing opposition and setbacks, like the Church now, these were parables of encouragement. Sow the seed and trust God. The faith spread, the Church grew, the kingdom increased against opposition and persecution. This happened because the early Christians continued to sow the word of God in the hearts of people and the society in which they lived.

Illustration

Jonathan Chapman used to travel around farms in America with his Bible. In the evenings he would read to the family; not many of them could read themselves. They looked forward to his visits and they called him 'Johnny Appleseed'.

This is how he got his nickname. On some farms he noticed the men busy making cider. The apples were pressed and when the juice was extracted the pips were thrown away. 'What a waste,' thought Johnny: those little pips could grow into fine trees. So Johnny asked if he could have some seed. The man replied he could have as much seed as he wanted. Johnny filled his saddlebag with seeds. When he visited a farm, in the evening he read from the Bible, then before he left he would make some holes in the soil and plant some apple seeds. He then made a little fence around them to protect them and to give them the chance to grow. For over 40 years Johnny did this work, sowing the word of God in the hearts of people and sowing apple seeds in the ground. Everywhere he went he left something behind to give pleasure and nourishment to the farming people. He understood well that seeds could not grow unless they were planted.

Proper 7

Sunday between 19 and 25 June inclusive (if after Trinity Sunday)

Aim

To learn to turn to Jesus in the storms of life.

Readings

1 Samuel 17:(1a, 4-11, 19-23) 32-49
or 1 Samuel 17:57–18:5, 10-16 or Job 38:1-11
Psalm 9:9-20 or Psalm 133 or Psalm 107:1-3, 23-32
2 Corinthians 6:1-13
Mark 4:35-41

Thought for the day

Jesus was exhausted. People had been coming day and night. He had hardly had time even to eat. He had been pouring himself out until there was little left and he needed space and refreshment. He got into the boat and was asleep almost straightaway. There he is in the stern sleeping.

Peter scans the sky and does not like the look of it. The wind is rising; the sea is becoming restless. From the heights of Mount Hermon and the hills and valleys around, funnelled through the ravines, winds descend without warning and with great force. Voyagers on the Sea of Galilee often met such storms. The disciples understood that only God could still the storm and bring calm; humans would do best to stay out of it if they could.

Suddenly the storm hits the little boat. There is little the fishermen can do. They cannot escape and their boat is filling with water. Jesus continues to sleep. The boat is in the midst of chaos: the canvas is out of control, the helm won't respond, timber and tackle groan. Like many before them it seems they could be lost at sea. They are fighting for survival and they call upon Jesus, 'Teacher, do you not care that we are perishing?'

Jesus wakes up and rebukes the wind and says to the waves, 'Peace! Be still.' Then the wind ceases and there is a dead calm.

(Read from Psalm 107:28-29.) The words of the Psalm were applied to God only. No wonder the disciples were filled with awe and asked, 'Who is this that even the wind and the sea obey him?' To this there is one answer only: Jesus is God.

Illustration

Do you know the story of Aladdin and his lamp? The lamp had wonderful powers but most people did not recognise it. The lamp standing unused was no better than any other. It could give out a little light but its great power remained untapped. It is no use having a wonderful power if you do not use it. In the same way, it is no use saying you believe in a Saviour if you do not call upon him.

Too often we allow Jesus to sleep in our lives. We struggle on alone and are often overwhelmed because we do not call upon him in the storm. While we allow fear to mount and energies to be overpowered, we fail to call upon the greatest power, which is our Lord.

In the storms of fear and sorrow, when we are feeling overwhelmed, we need to know the presence and the power of our God. We need to know again that God can bring order out of chaos and that Christ can give us his peace. Do not let Jesus sleep in your life; call upon him each day. Take heed these words from Julian of Norwich:

> He said not: 'Thou shalt not be tempest-tossed; thou shalt not be work-weary; thou shalt not be distressed.' But he did say: 'Thou shalt not be overcome.'

Proper 8

Sunday between 26 June and 2 July inclusive

Aim

To show Jesus is the giver of hope and life.

Readings

2 Samuel 1:1, 17-27 or Wisdom of Solomon 1:13-15; 2:23-24
Psalm 130 or Psalm 30 or Lamentations 3:23-33.
2 Corinthians 8:7-15
Mark 5:21-43

Thought for the day

Here are two sad stories, one of a young girl and the other of an older woman. It would seem the young girl was an only child. She would be the light of her parents' life, their joy and a living expression of their love. Now it would seem that light was about to go out. What darkness and pain it must have caused the loving parents that their child was so ill.

This young girl was 12. That is to say she had grown into a woman. In the land where Jesus lived when you were 12 years and a day you were counted as grown up and could even get married. (Maybe all the girls over 12 would like to stand for a moment.) Sadly, just as she should have been starting her adult life, she was going to die. Her father called doctors and healers but the girl could not be made well. He was desperate and that made him go to Jesus.

The man was called Jairus and he was the ruler of the synagogue. He was the administrator: he saw to the good running of the synagogue and to the list of who would take services and preach. He was an important man, respected and of good standing. Now he threw himself at the feet of a wandering preacher. No doubt he was not sure of Jesus and maybe even thought Jesus was a heretic, but he threw himself down before Jesus. He put aside any prejudice. He put aside any pride and begged repeatedly, 'My little daughter is at the point of death. Come lay your hands on her, so that she may be made well and live.' Jesus went with him immediately.

The crowds held up their progress. People were all around and seeking to see Jesus or hear him. It was a slow journey and suddenly Jesus stopped. Everyone stood still. Jesus turned and looked at the crowds and asked, 'Who touched me?' The disciples said, 'Look at the crowds. How can you ask such a question? Lots of people must have touched you.' But Jesus knew power had gone out from him to someone. He asked again, 'Who touched me?' and looked at the faces in the crowd. A woman came forward and confessed. She suffered from haemorrhages and should not even have been there. Any contact with people would render them unclean by the law. She should not have touched Jesus. Maybe she thought she could steal some power. It sounds as if she was rather superstitious but, whatever she was, she was desperate for healing. Jesus said to her, 'Daughter, your faith has made you well. Go in peace, and be healed of your disease.'

This was wonderful but it was a delay, and while Jesus was there a message came that the daughter of Jairus had died. Jesus looked at Jairus and said, 'Do not fear; only believe.' At the house the professional mourners were weeping and wailing, the flute players were playing sad songs. The girl was dead. Jesus said to them, 'The child is not dead but sleeping.' They didn't believe him and continued their wailing and crying. Jesus put everyone out of the house except the girl's parents. Then with Peter, James and John he went up to where the girl was and taking her by the hand he said to her, 'Talitha cum.' This was the local Aramaic language that the child would know; it meant, 'Little girl, get up.' Immediately, with Jesus holding her hands, she arose. Jesus told them not to tell anyone – they would know soon enough. The girl needed rest and food.

Illustration

How often do we lose contact with friends because we do not make the effort? To maintain a relationship with anyone we need to meet them and talk to them. If they are far away we can at least write, telephone or send an e-mail. A once-a-year Christmas card could hardly be called contact.

In a car the contacts give a vital spark that fires the engine. If the contacts are broken, the engine will not fire properly. Even if we have plenty of fuel and the battery is charged, the car will not go if there are no contacts at work.

When Jesus asks, 'Who touched me?' could you say, 'It was I, Lord'? Do you keep in proper contact with Jesus? When the woman touched him, power travelled from Jesus to her. We so often fail to achieve because we go it alone and do not touch base with Jesus.

(You might like to use the hymn 'What a friend we have in Jesus'; let the people read it during a silence.)

Proper 9

Sunday between 3 and 9 July inclusive

Aim

To show Jesus has work for us but will not force himself or his work upon us.

Readings

2 Samuel 5:1-5, 9-10 or Ezekiel 2:1-5
Psalm 48 or Psalm 123
2 Corinthians 12:2-10
Mark 6:1-13

Thought for the day

Not everyone welcomed Jesus: that should be obvious from the crucifixion. Jesus was often scorned and rejected and not always popular. It is to be expected that if Jesus was not popular, then his disciples and followers would not be popular either.

Often what stops people accepting Jesus is their pride and prejudice. Jesus is not given a chance because people have made up their minds before they meet him.

It was quite natural for Jesus to turn up at Nazareth where he lived most of his life. He went to the synagogue and taught but the people could not hear him because of their prejudice. 'How can he preach? Is he not a carpenter? Let him get back to making furniture.' They saw Jesus as a craftsman, but could not see him as a preacher. They could see him as he was, but could not accept him for what he had become. He had changed but they were unwilling to. Sadly, some would think he could not have a great message because he was just a working man. Where did he get his wisdom from, for he was no scholar!

They knew his family, his mother Mary, his four brothers James and Joses, Judas and Simon, and his sisters. Here we get a glimpse of home at Nazareth. Jesus was not an only child. He grew up in what we would consider a large family. Joseph is not mentioned so it is likely he was dead. As Jesus was the first-born, he probably had to work hard to help to bring up this family, and that is why he is still at Nazareth until he is about 30 (Luke 3:3). The people who knew his family would not accept that Jesus could achieve anything special because he was so ordinary in their eyes, and so they rejected him. How can a carpenter preach? Such prejudice has hindered many a good man or woman. Even though Jesus cured some sick people, the people of Nazareth could not see his power. There is none so blind as those who do not want to see.

Jesus was amazed at their unbelief. He knew them and did not expect it from them. Before he left he said, 'Prophets are not without honour, except in their home town, and among their own kin, and in their own house.' This is a very sad statement from Jesus.

When people refuse to hear, Jesus moves on; he goes to other villages. Jesus never forces himself on anyone. We all have the choice to accept him as our Lord and our Friend or to ignore him. Many are not antagonistic to Jesus; they just cannot be bothered to put themselves out. When Jesus is ignored or rejected he will move on unless we call him back.

He also sent his disciples out in twos giving them some of his power over unclean spirits. They were to go out in his strength, not their own. They were to go out in faith without taking provisions, financial protection or the security of extra clothing. They were to travel light. Likewise, we do not need degrees or theological training; we do not need special qualifications. We need to know Jesus. We need to be sent by him. This is what makes an Apostolic Church: people who are called and sent by Jesus. They were not to take a collecting bag because they were to give rather than seek to receive. The Church needs money to survive but if raising money is its priority, it is giving out a wrong message. Like our God, we are to give more than we demand.

The disciples were not sent out to create a message. They went out as Christ's messengers; evangelists are 'good news tellers'. In a sense all are called to be 'angels' – that is, God's messengers. The mission of the disciples is to share in the mission of Jesus. 'As the Father has sent me, so I send you' (John 20:21).

The message of the disciples begins as Jesus began: 'Repent' (Mark 1:15). It is a call to turn around: turn around because you are going in the wrong direction. This is a call that disturbs, a call to be aware of where we are going and to accept that we can change.

The disciples revealed the mercy – the loving kindness – of God in bringing liberty and healing. Like Jesus, they were not to force themselves on anyone. God respects our freedom. 'If any place will not welcome you and they refuse to hear you, shake off the dust that is on your feet as a testimony against them' (Mark 6:11).

Illustration

In the totalitarian state you are not allowed free choice. You must do as you are told. If you do not open your door to the officials, it will be broken down. You cannot hide because they will seek you out and make you do what they want.

Jesus is different. He has the power but he will not force himself upon you. The choice is yours: he respects your free will. You can edge him out of your life and home if you so choose. You can be too busy to bother to keep in contact with him if you so desire. He will not force you.

Have a large print of Holman Hunt's picture 'The Light of the World'. If you look at it you will see the door has not been opened for a long time. Jesus stands there knocking and waiting to bring his light upon those who live within. There is no means of opening the door from the outside. If he is to enter, you have to let him in. It is good to think of these words of Jesus every day: 'Behold, I stand at the door and knock' (Revelation 3:20).

COMPLETE COMMON WORSHIP

Sermon Illustrations

Proper 10

Sunday between 10 and 16 July inclusive

Aim

To compare the rule of Herod with the rule of Jesus.

Readings

2 Samuel 6:1-5, 12b-19 or Amos 7:7-15
Psalm 24 or Psalm 85:8-13
Ephesians 1:3-14
Mark 6:14-29

Thought for the day

You could present today's Gospel as a history lesson and show the dangerous times John the Baptist and Jesus lived in. But on its own none of that is very uplifting. As Mark and Matthew put the feeding of the 5000 next to the murder of John the Baptist, it is good to compare the events. We can look at the rule of Caesar compared to the rule of God: a way of death compared to the way of life.

Herod Antipas was the puppet ruler of Galilee. He served Rome and used military force to make his rule work. If anyone opposed him, he had them imprisoned or even put to death. John the Baptist had two faults in the eyes of Herod. First, John was popular with the people. Herod was afraid he might lead a rebellion. Like all tyrants he lived nervously and was suspicious of any popular person. Second, he saw John as dangerous because he spoke out against him and told the truth. Herod did not want to know the truth. To keep himself secure in power he had John imprisoned in the Castle of Machaerus on the east side of the Dead Sea. It is perched up on bare rocks and is one of the grimmest castles in the world. You can still see the dungeons where John the Baptist was imprisoned.

On his birthday Herod threw a feast for the rich and the famous. It was for members of the royal court, political leaders and officials – for people of influence. Herod was out to get what he could. His wife Herodias, who had been his brother's wife, was there. She had a seething anger against John the Baptist because he had objected to her marriage, and she wanted him killed. Their daughter Salome was also there and danced before them. This shows how decadent the court was as it was usually only loose women and prostitutes who danced before them. The ordinary women and slaves were counted as nobodies, not people but things to use, and they waited on the company. For their entertainment Salome danced, and to add to the entertainment she is offered whatever she would like. At the direction of her mother, she asks for John the Baptist's head. John was beheaded in prison and his head presented on a platter to Salome and she in turn presented it to her mother. Obviously this is not a safe place to be. This is the rule of force where people count for little and life is cheap.

The feast Jesus has is for any who come. He does not want to force them to do anything. He looks on them with compassion, caring for their needs. The poor, the needy, the hungry, those whom the world counts as nobodies, come to him. He gives them his attention. Such people would not have got anywhere near Herod. Jesus treats the poor and needy like royalty. He asks them to sit down (the word he uses actually means lie down) and his disciples wait upon them. (You may like to read out Mark 10:42-44). Jesus practised what he preached. He came to give and to care; not to take life but to save life. Jesus came not to proclaim his own rule but to bring in the rule of God through his love and sacrifice. This is the rule of love where everyone is counted as important.

To proclaim God is King is to challenge that the earthly ruler is almighty. It acknowledges a greater power. For this, Jesus will meet death as John the Baptist did.

Illustration

So many rulers rule by force. They often think of their subjects as objects for their own selfish ends. If people do not obey, there are ways of dealing with them, which include torture, imprisonment and even death. Dictators throughout history have got rid of those who opposed them by exterminating them; there are many tyrannical governments in our world that still operate like this.

The kingdom of heaven is the free gift of God's presence and love to us. It is not forced upon us but is offered freely. God loves us before we even turn to him. We are not rejected from his kingdom. We leave it of our own free will when we do not obey the King in love.

Proper 11

Sunday between 17 and 23 July inclusive

Aim

To show that we need times of quietness and rest.

Readings

2 Samuel 7:1-14a or Jeremiah 23:1-6
Psalm 89:20-37 or Psalm 23
Ephesians 2:11-22
Mark 6:30-34, 53-56

Thought for the day

When the disciples returned from their mission they gathered around Jesus and told him what they had done and taught. The crowds of people had kept them so busy they did not even have time to eat. Jesus said to them they should now go to a deserted place and rest. Here we see the balance of the Christian life: The Christian life is built up of going to the presence of God for refreshment, renewal and guidance and then going to people. The Christian learns to go to God with people in their heart and to people with God in their heart. No human can forever pour themselves out; there needs to be time for rest and renewal. If we have not spent time before God, we will not be able to introduce others to him.

There are two main dangers for everyone. The first is one of constant activity – and some church groups are like that. No one can work without rest: we cannot proclaim God unless we spend time quietly before him. Many Christians run out of resources or even faith because they have not learnt to be still and quiet before God. Our God is unable to be our strength because we are not still enough and quiet enough before him.

The second danger is that of too much withdrawal – though most churches cannot be charged with this. Devotion should lead to action. Awareness of God and his love should make us proclaim his goodness: prayer should lead to work. To turn to God is not to turn away from our fellow beings but to prepare us for caring and sharing with them in a better way.

Yet the rest the disciples sought was not to be. The crowds noted the direction Jesus took and they followed. The boat had a four-mile journey to cross the lake: it was a ten-mile walk for the crowd. No doubt some of this crowd set off and actually got there as quickly as Jesus. The boat journey was their only time of rest.

It would be easy to get frustrated with the demands of the people but Jesus was sorry for them. They were like sheep without a shepherd. They needed a guide and someone to care for them. They needed someone to love them and look after them. Let us see what Jesus meant by thinking of people as sheep without a shepherd.

Sheep without a shepherd lose their way. How right we are when we say, 'We have erred and strayed from your ways like lost sheep.' We need a guide and a travelling companion to prevent us from getting lost. Sadly, for so many today there is no knowledge of guidance or a companion.

Sheep without a caring shepherd can soon starve. So often people are undernourished in spirit. They might look well-fed but there is an emptiness within that nothing can fill except a relationship with God.

Sheep without a shepherd are in constant danger. The sheep cannot defend itself against wild beasts or from robbers. There are many things that can take away our life unless we discover eternal life in Jesus our Lord.

Illustration

There was a famous General who met a poor shepherd. The shepherd was distressed because he had lost a lamb and could not find it. The General offered to help and sent his soldiers in search of the lamb. One by one the soldiers returned to camp hungry, muddied and feeling too tired to carry on. It was dark by then and they felt they could do nothing more. The next morning, just as it was getting light, the General was seen coming into the camp carrying the lamb under his greatcoat to keep it warm. This is what made him such a great leader: he was not put off and he did not think of himself too much. He only stopped looking for the lamb when he found it. (You can compare this to the Good Shepherd.)

Proper 12

Sunday between 24 and 30 July inclusive

Aim

To show the care and concern of Jesus.

Readings

2 Samuel 11:1-15 or 2 Kings 4:42-44
Psalm 14 or Psalm 145:10-18
Ephesians 3:14-21
John 6:1-21

Thought for the day

The feeding of the five thousand reveals a good deal about Jesus and his mission.

First, there is the compassion of Jesus. He saw the hunger of the people who had been with him for a good while. He felt for these people who were physically and spiritually hungry. It would have been easy to say, 'There are too many of them; we cannot hope to feed them.' But Jesus has compassion: his heart goes out to them.

Second, there is the challenge of Jesus. He asks Philip, 'Where can we buy bread?' It must have been quite a daunting question when Philip looked at the crowd. Philip estimated that it would take about six months' wages to raise the money to buy enough bread. Jesus was challenging Philip and the disciples to look at their potential and resources. Though our resources are small, they can be greatly transformed if put in God's hands. Andrew seems to rise to the occasion by saying, 'There is a lad here who has five barley loaves and two fish. But what are they among so many?' We often wonder if our small efforts make a difference; well, here we learn they do.

Third is the command of Jesus: 'Make the people sit down.' The disciples were asked to get the people ready for a meal, and then, after the prayer, to distribute it. Jesus does not work alone; he works through us and with us. Without Jesus, we cannot do any great works. Without us, Jesus will not work; he wants us willingly to share with him.

Next is the concern of Jesus. Jesus says, 'Gather up the fragments left over, so that nothing may be lost.' Who would have thought that Jesus, who could feed five thousand with five loaves, would be bothered about crumbs and scraps? Jesus does not want waste: he is concerned how we use the things around us and how we deal with the world. It is good to know Jesus is concerned for the leftovers and that which is lost: they are precious in his sight.

Lastly, notice the caution of Jesus. The people were excited. Some saw the feeding as a 'sign', saying, 'This is indeed the prophet who is to come into the world.' They wanted to take him by force to make him king. Jesus did not come for this kind of kingship or to be a puppet of the people. The people were after Jesus for what they could get out of him. Jesus once again withdrew to the mountain by himself. Yet even in doing this there are hints that Jesus is like Moses who went up on Mount Sinai.

Illustration

There is a story about a boy walking along a beach. All along the shore there were thousands of starfish washed up. You could hardly walk on the sand for them. The boy was putting a few in his bucket and taking them back to the sea. A man came along and said, 'There are thousands of starfish stranded. Why do you bother? You will hardly make an impression. You will only be able to put a few back into the sea.' The boy replied. 'It will matter for these few and it will matter to me.'

Though our effort may be small, it is counted as worthwhile, and who knows what God will do with it?

Proper 13

Sunday between 31 July and 6 August inclusive

Aim

To see Jesus as the Bread of Life.

Readings

2 Samuel 11:26–12:13a or Exodus 16:2-4, 9-15
Psalm 51:1-12 or Psalm 78:23-29
Ephesians 4:1-6
John 6:24-35

Thought for the day

The early Church met regularly for the breaking of the bread. It is not surprising that there is a deep interest in Jesus as the Bread of Life. Today's Gospel ends with Jesus saying, 'I am the bread of life' (John 6:35).

It is worth looking at the questions raised in today's Gospel and the response Jesus gives to each of them as he seeks to clarify what true faith entails.

'Rabbi, when did you come here?' allows Jesus to discuss the motives of those who seek him: 'You are looking for me, not because you saw signs, but because you ate your fill of the loaves.' We often fail to read the signs that point us to God. We journey on, ever seeking, and ignore the God who can satisfy our emptiness and who is in our midst. We fill our lives with perishable goods and forget the One who alone gives eternal life. 'Do not work for the food that perishes, but for the food that endures to eternal life, which the Son of Man will give you.'

'What must we do to perform the works of God?' The work of God is to believe in him and in whom he has sent. The Greek word for 'believe' is far more than an assent to certain ideas about God; it is to have 'faith' in him: that is, to have a living relationship with God. Faith is about our personal relationship with the living God and with Jesus whom he has sent. If we do not have a relationship with God, we cannot truly perform his works. We are asked to give our heart to God. The German word 'belieben' is the root of the English word 'believe' and it means 'to belove'.

'What sign are you going to give us, then, so that we may believe in you? What work are you performing?' They hungered for more signs and more excitement and failed to seek the relationship that Jesus was offering. 'Our ancestors ate the manna in the wilderness; as it is written, "He gave them bread from heaven to eat."' Jesus responds by saying it was God not Moses that fed them in the wilderness and God gives you 'the true bread from heaven': that is, Jesus who came down from heaven and gives life to the world (John 6:33).

'Sir, give us this bread always.' The 'always' on this occasion is the Greek work 'pantote', which means again and again and again. Once more they have missed the point. Jesus clearly says, 'I am the bread of life. Whoever comes to me will never be hungry, and whoever believes in me will never be thirsty' (John 6:35). By saying, 'I am the bread of life', Jesus is saying he is linked to the 'I Am' who is God: he is God. The love of God is revealed in Jesus Christ and he meets the needs of those with inner hunger and thirst. In whatever situation we find ourselves we can trust in the unfailing power and love of God. There is no doubt that in writing his Gospel John was aware of the sacramental implications of the bread.

Illustration

Throughout our world there are people who seem to have to fill their lives with food, with things or with activity. No matter how much they get, they are still not satisfied. When young people say they are bored, it is usually when they have plenty happening around them but they recognise emptiness within. Bored means having a hole drilled in you. There is something in you that things cannot fill, no matter how you stuff yourself or your days. God made us for himself and nothing else will really fill the space he created within us for himself. In each of us there is a space for the eternal and nothing less than the eternal God can fill it.

Proper 14

Sunday between 7 and 13 August inclusive

Aim

To show the calling of God and the stalling of our hearts.

Readings

2 Samuel 18:5-9, 31-33 or 1 Kings 19:4-8
Psalm 130 or Psalm 34:1-8
Ephesians 4:25–5:2
John 6:35, 41-51

Thought for the day

John's Gospel continues with the reactions of the people to the feeding of the five thousand. For John this is in the context of the Passover festival and of the Christian breaking of the bread meetings. The readings from John 6 obviously have a Eucharistic setting.

We begin today where last week's Gospel ended with Jesus saying, 'I am the bread of life.' Sadly the reaction of the people was to start 'murmuring', complaining about him (6:41). Jesus is offering himself to them and all they can do is grumble and complain. How often the great mystery of God's gift of himself to us is lost because of our attitude and prejudices. God has always worked through his creation and has come to us time and again through the ordinary, but we fail to see it because we are so prejudiced against it. We are forever looking for another miracle whilst God is actually offering himself to us. The people did not see that Jesus could be anyone special, and certainly thought he could not be God's Son, or the 'Bread of Life', because they knew where he lived. They refused to see beyond the obvious: that they thought they knew his mum and dad! Jesus tells them to stop murmuring, stop complaining and grumbling. The people with Moses had grumbled against him and therefore against God (Exodus 15:24; 16:2). It was believed that such grumbling prevented them coming into the Promised Land. 'Do not complain as some of them did, and were destroyed by the destroyer' (1 Corinthians 10:10). How often we miss out on the mystery and wonder of God's gift to us through our attitude of complaining and dissatisfaction. When

Jesus offers himself to us we spend our time debating what we think of him! Let us learn to talk to God more than we talk about him; to come before the mystery with a sense of awe.

Jesus says, 'No one can come to me unless drawn by the Father.' The word which Jesus uses for 'drawn' is the translation of the Hebrew in Jeremiah 31:3 (the Authorised Version has 'With loving kindness I have drawn thee'). The word implies the tugging of God but it also suggests some resistance. The same word is used for tugging a heavy net ashore (John 21:6, 11). God tugs at us in love but we always have the power to resist him. In verse 45 of today's Gospel, Jesus says how all are taught by God, not only the Jews. All are called but all do not listen; all do not react to the tugging of God.

Jesus then repeats how he is the bread of life. Here is an invitation to come to him. Analysis and debate can easily keep you away. With words we can avoid the Word of God. How great is your resistance to his call and his love? There are none so deaf as those who do not want to hear.

Illustration

There was a brilliant scientist who was keen on analysis. He wanted to get to the basic elements of everything. A meal was set before him and he was hungry. But he wanted to check where this food came from and what was in it. He went into his laboratory and started on a loaf of bread. He did not eat any. He checked what its constituents were. He discovered wholemeal flour, water, yeast, vegetable fat, preservatives, emulsifiers and vinegar. He checked out the preservatives and found calcium propionate and potassium sorbate. By now he was starving but research must go on. The emulsifiers kept him busy for ages. He found mono- and diacetyl tartaric acid, esters of mono- and diglycerides, fatty acids. He was kept very busy but he grew weaker and weaker. He still had to analyse the wholemeal and check out the grains. Sadly he died of starvation whilst looking at the loaf. There was food all around him but he died of analysis.

Proper 15

Sunday between 14 and 20 August inclusive

Aim

To seek to abide in Jesus and let him abide in us.

Readings

1 Kings 2:10-12; 3:3-14 or Proverbs 9:1-6
Psalm 111 or Psalm 34:9-14
Ephesians 5:15-20
John 6:51-58

Thought for the day

The Passover and the Eucharist are the setting for this discourse on the 'bread of heaven', and it takes place in the synagogue at Capernaum. At the Passover the Jews are required to eat the unleavened bread and the paschal lamb amongst other things. The Passover remembers the exodus from Egypt, the wandering in the wilderness, including the provision of manna. The reading begins with the last verse from last week's Gospel: 'I am the living bread that came down from heaven. Whoever eats this bread will live for ever; and the bread that I will give for the life of the world is my flesh.'

Many claims are here. Jesus is still purposely using the words 'I am', which are used as a naming of God. God comes to us in Jesus Christ. It is Jesus who is the living bread. This is a greater offer than Moses', for the children of Israel ate the manna and still died: those who eat this bread from heaven will live for ever. 'The bread that I give for the life of the world is my flesh.' Jesus is not giving us things; he is giving us himself. He offers himself *to* us and offers himself *for* us. He wants us to take of him. We who receive Communion can understand this, and that we abide in him and he in us. The Jews murmured – as ever, analysis prevents the mystery from entering into our lives. The Jews said, 'How can this man give us his flesh to eat?' Surely it is a good question. Do we understand that Jesus was replacing the Passover lamb with his own sacrifice?

Jesus insists, 'Unless you eat the flesh of the Son of Man and drink his blood, you have no life in you.' Unless we take Jesus' life into our life, we will lack the fullness of life. Jesus continues with the theme of mutual indwelling: 'Those who eat my flesh and drink my blood abide in me, and I in them.' This mutual indwelling is the purpose and the joy of every Communion and with it the knowledge that through him we live for ever.

Jesus is not a figure in a book, not even the Bible. He is the living Lord and wants to be one with us. When we abide in him and he in us we have eternal life.

Illustration

There was once a man who bought a beautiful box for his wife. The box had flowers on the top and they would glow in the dark. As it was for her birthday he hid it away in a drawer and left it there for a few weeks. On her birthday it was given to her all wrapped in a lovely parcel. She was delighted and could hardly wait until the evening. When it got dark she looked at the box but it did not shine; it had not changed at all. They both waited until it got really dark but the box never did shine. They felt a little cheated because the box was bought to shine. Then a little note fell from the packaging. It said, 'If you want me to shine all night, you need put me in the sun all day.' The box would only glow if it was left out in the daylight. They left it out all the next day and, true to the words, all night it glowed with a splendid light.

If we are to glow with eternal life, we need to be placed in the presence of the Son of God to let him abide in us and for us to know we abide in him.

Proper 16

Sunday between 21 and 27 August inclusive

Aim

To affirm our commitment to Christ.

Readings

1 Kings 8:(1, 6, 10-11) 22-30, 41-43 or Joshua 24:1-2a, 14-18
Psalm 84 or Psalm 34:15-22
Ephesians 6:10-20
John 6:56-69

Thought for the day

God does not force himself upon us. He has given us the freedom to choose whether we serve him or not. He gives himself to us in love and we can choose whether to return that love or to ignore him. Some definitely choose to ignore or go against God; others ignore him by default – that is, they let other things and people squeeze God out. If we are to love and serve God, we have to be sure we have made this a definite choice.

Joshua called the tribes of Israel together and asked them to dedicate their lives to the true God. If they were unwilling to serve the Lord, they should at least choose whom they were going to serve, whether it was the gods of Egypt or the gods of the Amorites. There is always the danger of not making a clear choice. Joshua gave a lead by saying, 'As for me and my household, we will serve the LORD.'

Once they were given a lead, the Israelites declared they would not desert the LORD and follow other gods. They then recited how the LORD delivered them from Egypt and from slavery: the LORD did great wonders in their sight and the LORD protected them. 'Therefore we will also serve the LORD for he is our God.' The Israelites made a definite decision to serve the LORD.

In today's Gospel we find two definite groups of people. Those who find the teaching too hard, who take offence and do not believe, belong to the first group. They turn away from Jesus and no longer go with him. There are many who do this. The second group are those who seek to stay with him and be loyal to him.

Amongst those are the disciples. Jesus asks them, 'Do you also wish to go away?' They are not forced to stay: if they want, they can leave. Judas will later prove the possibility of this. Simon Peter replies for the disciples and says, 'Lord, to whom can we go? You have the words of eternal life. We have come to believe and know that you are the Holy One of God.'

We are given the opportunity of turning away from him or committing ourselves to follow him. This is not just a one-off choice; we have to make it every day and sometimes many times in a day.

Illustration

Here is a story of loyalty. A man and his dog walked in the hill country. The man saw an old mine in a hillside and went in. Whilst inside, the roof collapsed and trapped the man by his leg. For a while the dog stayed with him but it then went outside the mine and stood at the entrance. There it began to howl to attract attention. No one took any notice at first. The dog became hungry and thirsty but it did not leave its post. The weather became bad; the dog got wet and cold but it stayed put and continued to howl. Finally a nearby farmer decided there was something wrong with the dog and he climbed the hillside to find it. When he arrived, the dog stopped howling but would not let him touch it or even feed it. It tried to lead him into the mine. The farmer made to go away but as soon as he did this the dog started to howl and to walk towards the mine again. At last he decided to go to the entrance and call to see if there was anyone there. He heard a voice and so went cautiously inside. He saw the man was trapped and went for help. The dog seemed to understand because it now stayed with its master and remained with him until help came and he was rescued.

Proper 17

Sunday between 28 August and 3 September inclusive

Aim

To make sure our traditions do not hinder our relationship with God.

Readings

Song of Solomon 2:8-13 or Deuteronomy 4:1-2, 6-9
Psalm 45:1-2, 6-9 or Psalm 15
James 1:17-27
Mark 7:1-8, 14-15, 21-23

Thought for the day

It is hard to believe that the Pharisees would travel all the way from Jerusalem to Galilee to tell Jesus that he and his disciples had dirty hands. This meeting is about confrontation and it shows how Jesus was challenging the attitudes of the established church.

The Pharisees say that Jesus and his disciples are unclean. They have not washed properly before eating bread. Very often Jesus did things that made him unclean in the eyes of the Pharisees. He touched a leper; he touched a bier on which there was a dead man. A woman who was suffering from a haemorrhage touched him. Jesus was declared unclean by each of these acts, and anyone who was in contact with him became unclean also.

The Jewish rituals of washing were mainly good common sense. They were safeguards against infection and harmful contacts. In the same way, we know we ought to wash after doing a dirty job or going to the toilet. But with the tradition becoming fixed there was a danger that someone felt they could do something they ought not to and then just wash their hands and be clean. Within the Christian Church some people have misused the sacrament of confession. We cannot truly seek forgiveness of a sin if we intend to go on committing it. We cannot come to church on a Sunday for absolution if we intend to do the same things again.

Jesus replied that it was no use going through outward rituals if the inside is not cleansed. A show of being clean is just pretence. Jesus calls the Pharisees hypocrites. Originally a hypocrite was a play actor; it meant one who pretends or gives a set reply. It came to mean a person whose life was an act without depth or sincerity. Anyone who goes through the religious acts or rituals without a relationship to God is a hypocrite. Cleanliness does not depend on whether you have washed or eaten; it depends on your inner attitude, on your thoughts and your heart. It is no use being present at worship if we do not give ourselves to our God. This is why the Psalmist prayed, 'Make me a clean heart, O God, and renew a right Spirit within me.' We must be sure our human traditions do not come between God and us. Maybe this would make Christians take a careful look at how we keep Christmas.

Jesus lists among the things that defile a person evil intentions or designs. Every outward act of sin comes from an inward choice. We need to keep watch on our thoughts and our decisions. Very often our departure from goodness and from God begins with the attitudes and choices that we make. If we fail to give God the central place in our thinking, we will soon push him to the edges of our life.

Another word Jesus uses about defilement is translated as 'fornications'. It is from the Greek word 'porneiai' and means every kind of sexual vice. We must include all pornography and wrong attitudes towards sex. Anything that degrades others or ourselves makes us unclean. We need keep a close watch on our attitudes and what we expose our minds to.

Illustration

A devout Muslim carries his prayer mat around with him and prays a fixed number of times each day. At the fixed times he will unroll his mat and turn to God. This is a wonderful way of keeping in contact with his creator.

There was a certain Muslim who had great anger in his heart. He was in hot pursuit of a man whom he wanted to kill. He had a dagger and was intent on murder. Suddenly the call to prayer rang out from the mosque. The man stopped for a moment, rushed his prayers, then continued on his murderous chase. The prayer was part of his daily ritual but he did not let it touch his heart. This man could be seen to be a hypocrite.

Proper 18

Sunday between 4 and 10 September inclusive

Aim

To encourage our church to be open and welcoming.

Readings

Proverbs 22:1-2, 8-9, 22-23 or Isaiah 35:4-7a
Psalm 125 or Psalm 146
James 2:1-10 (11-13) 14-17
Mark 7:24-37

Thought for the day

The Pharisees had declared Jesus and the disciples to be unclean. This was a way of banning them and any who had contact with them from their synagogues. Therefore it is not surprising that the stories following this event come from a non-Jewish area.

Tyre and Sidon are famed for their Phoenician sailors who were the first to navigate the seas by the stars. Tyre is 40 miles north of Capernaum and Sidon is 60 miles away. Both cities looked to the sea and overseas for their trade.

Jesus is in Gentile territory. Just as the Jews would not soil their lips with unwashed pots, so they avoided contact with the Gentiles for that would also make them unclean. As Jesus challenged the distinction between clean and unclean foods, he is now challenging the distinction between clean and unclean people. The Jewish people survived through their exclusiveness. Jesus wanted to show that the love of God is inclusive. The rest of the world, the Gentiles, also have a place in God's kingdom.

Whilst there, Jesus is approached by two Gentiles. A woman comes asking help for her daughter and a man who is deaf with an impediment in his speech is brought to Jesus. The woman was a Greek, and adding to this that she was a Syrophoenician evokes the idea of the fractiousness there was between the Jews and the people of Tyre. There was a definite animosity between these groups. Jesus takes no notice of this division.

When Jesus replies to her plea for help, 'Let the children be fed first, for it is not fair to take the children's food and throw it to the dogs', he would have found many a Jew rejoicing, for they use the term 'Gentile dogs' as a term of contempt. Jesus used a diminutive word for 'dog' to soften this and there is no doubt his voice did not imply his rejection of the woman. Israel may be 'first' but only first; many others from the rest of the world would also be fed with the 'Bread of Life'.

The woman had sought Jesus out, and now from the Greek-speaking area of the Decapolis they brought to Jesus a man who was deaf and had an impediment in his speech. Again Jesus is to offer the healing and love of God to this Gentile. Isaiah said that a sign of God's kingdom would be when 'the ears of the deaf (are) unstopped . . . and the tongue of the speechless sing for joy' (Isaiah 35:5-6). On a deeper level we need to consider the Jewish idea of hearing and speaking. Hearing was the most important sense because it was through hearing and speaking that the covenant was given. It was Israel who heard; the Gentiles were deaf. The Gentiles cannot hear the word of God or sing his praises. Once more Jesus challenges this view by accepting the man who is brought to him. Jesus acts out the miracle as the man would not hear the words. When Jesus says, 'Ephphatha' – that is, 'Be opened' – it can be a call not only to the man but also to the opening of the Gentiles to the Christ. The ears of the Gentiles are opened to the Word of God. The man, representing the Gentiles, zealously proclaims what Jesus has done. The response is 'He has done all things well; he even makes the deaf to hear and the mute to speak.' The whole world is being opened to the Christ. Let not the Church act in exclusive ways.

Illustration

There was once a very famous church. Every Sunday it was fashionable to go there and be seen. People came in their finery. Some of the most important people of the land attended it. The music and the choir were superb, the ordering of the service was of a very high standard; everything done was to the highest degree of excellence and in the best possible taste. For a good few Sundays a poorly dressed and shabby-looking person turned up at the door but was turned away for one reason or another. After a few weeks of trying to get in, the woman sat on the lowest step and prayed to God, 'Lord, why can I not get entrance into this church?' The Lord replied, 'My daughter, how do I know? I have been trying to get into this church for years.'

Proper 19

Sunday between 11 and 17 September inclusive

Aim

To encourage a personal relationship with Christ the living Lord.

Readings

Proverbs 1:20-33 or Isaiah 50:4-9a
Psalm 19 or Wisdom of Solomon 7:26–8:1 or Psalm 116:1-9
James 3:1-12
Mark 8:27-38

Thought for the day

Jesus and the disciples are 25 miles north of the Sea of Galilee in an area that was well known for pagan worship. They are travelling around the villages of Caesarea Philippi. This area was famous for the worship of the god Baal in ancient times. The Greeks said it was the birthplace of Pan, the god of nature: the pipes of Pan could be heard in the woods and wood nymphs were to be seen dancing. It was here that Herod the Great built a gleaming white temple for the worship of Caesar. Herod's son Philip beautified the temple and added his name to the town, so that it became known as Caesarea Philippi. It was here, most likely under a starry sky by a campfire, that Jesus asked the disciples about their thoughts towards him.

Jesus asks first, 'Who do people say that I am?' Some were saying he was John the Baptist returned from the dead. No doubt this caused some amusement in the camp. Others were saying he was Elijah returned to herald in the coming of the Messiah. Yet others were saying he was a prophet, a good man and a wonder-worker. People still suggest all sorts of ideas about who Jesus is.

Jesus then asks, 'But who do *you* say that I am?' This is what Jesus wants to know from each of us. Not a summary of other people's ideas. He wants the reply from those who have spent time with him, the personal conviction of a disciple. It is not enough to be able to recite creeds or what others have said about Jesus. A person can be an atheist and still pass exams in theology. You can be able to recite stories about the historical Jesus and not be a Christian. Jesus seeks a personal response from each of us. He wants us to know him, to talk to him, and only then talk *about* him.

Notice how personal Jesus is in his invitations:

Come to me.
I will refresh you.
Abide in me and I will abide in you.

We can only be true disciples if we spend time with him, if we get to know him. Then we can respond as Peter does by saying, 'You are the Christ, the Messiah.' When we personally come to know Jesus as the 'Anointed One of God' we will acknowledge him as our Lord and Saviour. One of the reasons Jesus told the disciples to tell no one is that people had wrong ideas about what the Messiah should do. They would learn through Jesus that being the Messiah would involve his suffering, and they would discover that they will be called to suffer like him.

Peter tried to sway Jesus away from any conflict but Jesus knew he could not escape the battle if he had come to win people to God. He knew the powers of evil would rally against him and he could not run away. He did not want to suffer; that's what made Peter's words all the more dangerous. The Tempter often seeks to weaken our resolve through our friends. We need to learn to stand firm.

Illustration

In his poem 'Gareth and Lynette', Tennyson tells of the struggle Gareth has to leave home. He wants to become one of the knights of Arthur but his mother does not want him to leave home. She has already lost two of her sons to Arthur's court. 'Hast thou no pity on my loneliness?' she asks. 'Stay, my best son, ye are yet more a boy than a man,' she pleads. The mother produces excellent reasons for Gareth to stay at home and ignore his vision. Here, the tempter is using someone who loves him dearly to stop Gareth serving his vision. Gareth replies:

O Mother,
How can you keep me tethered to you – Shame.
Man I am a grown, a man's work I must do.
Follow the deer? Follow Christ the King,
Live pure, speak true, right wrong, follow the King –
Else, wherefore born.

Gareth was not tempted through his mother but followed the vision as he saw it.

Jesus could not allow Peter to sway him from his purpose.

Proper 20

Sunday between 18 and 24 September inclusive

Aim

To show that Jesus calls us to serve each other rather than to lord it over people.

Readings

Proverbs 31:10-31 or Wisdom of Solomon 1:16–2:1, 12-22 or
Jeremiah 11:18-20
Psalm 1 or Psalm 54
James 3:13–4:3, 7-8a
Mark 9:30-37

Thought for the day

Today's Gospel splits into three parts. In the first part (9:30), Mark shows Jesus seeking to keep his whereabouts a secret. The reasons are twofold. It was a time for teaching his disciples and getting them to understand his purpose and message. It was also necessary to avoid conflict before the disciples had time to understand. This was a precious and important time for Jesus.

In the second part Jesus is predicting his death and resurrection. He is seeking to warn his disciples of what lies ahead, the dangers and the suffering, his death and resurrection. This is important for the disciples to grasp and it is repeated three times (9:31, 8:31 and 10:32-34). We are told that the disciples did not understand what Jesus was saying and were afraid to ask him. No doubt this is part of the reason for the repetition. The disciples found it hard to grasp that God's Anointed One, the Messiah, could be rejected and killed by his own people. To understand the idea of a suffering Messiah was beyond their comprehension. There are still some Christians today who suggest that if only we had more faith we would escape suffering. That is not the way of this world.

The third part is the turning towards Carpernaum and back towards Jerusalem and danger. The disciples still think in worldly terms of power – hence their rejection of any idea of the cross or a suffering Christ. They still expect a display of might and when they will share in ruling. When they were on the way back to Capernaum they argued with one another who was the greatest

(9:34). In the ancient world, social position was highly ordered; people were expected to stay in 'their place'. The disciples wanted to know their place in the kingdom so that they could get the greatest gain from it. The phrase 'on the way' (33) is the same word as used in Mark 4:14 to describe the seed that got no entry because of Satan taking away any chance of growth. This must have been a very sad time for Jesus. He is willingly going to Jerusalem to offer his life for others and his disciples are arguing among themselves about position and power. Perhaps Judas believed that by betraying Jesus he would make Jesus use force against his enemies.

In 9:35 Jesus assumes the teaching position of a rabbi by sitting down and calling his disciples to him. What Jesus says turns their striving for position upside down – we do well to heed it. Standing, security, satisfaction are not gained by power struggles or beating the Joneses, but by serving. Not from getting and gaining but from giving and grace. The followers of Jesus are called to serve and to give their lives for others as he did.

Jesus illustrates what he means by picking up a little child and taking it in his arms and saying, 'Whoever welcomes one such child in my name welcomes me, and whoever welcomes me, welcomes not me but the one who sent me.' Children had no rights and could make no demands; they had the lowest place in the social order – of course, love made nonsense of such a statement. Being a follower of Jesus means to be willing to give of yourself and to serve. It is not being servile but choosing to give your life to others and for others. By this welcoming of children, or the least, we welcome into our lives not only Jesus the risen Lord but also God. Jesus will emphasise his own desire to serve when James and John are still seeking positions of power. Then he said, 'The Son of Man came not to be served but to serve, and to give his life as a ransom for many' (Mark 10:45).

Illustration

There is a story about a fourth wise man who wanted to come and see the Christ. He started off well. He dressed in his best clothes, rode a fine horse and brought a present of precious stones. On his journey he met a group of poor people who were hungry, so he gave away half of his jewels for them to trade for food. Then he met a family who were taken into slavery because of a debt. He used the rest of his precious jewels to buy their freedom. Further on he found a merchant in deep distress. His horse had died on him and he would not get his goods to be sold on time. The generous wise man gave him his horse and all its trappings. Now he had to walk on foot and the going was slow.

He was old and very weary. He wondered if he would ever see the Christ. The way was very muddy and he met a young family trying to get their cart out of the mud. The wise man helped them but ended up very dirty. He now wondered if he should give up and go home. In a dream he was told, 'The Christ you seek is now only a little distance away. He will welcome you because he knows you. You have met him many times on your journey in the poor and the needy. You soiled your clothes in caring for him. Tomorrow you will meet him and he will welcome you.' And so it was.

COMPLETE COMMON WORSHIP

Sermon Illustrations

Proper 21

Sunday between 25 September and 1 October inclusive

Aim

To express the unity of all believers, as there is only 'One Church, one faith, one Lord'.

Readings

Esther 7:1-6, 9-10; 9:20-22 or Numbers 11:4-6, 10-16, 24-29
Psalm 124 or Psalm 19:7-14
James 5:13-20
Mark 9:38-50

Thought for the day

Pride and prejudice or a feeling of our own insecurity and uncertainty often make us set ourselves against others. We see people as rivals, when in reality they are seeking the same good that we are. Sadly, the history of the Church is often one of rivalry and bitter factions. We set rules and regulations to say we are special and suggest others are not, especially if they do things in a different way. Many a church is afraid of, or incapable of, change or taking on something new. There seems to be a built-in fear of anything different. This was often the trouble with the Scribes and Pharisees when they met Jesus: they could only accept Jesus on their terms; they could not see that he had anything to offer.

In today's Gospel, John expresses a feeling of being scandalised by an exorcist who was casting out demons in the name of Jesus. In the ancient world there was a universal belief in demons. Everyone believed that physical and mental illness was the work of demons. Anyone who was ill was under a malign influence. The commonest way to exorcise a demon was to find a more powerful spirit and command the demon in that name to come out of the person. The demon could not stand against a more powerful name. John had found a man driving out demons in the name of Jesus and had tried to stop him. The reason he gave was that he was not one of them – that is, the little company of men around Jesus. Jesus said the man should not be stopped. We need to learn that those who are not working against us are for us.

We need to learn there are more ways than we can understand in which God comes to us and we come to God. We should not stop anyone because it is not our way. God is far bigger than our little understanding and works in many ways. We must guard against being exclusive. Heed these words:

He drew a circle that shut me out –
Rebel, heretic, a thing to flout.
But love and I had the wit to win;
We drew a circle that took him in.
Edward Markham (1852-1940)

Let us rejoice in the other churches that are around us and in the work they do.

Illustration

Hospitality was of great importance in the ancient world. By being open to others, the great Other, who is God, was given the opportunity to enter into your life. See the example of Abraham and Sarah when visited by the Lord (Genesis 18:1-15). In the story it is hard to decide whether we are dealing with three men, three angels or the three-person God. Ask the congregation who visited Abraham: was it men, angels, God? (Be careful how you phrase the question for it is not an 'either/or'. All visited Abraham at Mamre. The person that replies 'Yes' to the question or says, 'All three' would get top marks!)

There is a Celtic poem which expresses the Other approaching us through others.

I saw a stranger yestere'en
I put food in the eating place,
drink in the drinking place,
music in the listening place
and in the sacred name of the Triune
he blessed myself and my house,
my cattle and my dear ones,
and the lark said in her song
often, often, often,
goes the Christ in a stranger's guise.

Proper 22

Sunday between 2 and 8 October inclusive

Aim

To show that our relationships are important.

Readings

Job 1:1; 2:1-10 or Genesis 2:18-24
Psalm 26 or Psalm 8
Hebrews 1:1-4; 2:5-12
Mark 10:2-16

Thought for the day

In Genesis we hear that it is not good for a human to be alone. The Three Persons God values relationships and love. Human beings are to have a relationship with the world around them. We are put in charge of a world and we are accountable to the Creator for it. God created all out of his love and wants us to love it also. We are to express our relationship with God through our relationship with his creation. We have a responsibility to God for our use of and our sharing in creation. The human cannot survive alone and needs a helper and a partner. We are responsible for and to our partner in all our dealings. Through the love and understanding we share, with each other, we will grow in our love and understanding of God. Our relationship with God is expressed through our relationship with each other. If we do not treat each other with respect and the world with respect, it is not likely that we will respect God. In the same way, if we betray our God, we are as likely to betray each other! When our relationships break down it is bound to affect our relationship with God who loves us equally.

In Job we see a wife who feels deeply for her husband and his suffering. She suggests he should curse the Creator for what has happened to him. Obviously she underestimates his relationship of trust with God. Job understands that life in this world is not all sunshine and roses.

We disturb the relationship with creation when we act through selfishness and greed; by doing so we act irresponsibly. The destruction of so many creatures and plants in the name of so-called progress is a good example. What is happening to the rain forests and what is happening to the poor of our world are reflections of our relationships. There is a danger we just use people and creatures for our own gain, regardless of the results.

The most testing relationships are those we live with. It is said of a home that it is where we are treated the best and react the worst. Do not let that be true of us.

Relationships must be worked at, must be maintained. We must never take each other for granted, or deal with each other as if we had a servant or a slave. Relationships are meant always to reflect love. When our hearts are hardened we are already beginning a divorce, a break in our relationships. This is as true of neglecting our prayers as of taking each other for granted.

The disciples did not want to be bothered by the children or those who were bringing them. Jesus saw a desire for a relationship with himself and with the Father.

Illustration

Once a bird flying high overhead saw how our world was becoming polluted. The bird saw the rubbish dumped into the sea and fish struggling to survive, great tracts of land being robbed of trees, the ice-caps slowly melting. So it decided that it must tell the humans about what was happening. The first group would not listen – well, who would believe a bird! The next group were making good profits and did not want anything to be disturbed. A third group said they would happily talk about it for years. No one wanted to do anything. Yet the bird knew that all things were linked together. If the humans destroyed the environment, all the birds and all the animals would also suffer. Why were the humans so insensitive to their surroundings and to each other? The bird learnt that the humans had lost a sense of awe and wonder because they had broken their relationship with the Creator God. If they would not listen to the cries of creation, if they would not listen to the voice of God, they were not likely to hear a bird.

Proper 23

Sunday between 9 and 15 October inclusive

Aim

To show that God wants all of us and not just gifts and prayers.

Readings

Job 23:1-9, 16-17 or Amos 5:6-7, 10-15
Psalm 22:1-15 or Psalm 90:12-17
Hebrews 4:12-16
Mark 10:17-31

Thought for the day

It seems some people have everything going for them. Today we hear of a rich man coming to Jesus. St Matthew tells us the man is young (19:20). St Luke tells us he is a ruler (18:18): he is a rich young ruler – obviously God has blessed him. We also learn that he keeps the commandments. Now he comes asking what he should do to gain eternal life. He comes running to Jesus and throws himself at his feet. Surely here is a chance of a useful disciple. There is something startling about this situation when this rich young man of authority throws himself at the feet of a penniless wanderer from Nazareth.

Jesus seems to be hard on this man. Maybe it was the way the question was phrased. First, there is a bit of flattery – 'Good Master' – and then 'what must I do to gain . . .' It would seem this man was in the business of making a profit. He did not come to give of himself but to gain for himself. He already had many blessings but he wanted more. No doubt he was willing to give something for it. But Jesus replies that the man cannot pay the price. God does not want things instead of ourselves; he does not even want prayers or sacrifices unless we can give ourselves to him. Obedience to commandments is good but God wants more: he wants our love.

There is always the danger of being possessed by things. Instead of owning things, they begin to own us and we become possessed by our possessions – or some of us are possessed by the lack of them! We spend much of our lives seeking to gain, to get, to have, and we can be in danger of losing sight of loving and giving of ourselves. Money can be a good reflection of this. Some people's pockets are as hard to touch as their hearts.

Here was a man given a glorious opportunity; the same one that was offered to Matthew when he was at the tax desk: 'Leave it all and follow me.' Jesus invited this man to a great adventure, offered him the way to eternal life. But he went away grieving, and it is possible he would grieve for ever. Why did he grieve? Because 'he had many possessions'. He could not enter into the fullness of life because of the things that were around him. This is surely one of the most tragic stories of the Gospels and a warning to all of us.

Illustration

Imagine a table. I want you to put on it all the things you want to give to God: your time, talents, money; your home, your friends, your loved ones; your job, your plans, your future.

You are going to need a great big table. We raise up the things we want to give to God and say, 'All things come from you, O God, and of your own do we give you.'

But wait, one thing that God wants is still missing. Who knows what it is?

GOD WANTS YOU.

More than any gift, more than gold or silver, God wants you.

God wants you to give yourself to him.

God wants you to give your love.

God wants you more than anything.

St Paul said, 'If I give away all my possessions . . . but do not have love, I gain nothing' (1 Corinthians 13:3).

Proper 24

Sunday between 16 and 22 October inclusive

Aim

To compare the ambition of James and John and the servant role of Jesus.

Readings

Job 38:1-7 (34-41) or Isaiah 53:4-12
Psalm 104:1-9, 24, 35c or Psalm 91:9-16
Hebrews 5:1-10
Mark 10:35-45

Thought for the day

Jesus is on his way to Jerusalem. He has turned towards the opposition, towards the cross and death. He wants his disciples to understand and be prepared. It must have been so hard for Jesus when they failed to grasp what he was saying.

James and John had just heard Jesus talking about his death and yet they were still thinking in terms of power and rule. They still did not understand what sort of Messiah Jesus is. They could only think in earthly terms. Only after the crucifixion would they see in a different way.

James and John were after position and promotion: they wanted personal gain and power. Their thoughts were on getting not giving, on success rather than sacrifice. The other ten disciples were angry with James and John because they thought they had tried to steal a lead on them. The twelve could only see the rule of Jesus and his kingdom in earthly terms of power and force. The Messiah the Jews hoped for was the Lion of Judah, a king like David who would drive out their enemies.

In today's reading from Isaiah we get a glimpse of a different Messiah: not so much the Lion of Judah but the Lamb of God. We see the portrayal of the Suffering Servant who gives his life for the sins of the world.

Jesus wanted the disciples to understand that he is about to fulfil the role of the Suffering Servant (see Mark 10:32-34). There may be a triumphal entry but soon the road will lead to the cross.

Jesus did not come to win by force or to wield power. He came to win by love and to give his life as a ransom for many. Jesus could call on all the power and might that he desired but he chose the way of self-giving and love. Jesus understood you cannot force people into the kingdom, you cannot make people love God; you can only win them by love and grace. It is for this reason he calls his followers to do as he does, to give of themselves and to serve. A Christian can be seen as someone who has come down in the world. We should be able to step off our pedestal, relinquish our hold on power and possessions, and give ourselves in love and service. The question will not be how much you have gained but rather how much you have given of yourself.

The church that wields power and strives for position, that is full of pomp and possessions, is in danger of betraying the Servant King.

Illustration

When Toyohiko Kagawa, who lived in Japan, met Christianity he was captured by its call to serve. He prayed, 'O God, make me like Christ.' To become like Christ he went to live in the slums of Tokyo to care for others. He chose to live in a shed that was about two metres square. On the very first night he was asked to share his room and bed with a man with a contagious itch, the first test of his aim to serve. He welcomed the poor man. Then a beggar asked for his shirt and he gave it. The next day the beggar came back for Kagawa's coat and trousers. Kagawa gave them and was left wearing a ragged kimono. At first the slum dwellers laughed at him but they soon came to admire him. Kagawa wrote:

> God dwells in the lowliest of men. He sits on the dust heap among the prison convicts. He stands with the juvenile delinquents. He is there with the beggars. He is among the sick; he stands with the unemployed. Therefore let him who would meet God visit the prison cell before going to the temple. Before he goes to church let him visit the hospital. Before he reads the Bible let him visit the beggar.

Proper 25

Sunday between 23 and 29 October inclusive

Aim

To show that Jesus opens our eyes to the reality of the world.

Readings

Job 42:1-6, 10-17 or Jeremiah 31:7-9
Psalm 34:1-8, 19-22 or Psalm126
Hebrews 7:23-28
Mark 10:46-52

Thought for the day

Jericho is the lowest town in the world at about 700 feet below sea level. Here Jesus meets two people who were counted among the lowest of the low – a blind beggar and Zacchaeus, an inspector of taxes.

Jesus is on his way to Jerusalem, which is 17 miles from Jericho. This last journey is uphill nearly all the way. The Son of David is coming to the city of David and neither will be the same again from this encounter. In just over a week Jesus of Nazareth will be crucified. But at the moment Jesus is passing by.

Bartimaeus sees this as a once-in-a-lifetime opportunity not to be missed. The people had come out to see the miracle worker, the rabbi, the wandering preacher. Here is a man more perceptive than them all. He can see his own need and he can see an opportunity when it presents itself. With both eyes closed he can see what the crowds do not. Here among them is the Messiah, the Son of David. The crowds are blind to this fact and try to keep the blind man quiet. But the man knows his urgency and cries out, 'Jesus, Son of David, have mercy on me.'

Jesus stands still and says, 'Call him here.'

When he is called the man throws off his cloak; not to be hindered, he springs up and comes to Jesus.

Jesus asks, 'What do you want me to do for you?' We all feel the answer is obvious – but not Jesus. He does not offer a cure without the man pointing out his need: there is no prescription without talking to the patient. The Saviour meets each need personally.

The man's sight is restored and he then follows Jesus in the way. He did not just come to get what he wanted and leave; he became a follower of Jesus.

One of the signs of the Messiah and the coming of God's kingdom would be the opening of the eyes of the blind (Isaiah 29:18; 35:5). Those who are saved will see properly (Isaiah 52:10). Sadly there is a blindness of those who do not see God (Isaiah 43:8; 56:10; 59:9-10). Vision is about how we see the world and how we perceive our God. Without vision, people and nations perish (Proverbs 29:18).

One of the great moments of our life is when our eyes are suddenly opened and we see as if for the first time. We see a world that is full of wonder and mystery, and we see a world that is God-filled and not empty. Let us make these word of Origen ours: 'May the Lord touch our eyes, as he did those of the blind. Then we shall see in the visible things those that are invisible.'

Illustration

The comic character Mr Magoo is funny because he is short-sighted, though in real life he would be a tragic person. He walks across crocodiles thinking they are logs. He steps out of a window in high-rise flats just as a window cleaner's hoist reaches the window. He steps off the side of a pier as a boat pulls level alongside. He does not come to harm but he often leaves a trail of chaos and disaster behind him.

Can we see what is happening around us, to our communities and the way we are shaping the future? Or are we content to leave it in the hands of those who are blind to many of the finer things of life? If we allow the blind to lead us, will we not both fall into the ditch?

It is of extreme importance that we make sure we are led by men and women of vision. It is no use having a quick fix or a laugh now if we are destroying our future. Pray for vision for yourself and your leaders.

All Saints' Day

1 November or Sunday between 30 October and 5 November inclusive

Aim

To rejoice in God's saints.

Readings

Wisdom 3:1-9 or Isaiah 25:6-9
Psalm 24:1-6
Revelation 21:1-6a
John 11:32-44

Thought for the day

When a child was asked what is a saint, she replied, 'Someone who lets light in.' She was probably thinking of a stained-glass window. But in a sense she was absolutely right. Saints are like bright lights in a dark world. Through them the light of the Gospel and the glory of the presence of God is revealed. As we look at the lives of the saints we get glimpses of how life ought to be. The saints challenge us in our way of living: they invite us to risk and adventure. The saints challenge our way of looking at the world, our attitude to life and our priorities. Through them we get a glimpse of how we can live to the full and serve God. The saints are not people who diminish their lives but who show us the glorious freedom of the children of God. The saints live their lives to the full to the glory of God. They challenge us to do the same now: to live for God now and to reveal his glory now.

If we make our heroes from the world of sport and the film industry or the fictional characters of the soaps, we may find we are not getting good examples of how to live. To be a good footballer does not guarantee the wisdom to lead a good life. We need men and women of deep and courageous faith to be our guides. We need to know how the saints have lived. We need also to know that there are many people now who are saints revealing God to the world.

Because God wants us to live our lives to the full we often see God choosing people who were far from perfect but had a zest for living. St Francis was called from being a carefree partygoer to show how we can enjoy living for God. Augustine of Hippo was called from living a passionate life with a mistress and a son born out of marriage to show us how to use our passion for God. To be a saint means to have a great appetite for living life to the full.

The saints reveal the love and glory of the Trinity. They share a common union with Father, Son and Holy Spirit and in so doing are part of the Communion of Saints. We are called to be part of that communion. The saints we remember today are not just the great and well-known but those who have no memorials but who lived their lives revealing God's glory and their love for their fellow beings. We rejoice that the souls of the righteous are in the hands of God.

Illustration

The Lantern Saints were a group of early Methodists who lived on the North Yorkshire Moors. They had a meeting place on one of the highest points of the moor at Trough House at the head of Fryup Dale. And people came from outlying farms and hamlets, from the dales of Westerdale, Danby Dale, Farndale, Glaisdale, Rosedale and Great and Little Fryup. It made Trough House look like the centre of a web that spread out into each moorland valley. Often in the winter they struggled up to the moorland height and met in a shuttered room. As each family entered they would light their lantern (a good symbol of receiving the light of the Gospel and the Light of Christ). Once the service was over they would set off in every direction. You could see the light they had received and carried with them travelling to each dale, to farms and homes. From that light they would see in the dark and light other lights. This light was a symbol of how they sought to live by the Light of Christ. These ordinary folk were rightly known locally as the 'Lantern Saints'.

Fourth Sunday before Advent

Sunday between 30 October and 5 November inclusive; for use if the Feast of All Saints was celebrated on 1 November and alternative propers are needed

Aim

To encourage love of God and of each other.

Readings

Deuteronomy 6:1-9
Psalm 119:1-8
Hebrews 9:11-14
Mark 12:28-34

Thought for the day

The opening scene is a typical one: religious authorities disputing with one another. So often the Church is seen in dispute with itself, talking about God rather than talking to him.

One of the scribes comes and asks Jesus which is the greatest commandment. The answer Jesus gives is the traditional Jewish answer: 'Hear, O Israel: the Lord your God is one; you shall love the Lord your God with all your heart, and with all your soul, and with all your mind, and with all your strength.' The emphasis is that there is only one God and that God asks us for our love. There is no conflict here: this is a Jewish student bringing a question to a teacher and receiving an answer. Jesus is quoting from Deuteronomy 6:4-5. This is known as the Shema, which is the imperative Hebrew word for 'hear' or 'listen'. So the whole gets its name from the first word. This hearing demands attention and obedience, two things we can often be weak on. It is with this sentence (Deuteronomy 6:4-5) that the service in the synagogue begins every day. 'You shall love the Lord your God' is part of the daily prayers for every Jew.

In this account by Mark, the words 'with all your mind' have been added to the original. As Mark's community contained many Gentiles, it was obviously felt important to offer the mind along with the rest of us. In fact, God wants us to offer our whole self to him in love.

These words were also contained in little leather boxes called phylacteries (Matthew 23:5), which the devout Jew strapped to his hand and his forehead when he was at prayer (Deuteronomy 6:8). In the same way the words were put into a little cylindrical box called the mezzuzah and fixed to every door of a Jewish house. It was to remind them that God was ever with them in their going out and coming in (Deuteronomy 6:9). These were words that they were to keep in their heart, recite to their children and talk about. It would do us well to know them and to practise what they say.

To this first commandment Jesus added another commandment: 'You shall love your neighbour as yourself.' This is a quotation from Leviticus (19:18b). The Jews were to love fellow Jews and allowed to hate Gentiles. Here with Jesus this love is to be all-inclusive and applies to everyone.

Jesus was the first to put these two commandments together and show how they were dependent on each other. St John will say:

> Whoever does not love does not know God, for God is love (1 John 4:8).
>
> God is love and those who abide in love abide in God and God abides in them (1 John 4:16b).
>
> Those who say, 'I love God', and hate their brothers or sisters, are liars; for those who do not love a brother or sister whom they have seen, cannot love God whom they have not seen (1 John 4:20).

Jesus makes these two commandments into one and shows how we cannot love God if we hate any of his creation, and we cannot truly learn to love our neighbours if we do not love God. Very often in this world the love of another human is the way to reveal to us the love of God.

Illustration

My Dearest,

I love you with all my heart.

I think of you every minute of the day.

I would do anything for you. I would swim shark-infested rivers to get to you. I would climb the steepest of mountains. I would travel the whole earth to be with you. I would brave fire and frost, wind and hail to be at your side.

But I cannot see you this week. I was coming tonight but it is too cold and damp for me to bother. Tomorrow I have fitness training and I am out with the lads the day after. I have a new computer game I want to try out on Wednesday, and a match to go to on Thursday. Friday as ever is swimming, and on Saturday the finals are on the television. I would do anything for you but it is a busy week. Sorry.

Keep in touch,
Yours always.

Not what I would call a promising relationship but is this the way we often deal with God and our prayers? Do we really love the Lord with all our heart?

(Extra illustrations can be found in Proper 20.)

COMPLETE COMMON WORSHIP

Sermon Illustrations

Third Sunday before Advent

Aim

To show that God calls each of us and we all have an opportunity to answer that call.

Readings

Jonah 3:1-5, 10
Psalm 62:5-12
Hebrews 9:24-28
Mark 1:14-20

Thought for the day

The Sea of Galilee is 13 miles long by 8 miles across at its widest from east to west. St Luke never calls it a sea but only a lake. The Sea of Galilee lies in the rift of the Jordan valley and is 680 feet below sea level. The Jordan flows into it in the north and out in the south going towards the Dead Sea. In the days of Jesus, Josephus, who was governor of Galilee for a while, tells us that there were about 330 fishing boats that sailed Galilee. Galilee had at least nine populous towns. Bethsaida, the home of Andrew, Peter, James and John, meant 'the house of nets'; another had the name of Tarichaea, the place of salt fish. People ate little meat and fish was their staple diet. Fish was salted to keep it fresh and it was exported from Galilee to Jerusalem and Rome.

There were three modes of fishing. The first used line, hook and bait. The second was with a drag net that had ropes at the four corners and was dragged behind a boat, or, more often, behind two boats. The third method was a casting net which was circular and up to about nine feet across. This net was skilfully cast from the shore or from a boat in shallow waters. It was a casting net that Simon and Andrew were using as Jesus passed along the shore.

Mark gives the impression of a call from out of nowhere, but if we read John 1:35-40 we discover Jesus had contact with the fishermen before today.

Jesus had talked to them. They had listened. What Jesus wanted now was not discussion but reaction. At this moment it was time for the talking to stop and for them to answer his call. Very often when God or Jesus calls, man stalls. See the story of Jonah. The first time God called Jonah and asked him to go east towards Iraq, Jonah set off in the opposite direction and went west towards Spain. If we turn a deaf ear to the call, it does get harder to hear, yet God still calls each of us. Vocation is not for some people only; God has a calling for everyone.

Fish must have often escaped and slipped through the net of the disciples. They often went out and caught nothing. Sometimes they must have seen great storms and thought, like the Breton fishermen, 'Lord, the sea is so large and our boat is so small.' Jesus wanted men who had learnt patience and perseverance, who were courageous and who knew the right time to 'fish'. Jesus wanted them to use their expertise and their talents in his service. The word Mark likes using, and he uses it about the reaction of Simon, Andrew, James and John, is 'immediately' . . . they followed him. If we put off following Jesus, it gets harder to do it later. There are times when we must be aware of the immediacy of the call.

Illustration

The need to react to God's call is caught well in Shakespeare's *Julius Caesar*, Act IV:

> There is a tide in the affairs of men,
> Which, taken at the flood leads on to fortune;
> Omitted, all the voyage of their life
> Is bound in shallows and in miseries.
> On such a full sea we are now afloat,
> And we must take the current when it serves,
> Or lose our ventures.

Fortunately, our God will call us again and again. There is a time when we have to stop talking about Christ and set out to follow him.

Jesus calls us, whoever we are.

There was once a very ordinary man (if there is such a being) called Aeshines, who came to Socrates and said, 'I am a poor man. I have nothing to give you but myself.' Socrates replied, 'Do you not see that you are giving me the most precious thing of all?'

Jesus wants the gift of ourselves far more than talk and theory. Will we truly seek to follow him?

Second Sunday before Advent

Aim

To know that whatever happens in this world or to us, God is always with us and promises us the victory through Jesus Christ our Lord.

Readings

Daniel 12:1-3
Psalm 16
Hebrews 10:11-14 (15-18) 19-25
Mark 13:1-8

Thought for the day

The dark cold days are about here. It is as if darkness is triumphing over light. It is a time when people easily despair. So often the news of world events or what is happening nearer home does nothing to uplift us. We need to hear the Good News, we need to know that Christ is risen, that God is in control and that life is eternal.

Today's Gospel hardly sounds like Good News. As Jesus came out of the temple, the disciples admired the solidity and largeness of the stones and building. Surely the temple was a symbol of endeavour and lasting achievements. The temple, which Herod built, was one of the wonders of the world. It was begun in about 20 BC and was not completed when Jesus was alive. Josephus tells us that some of the stones were 40 feet long by 12 feet high and 18 feet wide. It was these stones that suggested strength and solidity to the disciples. Jesus, however, saw that they were not 'for ever'; in fact, he prophesied that the stones would all be thrown down and the temple destroyed. Salvation was not found in the temple.

In AD 70 Jerusalem fell after being under siege: over a million people died of starvation and the temple was destroyed. When the Gospel was written, Mark could have known this fact. This does not detract from the conversation of Jesus on the Mount of Olives; if anything, it enhances his prophecy.

It is too easy to trust in things we think will last when only God is eternal. All sorts will lead us astray promising us youth, fitness, peace, life: yet all these are dependent on God alone. False Christs abound, promising quick deliverance – beware. The world is in the grip of the evil one. There will be wars and rumours of wars, there will be famines. There will be all sorts of pain and suffering. You cannot escape them in this world. But these are only the beginning of the birth pangs of the new age, the new kingdom that is dawning. We may feel we are losing battle after battle (and this sadly can be true) but the final victory is assured us in Christ Jesus our Lord. Think again on the words from the hymn 'All my hope on God is founded':

> Human pride and earthly glory,
> sword and crown betray his trust;
> what with care and toil he buildeth,
> tower and temple fall to dust.
> But God's power, hour by hour,
> is my temple and my tower.

Our trust is not to be in any man-made thing, not even in the Church or prayer; our trust is to be in God alone. In the words of Julian of Norwich, 'He did not say, "You shall not be tempest-tossed, you shall not travail; you shall not be distressed." But he said, "You shall not be overcome."' It is this trust in God that made Julian to understand these words the Lord spoke to her:

> I shall make all things well.
> I may make all things well,
> and I can make all things well;
> and you shall see yourself that all things shall be well.

No matter how dark the days, the Light of Christ is with us: we are never alone or left in the dark. Victory is ours through him who loves us.

Illustration

When you go to an airport there are two places with frightening names. There is the 'departure lounge' and the 'terminal'. One is for those who are departing from us and the other is where it all ends! Well, you could look at it that way. Sometimes the departure lounge is a sad place because we are seeing people off whom we might not see again for a long time. But usually it is full of excited people who are going on holiday or going somewhere special.

When we come to the terminal, it is not that we are going to stop there. It can be where all traffic is halted but we are going on to a better place. We are not going to stop at the terminal.

I tell you this because Jesus was talking about the end of the world, as we know it. He was pointing out that there are certain signs that point us towards what seems to be the end. But for us it is the beginning of something new. All the troubles are but the birth pangs of the coming of the kingdom. It is easy to quake with fear when we do not know what lies ahead. But we do know who is waiting to meet us. We may fear that we are losing round after round of the battle but in Christ Jesus we are assured the victory will be ours. The terminal will be where we move on to a better kingdom.

COMPLETE COMMON WORSHIP

Sermon Illustrations

Christ the King

Aim

To show that Christ is King and seeks to rule in our hearts.

Readings

Daniel 7:9-10, 13-14
Psalm 93
Revelation 1:4b-8
John 18:33-37

Thought for the day

Jesus is brought before Pilate on charges of sedition, but Jesus does not look like a leader of a serious revolution. (How wrong Pilate was!) Jesus looks far more like a peasant. As yet the charge had not been made, so Pilate questions the prisoner: 'Are you the King of the Jews?' The question is asked with a tone of derision, implying that he surely could not be. Pilate cannot accept the idea. Jesus replies by asking how Pilate has come to ask this, as this was not the charge against him. Who had suggested this to him? 'Do you ask this on your own, or did others tell you about me?'

Pilate shows contempt for the Jews: he is not one of this despised race but a Roman, whereas Jesus is a Jew and his own people have brought him to this. He can hardly be their leader. 'What have you done?'

In reply Jesus talks of his kingdom that is not of this world. Not of this world's way of thinking or acting. If it were, his disciples would surely be fighting to rescue him. But a kingdom of love cannot use force to gain its ends. It is love that will keep Jesus on this track and on the cross, not weakness or lack of power. The kingdom of Jesus is the one that captures hearts and wills.

Pilate does not understand this talk of other-worldly kingdom and asks, 'So you are a king?' To this Jesus cannot answer because of Pilate's limited idea of kingship, which involves power used to force people and to control people. Jesus has changed the whole idea of kingship by becoming the Servant King, and the Suffering Servant at that. Our terms are too limited when it comes to describing the majesty of Jesus. A sad comment comes from the chief priests when they say, 'We have no king but the emperor.' Only too true, for they, like Pilate, have found it impossible to accept Jesus as their king and lord.

Have we allowed Christ to be our King? Do we seek to let him rule in our hearts and wills, or do we let other powers and events control our lives? Let us pray earnestly, 'Your kingdom come, your will be done in us as it is in heaven.'

Illustration

The school bus is at the top of a steep hill when the driver slumps at the wheel. The bus starts to swerve all over the road and is picking up speed. There is general panic on the bus for it is out of control. Two lads rush forward and move the driver off the seat. A girl grabs the steering wheel and gently applies the brakes. She has never driven before but knows what to do. One minute everything was out of control and the next the busload of children was rescued by the quick thinking and acting of three young people.

The world seems to have a tendency to run out of control; wars and rumours of wars, famine and earthquakes, violence and force seem to take over. Last week's Gospel warned us that these things would happen but that we should see them as the birth pangs of the new age, the coming of God's kingdom. We should celebrate that God is in control, that Christ is our Redeemer and King.

YEAR C

First Sunday of Advent

Aim

To affirm that whatever happens our God is with us.

Readings

Jeremiah 33:14-16
Psalm 25:1-9
1 Thessalonians 3:9-13
Luke 21:25-36

Thought for the day

Apocalypse now

St Mark wrote his Gospel believing that the world would soon end. St Luke, in his Gospel and in Acts, anticipates that the Church will go through a protracted time of delay (Luke 21:9) and suggests that we cannot know when the end will come. Yet Luke does expect the apocalypse (see Luke 10:1-23, 12:1–13:9, 16:19-31, 17:20-37, 20:27-40).

In 21:5-24 Luke uses the traditional language to tell us of the time when the world as we know it will come to an end. Already some of the events had taken place, like the destruction of the Temple in Jerusalem.

At the climax of the apocalypse the sun, the moon and the stars and other 'powers of heaven' will be shaken – that is, destroyed. There will be distress among the nations and the roaring of waves. The rule of Rome, which is seen as an agency of chaos, must be replaced by God's rule and peace. Underlying the idea of 'the end' is that the power and love of God never fail. Whatever happens to the world or to us, God is with us. God does not leave us.

For some people today the apocalypse came with the storming of the Twin Towers, with the tsunami on the day after Christmas, with the hurricane that overwhelmed New Orleans. But amidst all of this distress God was still present and caring for his people. God comes to us and is with us now.

The fig tree (Luke 21:29-31) is unusual in that its fruit appear before its leaves. By the time the leaves show summer is near and there are fruit on the tree.

Luke 21:34-36 gives advice on how to be ready to face disasters. Do not take to drink, for it is not really an escape. Do not try and insure yourself with money or amass riches against that day, for they will be of no use; rather use your material resources for the benefit of the community.

Turn to God in prayer, for God is your hope and your strength. Remember the world is not permanent but God is. When troubles come, as they will, God will not leave us alone. We belong to eternity and are being prepared to come before God.

Illustration

Airports can be sad places for it is where we often say farewell to friends and loved ones who are not coming with us. We see them off and then we go to the 'departure lounge' before going to the 'terminal gate'. Don't you find those words a little threatening, if not downright depressing? You are among the departing and have come to the terminal – it sounds awful! What lifts the spirit is what is beyond. You are not stuck there, for you are off to be with a loved one, to a richer and a fuller life, or escaping from the pressures of work. The terminus is not the end but a place where we get off or set off for somewhere better.

St Luke seeks to tell us that when *things* come to an end *we* do not, for our God cares for us and is with us.

Second Sunday of Advent

Aim

To look at the Benedictus and to rejoice in our saving God.

Readings

Baruch 5:1-9 or Malachi 3:1-4
Canticle: Benedictus – Luke 1:68-79
Philippians 1:3-11
Luke 3:1-6

Thought for the day

The opening chapter of St Luke's Gospel shows God working through the old priest Zechariah, Elizabeth and John the Baptist. To look at the Canticle set for today's readings and how it came about will help us to understand why John the Baptist suddenly comes on the scene.

Zechariah was a priest belonging to the section of priests of the line of Abijah. Both Elizabeth and Zechariah were descended from the priestly house of Levi. Zechariah was given the honour of a lifetime by being chosen to offer incense at the time the sacrifice was made. There, alone in the Temple, Zechariah meets an angel of God who tells him Elizabeth will have a son who will be the herald for the Messiah. Zechariah is truly lost for words – he cannot speak. He is meant to come out and bless the people but he cannot say anything. They wonder why he is delayed and then realise he has seen a vision.

Though Zechariah cannot speak, his mind is still able to work. During the nine months of his silence he composed the prayer of blessing we know as the Benedictus.

Luke 1:68-79 is sometimes called the Benedictus from the Latin for 'blessing'. It has the feel of the Old Testament and suggests that the story of John and of Jesus continue God's story of mission and redemption. The Benedictus is a typical Jewish prayer of blessing known as a berakah, which begins by blessing God and then tells of his gracious acts in creation and redemption.

The Benedictus begins by saying that the God who has been faithful throughout the history of Israel again comes to his people.

This is a God who comes and comes again and again; this is the God who comes to us today as he did yesterday. God comes to us that we may know the glorious liberty of the children of God, not so much a rule-imposing God but a freedom-giving God. Do we know the freedom that God offers to us?

This freedom is offered to us through a 'mighty Saviour' whom God has raised up in the house and lineage of David.

Through the prophets God promised us salvation, whether from the apocalypse or from the hands of our enemies, and death is seen as an enemy. This salvation is through God's mercy that is his loving kindness.

St Luke recalls God's promise made to Abraham and declares we should be free to worship God without fear, holy and righteous in his sight. We are called to live without fear before God for we are to know him as the God of love, to enjoy a relationship with the living God and to reflect his holiness.

The work of John the Baptist is explained in verses 76-79. These words echo the last book in the Old Testament (Malachi 3:1) and so offer a continuity and see John as the one who goes before the King to prepare his way. John will do this by calling people to repent, to turn around and find forgiveness.

The dawn that will destroy the darkness is coming through God's mercy and loving kindness. That dawn is Christ who is the Light of the World, who comes to shine on those who dwell in darkness and in the shadow of death and to guide our feet on to the way of peace.

Illustration

In the time of Jesus, when a king was about to make a journey a messenger was sent out before him. Each area would be told the king was coming. This was so that they could prepare properly. They would fill in any holes in the road and level off any awkward bumps so that the king's journey would be smooth and without hindrance.

The other task of the messenger was to make sure that people prepared themselves properly, and if the king was coming to stay, there would be room for him and that the people would give him attention.

John the Baptist was to prepare the way for Jesus, so that the people would be ready to accept him.

Third Sunday of Advent

Aim

To show that our faith is one of joy and love.

Readings

Zephaniah 3:14-20
Canticle: Isaiah 12:2-6
Philippians 4:4-7
Luke 3:7-18

Thought for the day

John the Baptist came out of the desert like a hell-fire preacher. He came warning people that the way they were going was wrong; they needed to turn around to repent. He warned them that words would not save them – only trying to do what is good. They could not say, 'We are Jews so we shall be saved.' Even with Jesus would come a time of judgement. This is hardly a Gospel: there is not much good news here, though there are plenty of practical warnings about the road we choose and about how our actions make us prepared or unprepared for the coming of Jesus.

In contrast with John the Baptist stands today's reading from the Letter to the Philippians (4:4-7). 'Rejoice in the Lord always.' Rejoice in his love and in his saving power. Rejoice in his birth and in resurrection. Above all, rejoice in his presence and his love. 'Again I say, rejoice.' As Christians, we need to show the joy of knowing the love and salvation of God. Christians who impose a heavy load on people do God a disservice. St Teresa of Avila rightly prayed, 'Lord, deliver us from sour-faced saints.' 'Let your gentleness be known to everyone.' This does not mean being made a fool of, but it does mean not imposing on others or forcing them to do things. As God deals gently with us, we have to learn to deal with others in the same way.

'The Lord is near' is the message of John the Baptist and of Advent. Do you accept the reality of it? The Lord is not far away from you but close at hand. Prayer is not a long-distance call but talking to a loving God who is close to you and with you. Learn to relax in the presence and in the love and power of God. Do not worry – much of our anxiety stems from feeling alone and without help. You are not alone. The Almighty is with you and cares for you. Speak to him in prayer and supplication; let your requests be made known to God. Remember a thankful heart cannot be a sad heart! Appreciate the world, people and the abiding presence. Then the peace of God – it is his gift – will keep guard of your heart and mind in Christ Jesus. Now *that* is Gospel!

Illustration

There was once a young girl who was always told off at home. Whatever she did, she was criticised (a bit like Cinderella). Nothing could please her parents and they often seemed angry with her. Never did they show their love. The girl felt ugly, she developed asthma and eczema. Later still she went into a psychiatric hospital because she was so depressed and felt useless. It seemed no one could make her better.

One day a hospital orderly noticed that beneath her sad face was a beautiful young woman. When he talked to her she was intelligent and interesting. Soon he formed a relationship with her, bringing her presents and praising the artwork she did. At this she seemed to glow. The orderly got permission to take her out on the odd Saturday. Soon they were deeply in love. Once she knew she was loved she began to smile. Her work was appreciated and soon her eczema and asthma seemed to disappear. There was a new peace and joy in her life. I can tell you she married the orderly and became a good artist. The loving presence of another had transformed her life.

Fourth Sunday of Advent

Aim

To look at the song of Mary – the Magnificat.

Readings

Micah 5:2-5a
Canticle: Magnificat or Psalm 80:1-8
Hebrews 10:5-10
Luke 1:39-45 (46-55)

Thought for the day

Mary's song is born out of love for God and an awareness of the Scriptures. Mary's song is very like the song of Hannah in 1 Samuel 2:1-10. Both songs sound like psalms. Hannah gives thanks for the promise of a child, as she had been unable to bear children up to that point, and she gives thanks to God for his care of the lowly and the oppressed. Mary gives thanks that through her pregnancy the world will come to know its Saviour. By saying 'Yes' to God, Mary is seen as a model of obedience and trust. Mary's song begins by giving thanks to God for his redemption. The important thing to note is that the God who has acted in this way in the past acts now. Our God is not of the past alone or to be projected into the future; our God is of the now and is with each of us now. The Lord is with you.

Mary rejoices in the presence, in God her Saviour. Like the saints of old, Mary will be called blessed, for God has looked with favour upon her lowliness. Yet Mary has made this possible by saying 'Yes' to God. It is the mighty one who has done great things, and holy is his name. God has the same loving kindness for all who fear him from generation to generation. We need to take time to experience this loving kindness towards us.

God's presence is a revolutionary power: the presence of God changes things. In his power God scatters the proud in the thoughts of their hearts. Things do not happen in our own goodness or power alone but because God loves us. We are not chosen because we are clever or skilful but because God cares for us and loves us. This love cannot be earned, only accepted and responded to.

It is not to the powerful that God submits. God puts an end to the world's worship of might and prestige; God often raises up the humble and the lowly. God cares for all, and those open to his love are raised up, rich or poor, common or royal. In fact, no one is common in God's eyes, for all are precious.

It is a strange experience to discover how happy many poor people are and how miserable are so many with lots of possessions and riches. Jewish belief was sometimes distorted to suggest that the more you gained on earth, the more God loved you. It was suggested that if you are very rich, then God favours you. But this is not so. You are not measured by what you possess. There are many so-called well-off people who are empty. You can even see it in their desire always to fill themselves with something. Those who know God are satisfied and realise their lives are filled with good things.

God acts as a God who keeps covenant: he keeps his promises and remembers to be merciful.

If we would learn the Magnificat and its attitudes to God and the present, our lives would be greatly enriched.

Illustration

Love matters more than riches. This is well illustrated by the story of King Midas. In his greed he accepted the offer that all he touched would turn to gold. Very exciting! He touched plates, leaves, statues and they all turned to gold. He would soon be the richest man in the world. But his food also turned to gold and he began to starve. He touched his daughter and she turned to gold and he lost her warmth and her love. He had sold himself for riches and now he was poor indeed. He had all the gold you could dream about but he was poor within. Fortunately, this condition was reversible. Midas could lose the desire for gold and become loving and happy once more. When asked if he would like this rather than gold his reply was 'Yes'.

Christmas Day

Aim

To celebrate the coming of the Saviour into the world.

Readings

Isaiah 9:2-7
Psalm 96
Titus 2:11-14
Luke 2:1-14 (15-20)

Thought for the day

It is important to capture both the ordinariness and the extraordinariness of the birth of Jesus.

Jesus was born at the time of registration ordered by the Roman emperor Augustus and enforced by Quirinius the Roman governor of Syria, which included Palestine. This registration was to determine how much backbreaking tax could be extorted from the community.

So Joseph had to travel from Galilee and Nazareth down to Bethlehem in Judea. The journey is almost 80 miles. There would be many people on the roads, either sleeping rough or seeking accommodation. The eastern inn would not provide food, only a fire to cook on, fodder for the animals and a shelter. The stable would be a better place for a mother about to give birth. Swaddling clothes was the normal way to wrap up a baby.

Up on the hills overlooking Bethlehem were shepherds. These men were despised by the orthodox people of the day. The shepherds could not keep the ceremonial rules of washing.

Taxes, journeying, stables, shepherds are things we know. But there is another world – or, to put it a better way, the hidden part of our world – breaking in. It is the world of angels, of God, of heaven. If we lose sight of this world, it is like trying to understand a picture by looking at a negative. The two worlds belong together. We have to open our eyes to the God who comes in Jesus and who comes to us. We have to make room for God in our lives and let him be born in us. If we fail to give time to the presence and say we are too busy, we descend to a world that is only a material world and so we have a distorted picture of what the world and life is. At Christmas we are invited to enjoy the reality that God loves the world and is in the world, that God comes to us in what we think is ordinary. The mystery of the Word made flesh is waiting to be revealed to us. Let us be still and give thanks for the birth of Jesus and welcome him into our lives and homes.

Illustration

There was a Scottish farmer who refused to believe the Christmas story. Though his wife and children went to church, he refused to and often mocked them. Why should God lower himself to be like us? It is foolish talk.

Once when it was snowing, the family went to church. The farmer noticed that the snow was getting much worse. Suddenly he heard a thump against his window and then another. He went out to see what was happening. There in front of him was a large flock of geese which had got lost in the storm.

The farmer was kind and felt for them. He wanted to help them. He realised that they could shelter in his barn. He got behind them and tried to drive them in, but they only scattered. Then he tried by laying a trail of food to the barn door, but the geese did not take any notice. There was nothing he could do to get them to enter the barn.

About to give up on them he said to himself, 'Why don't they follow me? If I were a goose, I could lead them into the barn. If I looked like one of them, I could save them.'

Suddenly he stopped and thought about what he had said: he could only save them by becoming like them. Suddenly he understood the great love of God for humankind. He fell to his knees in the snow and gave thanks to God for his great love.

First Sunday of Christmas

Aim

To encourage people not to 'suppose' the presence of Jesus but to seek to know he is with us.

Readings

1 Samuel 2:18-20, 26
Psalm 148
Colossians 3:12-17
Luke 2:41-52

Thought for the day

This story is the only glimpse we get of Jesus as a boy. Joseph and Mary used to go all the way to Jerusalem every year to celebrate the Passover. When Jesus was 12 it was time for him to go too, for at 12 a Jewish boy became a man. He then became 'a son of the law' and had to take the obligations of the law upon himself. So at 12 Jesus went up to the Passover festival for the first time.

The city would be crowded for the festival. Families and friends travelled there together, the young folk met up with friends and relatives and enjoyed being in each other's company. After the Passover the women usually set off earlier in the day for they would travel more slowly than the men. Later on the men would set off and the two groups would not meet up until the evening. Mary and Joseph supposed that Jesus was in the other's company. Joseph thought he was with Mary's group and Mary thought he was with Joseph and his group. They supposed him to be with one of the groups when in fact they had left him behind. Every mile they travelled took them further away. It was not until the evening when they had searched the camp that they knew he was missing. As they had travelled a day, it took another day to return to Jerusalem. By now Joseph and Mary were distressed and anxious for the safety of Jesus.

When they found him he was in the Temple. At the Passover it was the custom for the Sanhedrin to meet in the Temple to discuss religious and theological matters. And there was Jesus among them. It is wrong to think of Jesus leading this group; rather he was fascinated by them and their words. The Jewish phrase 'hearing and asking questions' is used for any student learning from his teachers.

You can feel the relief and anxiety in Mary's voice as she says, 'Child, why have you treated us like this? Look, your father and I have been searching for you in great anxiety.'

In his reply Jesus gently takes the title of 'father' from Joseph and gives it to God. As a good Jewish son, now that he has come of age, he must be about his Father's business. Here is a pointer to who Jesus really is. Being the Son of the Father does not free him from obedience to his earthly home. The references to growing in strength and in wisdom and in divine and human favour (Greek: charis = grace) are good Jewish qualities as reflected in 1 Samuel 2:21, 26 and Proverbs 3:5.

Illustration

There are so many ways that people can get lost. There is a lovely story of an absent-minded professor from Edinburgh. He used to travel regularly by train and all the ticket collectors knew him. Once by the gate he was anxiously going through his pockets and after a while the ticket collector asked if he could help. 'I have lost my ticket,' said the professor. 'That's all right, sir, we all know you. You can get on the train.' 'But,' said the professor, 'I need my ticket because I do not know where I am going.'

It is easy to get lost in this world. Do you know where you are going?

Second Sunday of Christmas

Aim

To continue to rejoice in the Word made flesh.

Readings

Jeremiah 31:7-14
Psalm 147:12-20
Ephesians 1:3-14
John 1:(1-9) 10-18

Thought for the day

St John's Gospel begins as the book of Genesis begins: that is, 'In the beginning'. John adds to Genesis by presenting Jesus as the 'logos' – the Word – through whom God created the world. Without Jesus the world is seen as a place of chaos and darkness. Jesus brings light and life to the world. This is a light that cannot be overcome, no matter how dark it gets. As he is the light of all people, he is our light. The great message of these opening words of St John is that we are offered light and life through Jesus Christ. Jesus himself will come to us and abide with us, protecting us from darkness and death. This is a wonderful offer.

But Jesus gets poor reception. 'He was in the world, and the world came into being through him; yet the world did not know him. He came to what was his own, and his own people did not accept him.' Time and again Jesus is given a poor reception: he is scorned and rejected, he is ignored and passed by. People are too busy for him. They have no time. There is still no room at the inn or in the heart. So many things crowd out Jesus. What about you? Have you given Jesus a good reception over this Christmas season?

Remember, 'to all who received him, who believed in his name, he gave the power to become children of God.'

Memorise John 1:14. You should be able to say, 'The Word became flesh and lived among us, and we have seen his glory.'

Illustration

Some people live in poor reception areas for television or radio. The signal cannot get to them so the picture or the sound is blurred, fuzzy and cannot be enjoyed properly. Many things can cause bad reception. People can live too far from the transmitter. Sometimes it is just that their aerial is pointing the wrong way and it needs to be turned around. Are you sure you are pointing in the right direction? At other times it is something close that destroys reception – a motor without a suppressor, or a lot of leaves on nearby trees that can block the signal. Then again it can be the opposite: there is too much interference because the set is too receptive. All sorts of sounds distort what we need to hear. We need to be able to finely tune to make proper contact. This is as true of prayer as it is of radio waves.

The Epiphany

Aim

To show we are all seekers and need to come to the Christ.

Readings

Isaiah 60:1-6
Psalm 72:(1-9) 10-15
Ephesians 3:1-12
Matthew 2:1-12

Thought for the day

We do not know where the wise men came from: we only know they came from east of the Holy Land. We do not know whether it was the Near East or the Far East. By tradition they are of different nations: one black, one oriental and one white. The important thing is that they were all Gentiles – they were not Jews. The Epiphany is about Jesus being revealed to the nations of the world. The Magi were the priestly leaders of Persia, now Iran, in the same way as the Levites were for the Holy Land. In leading these Gentiles to Jesus, God makes good the promise to Abraham and Sarah that their descendants would be a light and a blessing to the nations. These men were seekers. They may have been rich, they may have been clever, they may have been men of authority, but, above all, they were seekers. They needed something else in their lives. They needed a living relationship with their God. St Augustine of Hippo reminds us that we are all seekers when he says, 'You have made us for yourself, and our heart is restless until it finds its rest in you.'

In their quest these men searched the heavens and the earth, they spent time and energy, they risked their lives by travelling at night, they refused to be put off but journeyed on. Some must have laughed at them, others must have scorned their search, but they would not be put off.

In a sense they did not know where they were going but they did know whom they were seeking. They went to the wrong place by going to the obvious: they went to Jerusalem and to Herod. Herod's title was 'king of the Jews'. Fortunately, they realised their mistake and later did not tell Herod where Jesus was. From Jerusalem they journeyed on to Bethlehem. At last they were able to offer themselves and their gifts; their search was over and they could return home rejoicing. In them, the beginning of Jesus being revealed to the world had begun.

We need to know our lives cannot be really fulfilled if we do not know our God. We have to seek out his presence and come before him. Like the wise men, we may take a few wrong turnings, we may be laughed at, scorned or put in danger, but we must not be put off until we come before him and know him.

Illustration

(This can be said by three different people.)

I bring gold because I am a rich man. I have all sorts of wonderful possessions and I have a good mind. I really am well off. I can buy whatever I want. But there are some things money cannot buy. You cannot buy love or health; you cannot buy peace of mind or eternal life. I offer gold to the One who can give me what money cannot buy.

I bring frankincense, the precious gum of a tree. Incense is used in worship. I am well-off, with a good mind. But it is easy to feel self-sufficient or over-important. I need to look beyond myself, to look at the mysteries and wonders of life. I need to know God to be satisfied. In adoration I offer incense to the One who meets my needs and tells me God is here.

I bring myrrh that relieves pain, for I have tasted many sufferings. I am a clever man but I cannot escape pain or the fear of death. I offer myrrh for all the sorrowful people of the world, for all who are heavily burdened, for all whose labour is hard. I offer myrrh for all who are in pain or distress, to the One who tells us that God cares. God will give us freedom. God will relieve our pain. God will give us life eternal.

Together:
We offer our gifts to God who gives himself to us.

First Sunday of Epiphany
The Baptism of Christ

Aim

To affirm our belief in the Holy Trinity and in the mission of Christ.

Readings

Isaiah 43:1-7
Psalm 29
Acts 8:14-17
Luke 3:15-17, 21, 22

Thought for the day

Someone counted the phrase 'Do not be afraid' 365 times in the Bible – one for each day of the year. God says to each of us, 'Do not fear, for I have redeemed you; I have called you by your name, you are mine' (Isaiah 43:1b). God cares for us as individuals: He loves each of us personally. He is with us in our joys and in our sorrows. God never leaves us but is always with us.

Baptism not only celebrates our commitment to God; it also celebrates God's own commitment to us. Baptism is not just being immersed in water; it is affirming the reality of being immersed in the presence of God the Father, Son and Holy Spirit. A good way to start the day is to affirm:

> I am immersed in the light of God the Father.
> I am immersed in the love of God the Son.
> I am immersed in the leading of the Spirit.
> I am immersed in the Three in One.

We can use this affirmation with our children and godchildren.

The baptism of John was for the forgiveness of sins. Jesus did not need forgiveness but he needed to express his oneness with us. There are certain turning points in all our lives. St Luke shows Jesus as a man, 12 years old, deciding he needed to do his Father's – that is, God's – work. His baptism is another turning point: Jesus is now 30. Throughout the country, due to John the

Baptist, there is a movement towards God. Jesus identifies himself with these people.

At the baptism of Jesus something special happens. There is the voice of the Father speaking personally to Jesus and saying, 'You are my Son, the Beloved; with you I am well pleased.' These words can come from two texts. 'You are my Son' is from Psalm 2:7 and is understood to be the description of the Messianic King. 'Beloved, with you I am well pleased' is part of Isaiah 42:1, which is about the Servant of God and the description of the Servant reaches its peak in Isaiah 53 with the Suffering Servant. Jesus would have the dual role of King and Suffering Servant. Cross and crown go together.

It is worth noting that one of the few images of the Trinity is to be found in the baptism. There is the voice of the God from the heavens, Jesus coming up out of the water and the Holy Spirit descending in the form of a dove.

Illustration

There is a species of water fly which flies in the air but dives into the water for its food. It can survive in the water because, as it dives, it takes an air bubble with it. It moves around inside the air bubble until it gets what it wants and then returns to the air. It survives in the water because it is surrounded by air.

Our God surrounds us; we are immersed in his presence. St Paul tells us this when he says 'In him we live and move and have our being' (Acts 17:28). In baptism, our being immersed in water is an outward sign of our total immersion in the presence and power of God.

Second Sunday of Epiphany

Aim

To show that the presence of Jesus transforms our lives.

Readings

Isaiah 62:1-5
Psalm 36:5-10
1 Corinthians 12:1-11
John 2:1-11

Thought for the day

Epiphany is about Jesus being revealed to the world as someone special.

To the wise men he was revealed as 'the King of the Jews', a title used by Herod but kept by the Jews for the Messiah, the Christ, the Holy One of God.

The Baptism revealed Jesus as the Son of God, another title for the Messiah; and through the quoting of Isaiah 42 and 53 Jesus is also revealed as the Suffering Servant. With Jesus, Cross and Crown go together.

This week is the third part of the manifestations and that is through signs of power – what we usually call miracles. Miracles are wonderful events that defy full explanation – if they can be explained, then they are not miracles. Miracles point to Jesus as God's agent – as God himself – at work on earth.

Today's setting for the miracle is a wonderfully ordinary event, a wedding. Cana is a village near Nazareth and here a young couple are celebrating. It is good to know that Jesus, together with his mother and his disciples, is there and enjoying the wedding. For Jewish celebration, wine was essential. There was a saying of the rabbis: 'Without wine there is no joy.' For the wine to run out was a disaster for the couple. The joy and celebrations would drain away: the party would be over.

Into this situation Mary invites Jesus to do something. Jesus looked at the six water jars that were used for washing. Each jar held between 20 and 30 gallons. Jesus asked the servants to fill the jars and they did so. Now they were to carry them to the steward of the feast. Again they obeyed Jesus. When the steward tasted the water it had become good wine. A miracle! The steward did not know it was a miracle; only the servants knew. The steward congratulated the bridegroom on keeping the best wine till last.

Jesus could take ordinary water from the well and through his power it would become wine. He seems the sort of person a lot of people would like to follow. But we must not lose sight of the sign. The miracle points to Jesus doing only what God can do. This miracle and all miracles point to Jesus as the Son of God; that is, Jesus is God.

Illustration

The car was running well, there was nothing wrong with the engine or the electrics, but it suddenly came to a halt. It had juddered for a while and then came to a standstill. There was no way it would start again for it had run out of fuel.

The driver had to sit there on a lonely country road hoping for help. Fortunately there came a farmer on a tractor and he offered to give the car a tow. The driver was not keen as this was quite a new car. When the farmer looked he realised the car had run out of petrol. He had a full can on the farm, so he went away but soon returned and poured the petrol into the tank. He gave the petrol to the driver as a gift and said as he saw him off, 'None of us can run on an empty tank.'

There are times in life when our human resources run out. Then the harder we try, the worse it gets. There are many people who are drained or running near empty; now and again we all need our batteries recharged.

Listen to these words: 'Those who wait for the Lord shall renew their strength' (Isaiah 40:31); or these words of Jesus: 'Come to me, all you who are weary and are carrying heavy burdens, and I will give you rest' (Matthew 11:28).

Third Sunday of Epiphany

Aim

To show how Jesus begins his ministry through the Church and the Scriptures.

Readings

Nehemiah 8:1-3, 5, 6, 8-10
Psalm 19
1 Corinthians 12:12-31a
Luke 4:14-21

Thought for the day

Jesus was baptised by John and then spent 40 days in prayer and fasting. He was now ready to begin his mission and there were certain decisions to be made.

Where would he start, in what place?

What would he use for guidance?

Jesus began in Galilee. This was probably the least conservative area of Palestine because Gentiles, people of other nations, surrounded it. It was also very heavily populated: from here Jesus could reach many people and meet many needs. Josephus, who had been governor of Galilee, says it had 204 villages and towns and none with a population of less than 15,000. This means there could have been about three million people in Galilee. Jesus began where life was busy and there were many people. The beginning of his mission in a Gentile-friendly area points the way to the mission to the Gentiles in Acts.

He began by teaching in the Synagogue. The synagogue was the regular place of worship for every Jew. The law said that wherever there are ten Jewish families there must be a synagogue. The synagogue service was divided in three parts: worship, Scripture reading and teaching. Because there were no professional ministers anyone could be invited to teach. Here Jesus began and we are told all held him in high esteem. The positive reaction of the Jews shows that many of them were ready to embrace the Good News that Jesus brought.

He came to his hometown. Nazareth could not be called a village as it had a population of about 20,000. He went to the synagogue 'as was his custom'. The ministry and teaching of Jesus did not break with Judaism but grew out of it. There in the synagogue Jesus read Isaiah 61:1, 2 and 58:6 from a scroll, about God restoring the broken world and bringing in his kingdom:

> The Spirit of the Lord is upon me,
> because the Lord has anointed me
> to bring good news to the oppressed:
> to bind up the brokenhearted,
> to proclaim liberty to the captives
> and release to the prisoners,
> to proclaim the year of the Lord's favour.

When we are told Jesus 'sat down', this is what a rabbi, a teacher, did; he sat down to teach and that is why all eyes are upon him. How surprised they must have been when he said, 'Today, this Scripture has been fulfilled in your hearing.'

Do we see these words as the mission of the Church and the sharing with Christ of bringing in God's kingdom? Like Jesus we should start in our own area and bring the Good News to bear on what we do.

Illustration

There is the story of a Celtic monk who decided to give up study and only to pray. His abbess asked how his mind would be fed if he gave up study. The monk persisted and said that he would leave where he was and go and search for God overseas. The abbess replied, 'If God cannot be found on this side of the sea, by all means let us journey overseas. But since God is near all those who call on him, we have no need to cross the sea. The kingdom of God can be reached from every land.'

There is a great need for us to know that God is with us today and God desires to bring in his kingdom through us today. Psalm 95 need always be heeded: 'O that today you would listen to his voice!' (verse 7).

Fourth Sunday of Epiphany

(Also for use on the Feast of the Presentation)

Aim

To rejoice in the light of Christ that has come into our world.

Readings

Ezekiel 43:27–44:4
Psalm 48
1 Corinthians 13:1-13
Luke 2:22-40

Thought for the day

(If you want the Jewish background to this visit to the Temple, read Leviticus 12.) Forty days after Jesus was born, as was the custom, Joseph and Mary presented Jesus to the priest in the Temple. This is a service of thanksgiving for the birth of a child and an offering to God. As they are not rich, Joseph and Mary do not bring a lamb as an offering but two doves instead. This is all quite normal and every Jewish family in their time could be found doing this. Suddenly into the normal comes something strange. Simeon is a devout man who looked forward to the time when the Messiah would appear. He has spent his life in prayer and waiting for the promised time; he has waited patiently for the coming One. How wonderful that he is present when Joseph and Mary present Jesus. Simeon takes the baby in his arms and in an instant knows this is the Chosen One. A thrill runs through his whole being; what he has waited for is now fulfilled. The words of Simeon have become known by the Latin translation of the words he starts with – Nunc Dimittis – and have become one of the great songs of the Church.

In verses 32 and 34 Simeon gives a summary of the work and the actions of Jesus: 'a light for revelation to the Gentiles and for the glory to your people Israel . . . this child is destined for the falling and the rising of many in Israel and to be a sign that will be opposed.'

Here is another Epiphany, another revealing of Jesus and who he is. Jesus is not only for the Jews but for the Gentiles too. Yet this will meet opposition.

Let us this day rejoice in the light of Christ, the light that scatters the darkness of sin and death, the light that leads us to eternal life. Let us make sure we place our lives in that light each day and that we live by that light.

Illustration

As Simeon waited, his life was one of watchfulness and patience. We see a similar watchfulness in bird watchers. They place themselves where they believe things will happen. They prepare themselves with binoculars or telescopes. Then they wait, often in silence. This is an attentive waiting, a watchful waiting; they are alert and focused on their hoped-for sighting. There was a man who went in search of a rare owl this way. He waited for three days before it appeared. He saw it only for a few moments but he said he would remember it for the rest of his life. He just had to close his eyes to see it again. He knew what it really looked like. Many of us could learn to be more attentive and watchful towards our God.

Proper 1

Sunday between 3 and 9 February inclusive
(if earlier than the Second Sunday before Lent)

Aim

To show that if we are faithful in small things, then we will be trusted to do greater things.

Readings

Isaiah 6:1-8 (9-13)
Psalm 138
1 Corinthians 15:1-11
Luke 5:1-11

Thought for the day

Luke never calls the 'Sea of Galilee' a sea (thalassa) but only a lake (limne). He calls it the Lake of Gennesaret. It is also known as the Sea of Tiberias. This lake is 13 miles long and about 8 miles wide. The river Jordan flows into it from the north and it flows out to the Dead Sea in the south. In the time of Jesus there were at least nine cities around the lake with a population of more than 15,000. Josephus records that on one expedition he was able to commandeer 240 fishing boats. Fish was sent from Galilee to Rome.

Today we hear of Jesus taking the Good News outside the synagogue. He sits in a boat to teach because the crowd had been pressing in on him. The boats belong to Simon Peter (and his brother Andrew who is not mentioned) and to the brothers James and John.

Notice how gently Jesus deals with people. From most of us he asks small things first. It is only if we are willing in the small request that can we expect Jesus to ask us to do something greater. Jesus gets into Simon Peter's boat and says, 'Put out a little way from the shore – just a little way from the land.' It is not asking much, yet the tired fisherman could have said, 'No'.

After speaking to the crowd Jesus turns to Simon Peter and says, 'Put out into deep water.' This was only possible after being in the shallows. The word for 'deep' is 'bathos' and it is a symbol for chaos (Genesis 1:2; Psalm 66:6; Isaiah 5:30). The deep sea was a fearful thing for many Jews, an element that cannot be controlled.

Yet God calls into the deep of life and from the depths of our own being. Again Simon Peter could have refused. Discipleship comes through obedience.

Now Jesus says, 'Let down your nets for a catch.' Maybe at this moment the fisherman Simon Peter wonders what this carpenter knows about the sea. Fishing is done at night, and Simon Peter and his fellow fishermen have been out all night and caught nothing. It is interesting to discover how often God calls us through our emptiness or the fruitless tasks we have performed. (Isaiah experienced the empty throne before it was filled with the Presence.) Simon Peter answers, 'Master, we have worked all night long but have caught nothing.' How often is there a feeling of life slipping through the nets or through our fingers; is it all a waste of time? Yet Simon Peter continues: 'Yet if you say so, I will let down the nets.' Though reason and habit say, 'No', Simon Peter still obeys, and through obedience comes the miraculous catch of fish. A more miraculous catch is that of the fishermen. Once Simon Peter, James and John (and Andrew?) came to land their fish, Jesus said, 'Do not be afraid; from now on you will be catching people.' And they left everything and followed Jesus.

We must see this as a 'call narrative', where God calls someone to work for him (see Exodus 3:1-22; Isaiah 6:1-13; Jeremiah 1: 4-13). The call authenticates the person and their vocation. This will remind the readers after the death and resurrection of Jesus that the apostles had been called by him.

Illustration

Denzil was always talking of giving glory to God. The house he lived in was a tip. Every room was untidy if not unclean. Denzil continued to talk of praising God but gave little respect to the people around him. He seemed unaware of his surroundings or of others, only full of himself. One night he heard God in his dreams saying, 'If you want to serve me, start where you live. Give glory to me by tidying up your part of the world. You will hear me better if you learn to listen to others.' Denzil awoke, aware of how ugly his room looked. That day he started to clean up and get rid of rubbish. Soon he redecorated the room and added fresh curtains. He scrubbed himself and got new clothes. He seemed to be a different person: he actually glowed. If someone needed a person to listen or to care, Denzil was the one. By being attentive to small things, God had called him to do greater things for him.

Proper 2

Sunday between 10 and 16 February inclusive
(if earlier than the Second Sunday before Lent)

Aim

To show that God is our key to happiness.

Readings

Jeremiah 17:5-10
Psalm 1
1 Corinthians 15:12-20
Luke 6:17-26

Thought for the day

There is a sequence that is very like that of Moses in Exodus. Jesus is in the wilderness and he then goes up a mountain to be alone with God. By going up the mountain Jesus is saying, 'Pay attention, for the words I am going to speak to you are special.' We are meant to encounter the word of God in the teaching of Jesus and to receive the light of God's presence. Jesus comes down and chooses the twelve disciples (like the twelve tribes of Israel). Jesus gives the twelve the title of 'apostles' for they are not only to be learners; they are to be sent by him. In the same way as Moses (Deuteronomy 1:1). Jesus addresses the crowd on the plain. In Matthew, what follows is known as the 'Sermon on the Mount'; in Luke, it is the 'Sermon on the Plain'.

People had come to Jesus for teaching and for healing and they were aware that power came out of him. In Jesus there were signs of the kingdom of God at work.

Jesus tells them of the 'blessed'. Blessed is a good translation of the Greek word 'Makarioi', which can simply mean 'happy', though 'blessed' is also connected with the last times and the favour of God.

Jesus connects some strange things with happiness or the blessed, and the oddness of what he says should bring us up with a jolt. Happy are the poor, happy are the hungry, happy are those who weep, happy are those who are hated on account of the Son of Man. We make happiness dependent on external circumstances – 'I would be happy if I won the lottery'; 'I would be happy if I had a good drink'. Jesus wants us to know that true happiness comes from something deep within us. It is not about 'having' or even 'not having'; it is about our relationship with God. True happiness is not dependent on outward things, though they can help – happiness is dependent on God. The danger with riches or plenty is that they can make us self-sufficient and make us forget God and think we can provide for ourselves. Happiness comes from knowing that God provides for us and loves us (see Deuteronomy 8:1-18; 1 Corinthians 6:10).

Illustration

It is amazing how many products offer us more happiness, when in fact they are only seeking to fulfil our consuming passion to have more. The notice of 'Happy Hour' at some places is always amusing, for if that is the 'happy hour', what is the rest of the time?

There are many stories of people who have sold their heart or their soul to make money. At first it is wonderful, for money can buy all sorts of things. But possessions alone cannot fill our inner emptiness; we also need love and to know we are of some value. There is nothing worse than the person that has made it in the world but is poor in the sight of his neighbours or God. There is a very telling story from Matthew 19:16-22: the rich young man sought eternal life (did he think he could buy it?) but 'he went away grieving, for he had many possessions' (verse 22).

Proper 3

Sunday between 17 and 23 February inclusive
(if earlier than the Second Sunday before Lent)

Aim

To show that Jesus wants us to have the glorious freedom of the children of God.

Readings

Genesis 45:3-11, 15
Psalm 37:1-11, 40
1 Corinthians 15:35-38, 42-50
Luke 6:27-38

Thought for the day

In today's Gospel, Jesus continues his teaching after coming down from the mountain. Like Moses, he wants to lead his people to the freedom of the Promised Land. That freedom will involve a change in our attitude – a change of heart – towards much of life. We are to learn to love and not to hate. The word used for love is not 'eran', which is passionate love, or 'philien', which is family love, but 'agapan' – an active benevolence towards each other. This love is more about our will than our heart, though both are involved. If we are not to become slaves to hatred, greed, anger or resentment, we will have to have a positive attitude of will towards all people. This means whatever people do to us, we will seek to react in a good way to them; we will go out of our way to be kind and generous. Jesus gives us a summary of this attitude in the positive commandment 'Do to others as you would have them do to you' (Luke 6:31).

It is so easy to give up our freedom and become slaves to bad attitudes. We can become consumed by harbouring anger or resentment towards people who have done us wrong. Anger and hatred can use up so much of our time and energy and stop us from enjoying the freedom that God gives to us. We need to learn to be merciful as our Father is merciful; to forgive as we are forgiven. A critical attitude towards others can be so destructive to the community and us. It does not mean acting without discretion; it *does* mean an act of will that seeks the good for the person and in the person. Forgiveness can so often bring us to a new freedom. Possessiveness of things or of people can so easily enslave us; if we cannot give away, if we cease to be generous, then life no longer seems to be generous towards us. It is by giving that we make room in our lives to receive.

Let us seek to learn the glorious freedom of the children of God.

Illustration

In the Holy Land there are two seas, the Sea of Galilee and the Dead Sea. The same river, the Jordan, feeds both of these seas. The Sea of Galilee teems with life: there are fish in its waters, trees grow near its shoreline, birds visit it and their singing can be heard. The Dead Sea lives up to its name: it does not sustain life, it is too salty to allow plants to thrive and the birds do not like its saltiness. One sea has life and the other is dead, yet the same river feeds both. What is the difference? The answer is quite simple: the river Jordan flows into one end of the Sea of Galilee and out of the other. As the Sea of Galilee receives, so it gives out. The Dead Sea does not have an outlet. All the water that flows into the Dead Sea is kept; it does not give out. The sun evaporates the water and the salts are left behind. Because the Dead Sea does not have an outlet, it dies. By keeping all that it receives, it chokes itself of life. Sadly there are people just like that.

Second Sunday before Lent

Aim

To show that Christ is our peace among the storms of life.

Readings

Genesis 2:4b-9, 15-25
Psalm 65
Revelation 4
Luke 8:22-25

Thought for the day

Jesus is very like Moses who led the people to the Promised Land.

- Jesus receives a call at his Baptism (Luke 3:21, 22).
- Jesus is in the wilderness (4:1-12).
- Jesus goes up a mountain to be alone with God (6:12-15).
- Jesus comes down and teaches the people (6:17-49).
- Jesus rescues his disciples from an overwhelming sea (8:22-25).
- Jesus feeds people in the wilderness (9:10b-17).
- Jesus is leading his people to the promised kingdom of God. Jesus seeks freedom for his people.

Throughout all of this there is a feeling that Jesus is more than a second Moses, more than a good leader or a good teacher. He is the 'Son of God' (Luke 3:22). When the disciples are caught in the storm and Jesus brings calm, they ask the question, 'Who then is this, that he commands even the winds and the water, and they obey him?' (Luke 8:25). The answer can be found in the psalm chosen for today. Psalm 65, verse 7 is addressed to God alone and it says:

> You silence the roaring of the seas,
> the roaring of their waves,
> the tumult of the peoples.

And the next thing Jesus does after the stilling of the storm is to heal the mad man of the Gerasenes.

The same verse from Psalm 65 in the Book of Common Prayer is even more fitting:

> Who stilleth the raging of the sea: and the noise of the waves, and the madness of the people.

The only answer to their questions is, of course, God. It is important for the disciples and for us to realise that Jesus is God and not just a wonder-worker. As God, Jesus is able to control the chaotic elements of this world and to help us survive amid the chaos and dangers that life sends to us. Jesus reveals to us that in him light conquers darkness, order conquers chaos, love conquers hatred and life is stronger than death. In the power of Jesus we are able to survive whatever this world throws at us. We are given strength by having him as our constant companion (if we do not let him just slumber in our lives). To have faith is to have a relationship with him and then to be able to say with St Paul, 'I am convinced that neither death nor life, nor angels nor rulers, nor things present, nor things to come, nor powers, nor height, nor depth, nor anything else in all creation, will be able to separate us from the love of God in Christ Jesus our Lord' (Romans 8: 38-39). (You may like to begin at verse 18.)

Illustration

There was a man who, for some reason, raged against life. Because he did not start off with riches, he was angry with all rich people. He did not make friends easily and often got into trouble by his aggressive attitude. Everything he gained he kept to himself. Soon he was well-off and successful – but not happy. It seemed storms followed him around. He was not comfortable to be with. He was also very lonely. Then he became ill and he began to struggle; he needed the care and attention of someone. He could afford it and hired a group of carers. One was a nurse who was willing put herself out to help him. She did errands and stayed with him for company. She also told him that she gained great peace of mind from knowing Jesus. The man was embarrassed at first but then wanted to know more. He wanted to know why she cared for him and how Jesus brought peace. In time, as his health improved, he no longer needed carers but he felt he needed this nurse; in fact, he loved her and proposed to her. She accepted him, they married and lived very happily together. He also had a living relationship with Jesus and so he knew of love and peace in his life.

Sunday before Lent

Aim

To show that in Jesus is revealed the full glory of God, for Jesus is God.

Readings

Exodus 34:29-35
Psalm 99
2 Corinthians 3:12–4:2
Luke 9:28-36 (37-43a)

Thought for the day

The story of the Transfiguration is the story of the disciples seeing Jesus for what he really is. The story begins eight days after Peter saying that Jesus is 'the Messiah of God' and Jesus telling them how he must undergo suffering, death and resurrection (Luke 9:18-22).

The place of the Transfiguration has by tradition often been Mount Tabor but this is unlikely as there is a fortress on the top of it. It is more likely to have been Mount Hermon – 9,400 feet high and 11,000 feet above the Jordan valley. Hermon can be seen from the Dead Sea, a hundred miles away. If it is Hermon, then the action probably happened somewhere on the mountainside rather than the top.

The reason for going up the mountain was for Jesus to be alone to pray to God. This also reflects the time when Moses went up the mountain to talk with God and to receive the Law. When Moses came down from the mountain he did not realise that his face shone (Exodus 34:29).

Jesus took with him Peter, James and John. We are told that the disciples were weighed down with sleep. It seems they were often tired. It could also be that here is an attempt by Luke to show how the disciples' eyes were opened to the glory of Jesus: it is when their eyes are opened – 'when they are fully awake' – that they behold his glory.

With the vision of Jesus in his glory, the disciples see Moses and Elijah in glory. Jesus fulfils both the Law as given by Moses and the prophets as represented by Elijah, the greatest of prophets.

Both Elijah and Moses had encounters with God on mountains. Moses departed this life on Mount Nebo, and Elijah went up to God in the whirlwind with chariot and horses of fire (see Deuteronomy 34:5, 6 and 2 Kings 2:11).

These two great leaders talk with Jesus of his 'departure'. It would be better to keep the word without translating it, for it is his 'exodus'. Like Moses, Jesus is going to go through a time of trial to bring his people to the Promised Kingdom.

The cloud that overshadows them is like the 'Pillar of Cloud' that went with Moses and the Israelites through the desert (Exodus 13:21, 22). Like the cloud that covered the Tent of Meeting, when the glory of the Lord filled the Tabernacle (Exodus 40:34), this luminous cloud is known as the 'Shekinah' and it represents the hidden glory of God. It is the cloud that hides the glory, for humans cannot bear too much of the glory of God. As if to confirm this there is also the voice from the cloud, the 'Bath Qol'. The voice says, 'This is my Son, my Chosen: listen to him.' Once again it is affirmed that Jesus is the Son of God, that Jesus is therefore God in human flesh. 'Listen' has with it the implication of 'Listen and obey'.

Now the disciples are suddenly alone with Jesus. Everything is back to normal and yet the disciples who had seen this can never be the same again. You might like to look at statements like 'We have seen his glory, the glory as of a father's only son' (John 1:14) or 'The light of the knowledge of the glory of God in the face of Jesus Christ' (2 Corinthians 4:6).

Illustration

On the night of 31 August 651, the young man Cuthbert was guarding sheep against robbers and wild animals. He was only 16 years old but possessed a spear and a horse. While he stayed alert and watching, the shepherds slept. The night was clear and full of stars. During the night Cuthbert suddenly saw angels descending to the earth and then ascending, taking with them a holy soul to heaven. Cuthbert sought to awaken the shepherds but they missed seeing what he saw. This made Cuthbert say, 'What wretches we are, given to sleep and sloth, so that we never see the glory of those who watch with Christ unceasingly.' The next day Cuthbert learnt that Aidan had died and he then went and offered himself to become a monk at the monastery of Melrose. True vision nearly always demands obedience and a change of direction.

First Sunday of Lent

Aim

To encourage people to see Lent as a time for improving their lives and their worship.

Readings

Deuteronomy 26:1-11
Psalm 91:1, 2, 9-16
Romans 10:8b-13
Luke 4:1-13

Thought for the day

Jesus is full of the Holy Spirit after his Baptism, and it is this Spirit who leads him into the wilderness. It is the Spirit who initiated the encounter with evil. In the same way, the Church and its people need to confront evil as a witness to God. Too often the Church seems silent in the face of evil.

The wilderness is a dangerous place where food and water are scarce and wild beasts roam; it was also thought to be where evil powers roam – maybe a place for some to avoid. But God is also to be found there, as he was with Moses and the people of Israel in the desert; as he was with Elijah in the wilderness. The number forty implies a long time but it is also symbolic. The flood lasted for Noah for forty days (Genesis 7:4). Moses was on Sinai for forty days and nights (Exodus 34:28). Elijah travelled for forty days in the wilderness (1 Kings 19:8). Israel was in the wilderness for forty years (Exodus 16:35; Deuteronomy 2:7). On all these occasion we are told of the care and protection of God.

Testing or temptation often comes when our resistance is low. Then comes the desire to give up the struggle against evil and to give up striving for God's kingdom. We lower our sights and our aims and so miss the target. In the New Testament one of the words for sin means 'missing the target'. For Jesus the desert is where he sorts out his aims and priorities.

'Command this stone to become a loaf of bread' is a great temptation for a hungry man. More subtle is the implication: look after yourself. Fill yourself with the things you desire, for you have the power to do it. We spend much of our lives filling ourselves with one thing or another. Jesus reminds us that we are dependent on God for life.

Jesus says, 'One does not live by bread alone.' All his hearers would understand by knowing the full quotation that continues, 'but by every word that comes from the mouth of God' (Deuteronomy 8:3).

Jesus is then offered the whole world. Was it the devil's to give? All Jesus had to do was compromise a little; accept the 'fallen' life as normal. Jesus replies with Deuteronomy 6:13: 'Worship the Lord your God and serve him only.' Jesus rejects false worship. What we worship determines our character, whether it is footballers, pop idols, models, or soap stars. Only the worship of God is the road to eternal life.

The devil then uses the holiest of places and quotes Scripture to lead Jesus astray. Nowhere or nothing is safe in the struggle against evil. Scripture can be misused and so can the Church, as history often shows. Jesus replies from Deuteronomy 6:16: 'Do not put the Lord your God to the test.'

It is too easy to jump just because the suggestion seems to come from good quarters; we have to use our hearts and minds and seek to serve our God.

Notice the devil leaves 'until an opportune time'; the battle is not over. It never is, as long as we are alive. The struggle against evil continues.

Illustration

Anyone who is still alive is tempted, so do not say you are not tempted. If you are not tempted, you have never lived or you have let something in you die. There is always a tug of war between good and evil, between achieving and failing to do so. There is no place or person free from this battle. In the book *Rogue Herries,* Hugh Walpole tells of how Herries had come to the wild and lonely Lakeland where he met a travelling preacher called Robert Finch. Herries asked:

> 'How shall I like this place? It is cut off from the world.'
>
> There was a sudden odd note of scorn in the little man's voice as he answered, 'It is the world, sir. Here within these hills, in this space of ground is all the world. I thought that while I was with my Lord Petersham that the world was there, but in every village I have passed since then I have found the complete world – all anger and vanity and

covetousness and lust, yes, and all charity, goodness and sweetness of soul. But most of all, here in this valley I have found the whole world. Lives are lived completely . . .The mountains close us in. You will find everything here, sir. God and the devil both walk in these fields.'

Rogue Herries, Part 1, by Hugh Walpole

COMPLETE COMMON WORSHIP

Sermon Illustrations

Second Sunday of Lent

Aim

To show how God can be trusted to keep his promises.

Readings

Genesis 15:1-12, 17, 18
Psalm 27
Philippians 3:17–4:1
Luke 13:31-35

Thought for the day

In today's Gospel we see that not all Pharisees were opposed to Jesus. Here we have some Pharisees warning Jesus that Herod is out to kill him and advising him to flee for safety.

The very mention of Herod must have made the disciples quake with fear. Herod had already ordered the beheading of John the Baptist. He had shown disrespect for the dead by building Tiberias on tombs. Herod could easily have had Jesus killed.

Jesus shows no fear. He sends a message to Herod, saying, 'Go and tell that fox.' Now to the Jew the fox was a symbol of three things: it was the most cunning of animals, it was more destructive than other animals as it killed for pleasure, and it was a worthless and insignificant creature. Herod did not intimidate Jesus. As the devil could not sway Jesus from his course, neither could this tyrant. Jesus continues the work of the kingdom of God and says Herod cannot stop it (Luke 13:32, 33). The reference to the 'third day' contrasts Herod who puts to death, with God who brings to life, even from the dead.

Although Herod destroyed John the Baptist, and although by the time Luke was writing the Temple built by Herod had been destroyed, the movement towards bringing in God's kingdom will not cease. God's promises will be fulfilled. In a time when the idolatry of Rome, its destructive power and its injustices were rife, it is important to know God's promises will still be fulfilled. The outward symbols, even the officers of the church, may be attacked and destroyed, but God will still be there and continue his work.

The lament of Jesus over Jerusalem is that it has rejected his offer: God's offer of love. Like Herod, the city of Jerusalem had a destructive side: it rejected and killed the prophets. Jesus wanted to take Jerusalem 'under his wing', to give it love and protection, but it was unwilling. God fulfils his promises but he will not force them upon us. God offers us his kingdom but it is up to us to accept it and give it our allegiance.

Illustration

In a dream a man was told where there was treasure hidden in a nearby castle under a blue stone. The dream was quite clear and he could remember every bit of it. Yet he did not bother even to see if the stone was there in the castle. He told his dream to a friend. His friend went immediately and found a great treasure under the blue stone. He became very rich and although he was generous toward his friend, his friend realised that because he had not bothered when an opportunity was offered him he had missed out in a big way.

How often do we miss out on the fullness of life because we do not take up the promises of our God?

Third Sunday of Lent

Aim

To show how our lives have purpose and are meant to be useful.

Readings

Isaiah 55:1-9
Psalm 63:1-8
1 Corinthians 10:1-13
Luke 13:1-9

Thought for the day

To understand the parable of the fig tree, we need to know two things. We need to know that all parables are about us and the way we live. We also need to know something about the importance of the fig tree in the Promised Land.

In many ways the fig tree was the most popular of trees. The picture of the Promised Land was 'a land of wheat and barley, of vines and fig trees, of pomegranates, a land of olive trees and honey' (Deuteronomy 8:8). When the spies looked over the land to see how fertile it was, they brought back grapes, figs and pomegranates as proof (Numbers 13:23). When the Old Testament wanted to describe peaceful times and prosperity it is of someone sitting under his own vine and fig tree (1 Kings 4:25; Micah 4:4; Zechariah 3:10). The fig tree was used as a symbol for the covenant between Israel and God (1 Kings 4:25; Isaiah 36:16; Jeremiah 24:4-7; Joel 2:22). The lack of fruit was a symbol of a lapse in faithfulness (Jeremiah 5:17, 8:13, 24:8-10; Joel 2:12).

The fig tree is a lovely tree, though not terribly tall – it grows to about 15 to 20 feet high. The spread of its branches can be up to 30 feet and so it provides good shelter and shade. Jesus had seen Nathanael under the fig tree's shade. But, more than shade, the tree was valued for its fruit and it cropped twice a year. The first crop comes off the old wood in June and the second off the new wood in September. A fig tree takes about three years to reach maturity; if by then it has not fruited, it is not likely to. From a fig tree the owner expects figs; if it does not produce, it does not fulfil its purpose. A tree that does not fruit is taking up room, feeding off the land and not giving in return. In the parable the tree is given another chance but it will not go on for ever, for there will be a day of reckoning.

The fig tree in the parable was all promise and no performance. It had its leaves, maybe even flowers, but it did not produce fruit and that was its main purpose. To give shelter from the heat was not enough; it was there to produce figs and if it failed to produce fruit, then it was useless. Uselessness invites disaster, for all things have a purpose – and that includes us. The church is not only a place of shelter; we have to produce the fruits of the Spirit.

Profession without practice is condemned. It is no use saying we are Christian if it does not show in the way we live.

Thank God for the second chance. We are still here for another year. Heed the words of Jesus to repent: we are to turn around (Luke 13:5) and not proceed in the wrong direction. Let us bring forth fruit.

Illustration

Abraham Lincoln triumphed over many adversities to become the President of the United States. Here are some of his words and they are about all of life and not just gardens:

> Die when I may, I want it said of me that I plucked a weed and planted a flower wherever I thought a flower would grow.

Think of the purpose of our existence as expressed by The Shorter Catechism of 1647:

> What is the chief end of man?
> To enjoy God and to glorify him for ever.

Fourth Sunday of Lent
Mothering Sunday

Aim

To give thanks to God for our mothers and for all who have mothered us. We also give thanks to God for his loving care.

Readings for Mothering Sunday

Exodus 2:1-10 or 1 Samuel 1:20-28
Psalm 34:11-20 or Psalm 127:1-4
2 Corinthians 1:3-7 or Colossians 3:12-17
Luke 2:33-35 or John 19:25-27

Readings for Fourth Sunday of Lent

Joshua 5:9-12
Psalm 32
2 Corinthians 5:16-21
Luke 15:1-3, 11b-32

Thought for the day

What does every living creature have in common? They have a mother. If there were no mothers there would be no people to know of in the Bible. Moses, Samuel and Jesus all had mothers who cared for them and protected them. Do you know the name of the mother of Moses? She was called Jochebed (Exodus 6:20). His mother hid him from the soldiers of Pharaoh at great risk to herself.

Who was the mother of Samuel? She was called Hannah (1 Samuel 1:20). For a long time she had no children and promised if she had a child she would raise him to do the work of God. When Samuel was born Hannah sang a song for joy. When Samuel was old enough she took him to the priest Eli, so that Samuel could learn to work for God.

Who was the mother of Jesus? Mary; without her saying 'Yes' to the angel that visited her, without saying 'Yes' to God, the baby Jesus could not have been born into the world. In caring for Jesus, Mary helped to bring to the world a loving Saviour.

All of us are fortunate if we have a mother who has loved us, cared for us, fed us, worked for us and protected us. Even when we have done wrong things, our mothers still love us. Most of us can depend on the love of a mother.

Today we seek to give thanks for the constant love and care of our mother. We also give thanks for the care and nourishment we have received from the Church.

Let this be the day when we thank our mother by trying to make her work easier, by taking our share of the work at home, by washing up and tidying our room. Let it be a day when we give her a card, a letter of love, a posy or some present as a sign of our gratitude and love in return for her love.

Illustration

I want to tell you of a mother who had no children, yet she had a big family. Her name was Teresa and she was born in Albania. She became a nun and her work took her to one of the largest towns in the world, Calcutta. There are many people in that city and it is overcrowded. Many poor people have nowhere to go and they feed off scraps thrown out by others, often out of rubbish bins. They sleep on the streets, in doorways, under bridges. If they are ill, no one cares for them; there are not enough doctors and nurses. They have no home to go to and no mother to look after them. Teresa tried to help as many as she could and they knew her as Mother Teresa.

One day Mother Teresa saw a woman lying in the road. People were just walking past and ignoring her. Mother Teresa saw the woman was very ill. She tried to get people to help but no one wanted to know. Mother Teresa tried to get her into hospital but the doctor said there was no room for people so poorly. She went to see the health officer and he offered her two very small rooms where she could live with the woman and look after her. She did that until the woman died.

Mother Teresa got lots of women, mothers and nuns together and founded the Missionaries of Charity to care for the ill, the unwanted, for the old, for babies and for unwanted children. Mother Teresa may not have had any children of her own but many people called her Mother and she had one of the largest families on earth.

Mother Teresa often said, 'Let us do something beautiful for God', and this she did time and time again.

Fifth Sunday of Lent

Aim

To rejoice in the sacrificial love of Mary, which is a foretaste of the sacrifice of Christ the 'Anointed One'.

Readings

Isaiah 43:16-21
Psalm 126
Philippians 3:4b-14
John 12:1-8

Thought for the day

St John tells us it is only six days to the Passover, the time of sacrificing the sacrificial lamb. All male Jews who lived near enough were expected to go to Jerusalem for the Passover. Because the city was so crowded, Bethany was counted as part of the outer limits of Jerusalem and a place that could accommodate pilgrims. Jesus had been condemned by Caiaphas and 'outlawed' by the Pharisees (see John 11:47-53, 57). Jesus was not put off and went towards Jerusalem at great risk to his life. He stayed at the home of Lazarus, whom he had raised from the dead, and Lazarus sat at table with him.

Martha loved Jesus and served him as best she knew how by looking after his need for food and comfort. People like Martha made the ministry of Jesus possible.

Mary was an impetuous person and not afraid of showing that she loved Jesus. She came into the room and gave him the most precious thing she had – a pound of costly perfumed oil. She poured this perfume over the feet of Jesus. She did not presume she could anoint his head with oil (Psalm 23:5). She did the unusual act of anointing his feet.

As Messiah, or Christ, means the Anointed One, Mary's act has special significance. It is an act of love, and in love nothing is too costly to give to the beloved. Mary then probably scandalises some by wiping the feet of Jesus with her loose hair. (In Palestine no self-respecting woman would appear in public with her hair loose; this was a sign of a loose woman.) Jesus accepts this attention as a sign not only of her love but also as a preparation for his burial (John 12:7). He is in no doubt that his time is now limited. Love makes it possible to face the task ahead. Pain can be borne as long as we know we are not totally on our own. The extravagance of love enriches giver and receiver.

When we are told the house was filled with the fragrance, it is a little detail that must be obvious. Perhaps John wanted us to realise that the whole Church would be filled with the memory of this act (see Mark 14:9).

Judas then costs Mary's act of love. You can never do that – love cannot be measured by money. Here is a hint that some of the women understood Jesus better than some of the apostles.

Illustration

A nurse in hospital described how humans have a great capacity for accepting what is happening to them and for enduring pain as long as they have loved ones about them and people who truly care. Pain can be borne as long as we are not left alone. We need to know in our troubles that we are still loved and cared for. Worse than pain is the feeling of separation from loved ones or a feeling that we are no longer wanted.

When many were beginning to go against Jesus – including Judas – it is good to see the expression of love and affection that is shown him from the whole household at Bethany.

Palm Sunday

Aim

To rejoice at the entry of Christ into Jerusalem and to share in the Passion story.

Readings

Liturgy of the Palms
Luke 19:28-40
Psalm 118:1, 2, 19-29

Liturgy of the Passion
Isaiah 50:4-9a
Psalm 31:9-16
Philippians 2:5-11
Luke 22:14–23:56 or Luke 23:1-49

Let the dramatic readings of the Passion narratives replace the sermon today. Allow the Scriptures to speak for themselves. Use as many people as possible to share in the readings.

Thought for the day

Jesus was travelling from Jericho to Jerusalem, about 20 miles and uphill nearly all the way. This was a rocky and dangerous road, more dangerous for Jesus because the leaders of the church had already outlawed him. There was a price on his head (John 11:57).

Jesus would not be swayed from coming to celebrate the Passover in Jerusalem. It was all planned. He had made arrangements for the ass and the password was 'The Lord needs it'. Bethphage and Bethany were favourite places of Jesus and here he was well known and liked. These places were on the southeast side of the Mount of Olives and were counted as part of Jerusalem for festivals. Here Mary had anointed Jesus. Here he stayed at the house of Lazarus, Mary and Martha. Here he raised Lazarus from the dead. It was also where he had stayed at the house of Simon. And on this hillside was the Garden of Gethsemane. The Palm Sunday events started from here.

Jesus could have slipped into Jerusalem unseen but he co fronted the authorities by his action. Many people rode donkeys. The donkey was counted a noble beast. Kings rode horses to war or when they wanted to emphasise their might. When they came in peace they rode upon a donkey. Jesus would enter Jerusalem as the Prince of Peace, the promised Messiah. People would be given the choice to accept him or reject him, as is still the case. Already groups were polarising for or against Jesus. Jesus refused to be a puppet king who would dance at the whims of people. He refused to be a warlord and lead them to battle. He refused false dignity and pomp. Yet he would rule in the hearts of those who would allow him to.

Jesus rode on the donkey to fulfil the prophecy of Zechariah 9:9, 10 (read these verses out). He is your King. Will you accept him? It is by living his way that God's kingdom comes on earth.

Easter Day

Aim

To enter into the joy and wonder of the resurrection and the presence of the risen Lord.

Readings

Acts 10:34-43 or Isaiah 65:17-25
Psalm 118:1, 2, 14-24
1 Corinthians 15:19-26 or Acts 10:34-43
John 20:1-18 or Luke 24:1-12

Thought for the day

After the harrowing events of Good Friday, Mary could not sleep. One of the things that troubled Mary was that Jesus didn't have the usual spices placed by his body. She rose early while it was still dark and made her way to the tomb. Throughout the journey (maybe two miles) Mary kept asking who would roll away the stone. It would take a few men and the tomb was sealed. Who would roll away the stone? Mary wondered who could roll away the sorrow and heaviness that was in her heart; it would take a miracle for the weight to be lifted. Who will remove the stone? (Two or three people could quietly sing a few lines of the hymn 'The angel rolled the stone away'.)

Yet when Mary saw the stone rolled away it caused her to panic. Her reaction was to think that someone had stolen the body. She went to tell Peter. He would be delighted to be woken up before six in the morning! Perhaps Peter feared the authorities were now coming for him.

Now Peter and John run to the tomb. The young John outruns Peter, but is afraid to enter the tomb until Peter arrives. Peter goes into the tomb and so does John. The linen wrappings are there and the cloth that had been around the head. It is as if Jesus had just come through them. As yet they do not understand that Jesus must rise. The disciples return to their home.

Mary stays there weeping and wondering. In a vision of angels Mary is asked, 'Woman, why are you weeping?' She is weeping because she has been separated from Jesus, first by his death and now by not being able to see his body. Now Jesus asks her, 'Woman, why are you weeping?' Mary supposed the speaker to be the gardener as she looked up with tear-filled eyes. When Jesus said, 'Mary', she knew. No one spoke to her like that except Jesus. She replied, 'Rabbouni' (which means teacher) and reached out and clung to him. This was no ghost; this was a solid person. Mary was told not to stay there hugging Jesus but to tell the disciples that he was to be ascending to the Father. Yet another knock on Peter's door and this time the word of Mary astounded them all: 'I have seen the Lord' – and she meant the risen, living Lord Jesus. This new awareness would change Mary, the disciples and then the world.

Illustration

High up on the moors in the winter season, men go out and set fire to the old heather. By now the heather is all twisted and gnarled; it no longer produces food for the birds and even the moorland sheep are in danger of pulling their teeth out tugging at it. The heather has become useless to the life it usually sustains. So it is burnt, but with a controlled burning. In the flames it may look as if it is totally destroyed but it is not. Under the ground its roots are safe and the men make sure the fire is not too fierce to reach the roots. In the spring the old heather is gone but little shoots appear. The heather is rising from the earth and soon will appear as fresh and as useful as ever. What was destroyed is back with newness of life.

Second Sunday of Easter

Aim

To share in the joy of Easter.

Readings

Acts 5:27-32
Psalm 118:14-29 or Psalm 150
Revelation 1:4-8
John 20:19-31

Thought for the day

Some people are fortunate in that they are in the right place at the right time. Others only reach what they seek through their persistence and determination.

Thomas was not with the disciples on Easter Day when Jesus appeared. He could see their joy but he found it hard to enter into it. How could you just believe it if someone told you they had seen a person alive after a cruel death?

Thomas had a few habits that were not useful to his faith. He was a natural pessimist. When Jesus suggested they went to Jerusalem, Thomas said, 'Let us all go and we will die together.' Then he was a sceptic. He would not accept belief because he was told about it. He was aware of the joy of the disciples. They said they had seen the Lord. Thomas coolly said, 'Unless I see the mark of the nails in his hands, and put my finger in the mark of the nails and my hand in his side, I will not believe.'

Thomas stayed with the believers and talked with them. He prayed with them and ate with them. He did not separate himself from them. The surest way to belief is to stay with real believers; not with people who just recite creeds but with those who have met the risen Lord. Regular worship is the way our faith grows and is kept alive.

Thomas was not afraid to say when he doubted. 'Unless I see . . . and touch I will not believe.' Thomas said what he felt and not just what he was expected to say. Of such Tennyson wrote:

> There lies more faith in honest doubt
> than in a thousand creeds.

Thomas doubted but it did not stop him being a seeker. He did not write off the experience of the disciples. He stayed with them and questioned and sought the truth. He found because he was a seeker. Did not Jesus say, 'Seek and you shall find'?

Like Thomas, we need not fear doubts. We do need to fear not testing our doubts within the fellowship of the faithful. We need to seek until we find.

Illustration

Before he became Archbishop, Anthony Bloom was a young atheist, but he was a seeker. He heard a lecture on Jesus and just could not believe what he heard. He picked up a Bible and turned to the Gospels. He counted the chapters of each Gospel so that he could read the shortest. He chose St Mark and this is what he said:

> I started to read St Mark's Gospel . . . before I reached the third chapter, I suddenly became aware that on the other side of my desk there was a presence. And the certainty was so strong that it was the Christ standing there that it has never left me. This was the real turning point. Because Christ was alive and I had been in his presence.

Third Sunday of Easter

Aim

To see Jesus as the risen Lord on the shore of Galilee.

Readings

Acts 9:1-6 (7-20)
Psalm 30
Revelation 5:11-14
John 21:1-19

Thought for the day

Today's readings are very much about vision, of seeing the Lord. Saul sees Jesus on the Damascus road, and in Damascus, Ananias also sees the Lord. St John the Divine in his revelations sees the 'Lamb that was slaughtered being worshipped by the hosts of heaven'. Then the Gospel is about seven of the disciples seeing the risen Lord. It is wonderful to have a vision but with all visions comes responsibility; at the very least vision needs our attention and usually obedience to the call. See how both Saul and Ananias are asked to do something. Like Isaiah (Isaiah 6) Ananias says 'Here I am.' The Lord says to Ananias, 'Get up and go.'

Today's Gospel reading appears to be an addition to St John for it is almost certain that John's Gospel ended originally with chapter 20. As it has been added, there must be an important message.

Life has a habit of repeating itself. Things that we thought had passed have a habit of returning. We think we are making progress, then suddenly we find ourselves back where we started. H. E. Bates compared life to a game of snakes and ladders: sometimes you are climbing ahead and suddenly you drop back almost to the beginning.

It was like this for the disciples. They had left all to follow Jesus: they left fishing, the tax office and the field to share with him. Then it came to a sudden end with the crucifixion. They were knocked right back. The risen Lord made their spirits soar and they were full of new hope. But how would they make their living now? Naturally the fishermen went back to Galilee. Peter decided to go fishing and with him went six others – Thomas,

Nathanael, James and John who were the sons of Zebedee, and two other disciples. They toiled all night and caught nothing. As in all of life, when things go wrong, they go wrong in all sorts of directions. They couldn't even catch fish. There was a feeling that they had been here before.

Just as the new day dawned, Jesus stood on the shore. They did not recognise him at first. He directed their net throwing and they caught so many fish that they could not haul them all in. It was then that John realised who it was and said to Peter, 'It is the Lord.' Peter, who had only been wearing a loincloth as he fished, put on his tunic before he jumped into the sea – odd to put clothes on to jump into the water. Perhaps it can only be understood if you know that the Jews said a man had to be properly dressed to come and worship.

Jesus is not a ghost, not just a vision; he is real and he is solid. He has lit a fire and prepared food for them. He shared bread and fish with them. Now come the challenges of the story. 'Simon, son of John, do you love me more than these?' We do not know if Jesus was talking about the catch of fish or about the other disciples. More likely it was about the promise that Peter did not keep, for three times Peter had denied knowing Jesus. Now three times Jesus asks Peter about loving him. Each time when Peter says, 'Yes, Lord; you know that I love you', Jesus asks him to care for his lambs and sheep. Peter was given his task, his mission to be a pastor, to be a co-shepherd with the Good Shepherd.

The risen Lord brings forgiveness; love restores broken relationships. Peter is affirmed and then is able to affirm his task. If we are to be disciples, we have to listen to and follow the Master (John 21:19).

Illustration

It is told that, when Jesus returned to heaven, the Archangel Michael barred his way. The archangel said, 'How can you return to heaven? Your work is not yet completed. There are many who do not know about or who have not heard of your saving acts.' Jesus said, 'I have left my friends to complete what I have begun.' The Archangel was amazed. 'Do you mean those puny, often straying humans?' 'Yes,' said Jesus, 'I trust them and I know that through following me they will bring my gospel to all the world.'

Fourth Sunday of Easter

Aim

To explore our relationship with Jesus through the image of the shepherd.

Readings

Acts 9:36-43
Psalm 23
Revelation 7:9-17
John 10:22-30

Thought for the day

The tenth chapter of St John is very much about the image of sheep and shepherd. Jesus describes how the shepherd calls his own sheep by name and leads them out. In verse 8 Jesus declares he is the gate for the sheep. This describes not only our entry into his kingdom but also his protection of us, as the shepherd used to lie across the gateway of the fold to safeguard the sheep. This idea is continued in verse 11 where Jesus says, 'I am the good shepherd. The good shepherd lays down his life for the sheep.'

The Jews were arguing about these words. Some thought Jesus mad; others thought him to be wonderful. At this point today's Gospel begins. It is the Dedication Festival, the festival of Hanukkah, sometimes called the Festival of Lights. It was to celebrate the heroic victory of Judas Maccabaeus over the King of Assyria. In 170 BC over 80,000 Jews perished in the attack on Jerusalem and as many again were taken into captivity. Only six years later Judas Maccabaeus rescued Jerusalem, and the Temple was cleansed and purified. To celebrate this festival, lights were lit in every Jewish home as well as in the Temple. The festival takes place on the 25th day of Chislev, which corresponds to our December and so is very near to our Christmas. We are told it is winter and Jesus is walking in the portico of Solomon, which is a roofed-over colonnade in the first court of the Temple precincts.

The Jews ask Jesus, 'How long will you keep us in suspense? If you are the Messiah, tell us plainly.' There were two main groups: those who wanted to know and looked forward with joy to the answer, and those who sought to trap Jesus and accuse him of blasphemy or madness. Jesus replies by telling them he has already told them and that his works testify to this. 'But you do not believe, because you do not belong to my sheep.'

Jesus details then what makes believers. 'My sheep hear my voice. I know them and they follow me. I give them eternal life, and they will never perish. No one will snatch them from my hand' (John 10:27, 28).

To hear is to obey. Not only do his believers hear him, they obey him. He knows them. He has a relationship with them. He loves them and cares for them. They are his followers. Just as sheep follow their shepherd to new pastures, we follow Jesus into newness of life. Unlike ordinary sheep, those who follow Jesus will not perish: they receive the gift of eternal life. (Compare John 3:16.)

No one can take them from Jesus, not even death. One of the greatest comments on this is Romans 8:35-39; it would be worth reading this aloud.

Illustration

Two flocks of sheep had become intermingled. Night was coming down and it would be very difficult to separate them before it was dark. If men or dogs were sent in, it would cause a lot of fear among the sheep and greater confusion. The shepherd who came to care for his flock said, 'Leave them alone. Wait until it is almost the end of day, then I will call mine. They know me, they will hear my voice and follow me.' As evening came, the shepherd started to call. The reaction among the sheep was interesting, for some heard the voice and wanted to run away because they did not know it. The sheep that belonged to the shepherd recognised his voice. They heard a call that meant safety, shelter and sustenance. They knew of the love of the shepherd and came running to where he was.

Fifth Sunday of Easter

Aim

To explore how God's glory is revealed in the death and resurrection of Jesus.

Readings

Acts 11:1-18
Psalm 148
Revelation 21:1-6
John 13:31-35

Thought for the day

John reminds us that Judas has left the company. In a very telling way John declares Judas went out and 'it was night' (13:30).

Judas chose to go out into the dark rather than stay with the Light of the World. Jesus does not exclude Judas. Judas walks away from him and excludes himself. Judas excused himself from the company and went into the dark. Jesus knew what Judas was about to do and yet did not stop him. Jesus never forces any of us to stay against our will. The choice is ours. The dark clouds had been building and what was about to happen could be easily predicted. There was already a price on Jesus' head. Jesus wanted the disciples not to lose heart but to see that through the events that followed the glory of God is to be revealed.

The glory of Jesus is revealed on the cross. Jesus lays down his life for all who are willing to be his friends. St Paul tells us that while we were yet sinners Jesus died for us. Glory is seen through the willing sacrifice of his life for our lives. In the field of medicine we remember not those who make a fortune but those who gave their lives that others might live. The researchers into radiation, Pierre and Marie Curie, are a good example of this.

The glory of the Father is revealed in that he gave his Son for our salvation. God cares for the world and the state of the world. He is not unmoved by our troubles and sorrows. God loves us so much that he would go to extremes to help us and reveal his love. This is the love that is seen on the cross, yet is there for us to see from the incarnation through to the ascension. God's glory awaits us in all creation.

God will glorify Jesus in that the cross is not the end. Death is not the end. Jesus wins the victory over death. In the cross the glory of God is revealed but it is seen again in the resurrection and the ascension. Soon the disciples would be separated from Jesus by death but it is only for a little while. This farewell is only for the moment.

As part of his bequest, Jesus leaves the disciples a commandment: 'that you love one another, just as I have loved you'. And it is by this that people will know that we are his disciples: by our love for one another. If this is how our discipleship is measured, how our life is measured, we need take heed how we react to each other.

Illustration

Over 150 years ago no one cared for the lepers on the Hawaiian islands. They were driven out of their homes and even off their island. The lepers were taken to a special island called Molokai. Here they were abandoned on the beach, left to suffer and to die.

One man was anxious to do what he could. He was a Roman Catholic priest, Father Damien. He went to Molokai and was shocked at the state of the lepers. A collection of filthy ramshackle huts housed over 800 lepers. Many were helpless, weak and unable to do anything. Yet in their troubles they had built a small chapel.

Father Damien set to work. He encouraged those who were able to tidy up the mess they lived in, to build better homes and to provide a decent water supply. For 13 years he stayed with the lepers and in the end caught the disease himself. He said he was proud and privileged to be one of them. They wanted him to leave Molokai and receive better attention but he refused. Even in his last illness he gave his blankets to others in their need. He continued to show to the end his love of others, that they were not without hope and that the glory of God was for them as for others.

Sixth Sunday of Easter

Aim

To show that Christ offers us his peace and his presence.

Readings

Acts 16:9-15
Psalm 67
Revelation 21:10, 22–22:5
John 14:23-29 or John 5:1-9

Thought for the day

Jesus knows that his time is short. He is aware that there is a price on his head and he knows Judas has gone out to betray him. Soon Jesus will be taken prisoner and killed. All his earthly teaching will apparently come to an end. This must have been a very sad time in some ways. Today's reading sounds a little like the last will and testament of Jesus. He does not have possessions to leave with the disciples; he has no money but what he leaves will enrich them for ever.

First is the promise of the Spirit, 'whom the Father will send in my name'. The disciples of Jesus are not to be bereft for they are to be given the Spirit of God. The Spirit will be their guide and teacher. The Spirit will inspire them. The Spirit will remind them of Jesus, of his teaching and of his calling each of them.

Jesus leaves his disciples the gift of peace. This is not worldly peace, which is usually a cessation of war or when nothing is happening. This is the deep peace of God. This peace cannot be created by stillness or even meditation, for it is not of our making. It is a gift from Jesus: it is his peace. Whatever is going on in the world, even when troubles rage, his peace is there for us to accept. This peace is not dependent on circumstance but on us accepting it from the Lord.

The 'exodus' of Jesus is now near, yet he says to his disciples, 'Do not let your hearts be troubled, and do not let them be afraid.' This must have reminded the disciples of the words from Isaiah 43:1: 'Do not fear, for I have redeemed you; I have called you by your name, you are mine.'

Jesus tells them how he is going back to the Father and suggests they should be glad. Jesus is trying to widen the vision of the disciples. Life is larger than we can see. Though Jesus is going away from our sight, he still comes to us as he promised the disciples. The gifts of peace and the Presence are Christ's gifts to us all.

Illustration

In the old days crossing the Atlantic in a sailing boat left everyone to the mercy of the wind and waves. How those old wooden boats rocked about! People not used to the rolling of the boat could not walk on deck. Many had to spend most of their voyage below deck. Everything that could be was fastened firmly down to prevent it from being washed overboard. Today's journeys are a great contrast. Waiters can carry soup and children can play on deck. People lounge in the sun and hardly notice the rising and falling of the waves. Even in a storm the main body of the ship remains relatively calm – all because of the unseen gyroscope that maintains the balance of the ship. We have been offered the power of peace and calm in our lives through the presence of Christ. Do we accept this offer or neglect it at our peril?

Ascension Day

Aim

To rejoice in the presence of the ascended Lord.

Readings

Acts 1:1-11* or Daniel 7:9-14
Psalm 47 or Psalm 93
Ephesians 1:15-23 or Acts 1:1-11*
Luke 24:44-53

* *The reading from Acts must be one of the readings for the day.*

Thought for the day

'While he was blessing them, he withdrew from them and was carried up into heaven. And they worshipped him.'

Some things defy description and the Ascension is one of them. I do not like the paintings that look as if Jesus is levitating a little off the ground. I prefer to see the disciples and a bright cloud that represents the hidden glory of God. I do not like the idea of Jesus taking off as if rocket-propelled. The Ascension is not about having lost Jesus but of us having gained the way into heaven: it is about the eternal presence of Jesus in our lives.

Jesus had to be freed from the restrictions of space and time. There are examples in the Gospels of Jesus being needed but not being there. Mary and Martha were upset that Jesus was not there when Lazarus was dying. He did not even arrive in time, though the raising of Lazarus made a great difference. When the disciples were at sea in the storm Jesus had to go to them. The Ascension frees Jesus from the restrictions of time and space. Jesus can say at the end of St Matthew, 'I am with you always.' Though departed from our sight, Jesus is ever-present and with us. We should rejoice in the company of the risen and ascended Lord.

Jesus ascended because he had descended. He came down to walk among us as man but not just to be a friend. He came down with the purpose of lifting us up. He descended so that we might ascend and be part of his everlasting kingdom. He became man so that all of humanity might share in the Godhead. He seeks to lift those that are down. May we, in heart and mind, ascend to where our Lord is.

Illustration

A man was wandering carelessly without looking where he was going. The result was he fell into a well. The well was deep and dark, and the dirt and slime clung to the man. He knew that he could perish in this horrible place.

The God of the Old Testament, the God of the Law, came and said, 'If you had kept to the right path, you would not have ended up like this. You have strayed from the straight and narrow and now you are suffering for it. One day you will be given a rescuer.'

Allah then came and looked down at the man and said, 'It is the will of Allah. Fate has brought you here. You could not escape from this whatever you did. But it may be my will that you get out again.'

Buddha looked down on the man and said, 'Smile, for it is all in the mind. Cleanse your mind and everything will be all right.'

Jesus said nothing. He descended into the mud and mire. He experienced the dark, the pain, the discomfort. He was there in the depths taking hold of the man. Then, through great efforts that cost him dearly, Jesus rose and when he ascended he took the man with him.

Seventh Sunday of Easter

Aim

To rejoice that we dwell in God and he in us.

Readings

Acts 16:16-34
Psalm 97
Revelation 22:12-14, 16, 17, 20, 21
John 17:20-26

Thought for the day

Today's Gospel has the last words of Jesus before he goes out to the Garden of Gethsemane, to his arrest and crucifixion. This is a prayer of Jesus for his disciples and for all who come to believe through the disciples and the outreach of the Church. The prayer shows the trust Jesus puts in the disciples and in us. He knew the frailty of the disciples and that they hardly understood what he was saying. He still handed his work on to them and put his hope and confidence in them as he does in us.

Jesus prays for our unity but it is not a unity of our making; it is a unity through our dwelling in God and God dwelling in us. It is a unity that is about relationships, not only with each other but with God. It is a unity of love, that we love each other as Jesus loves us. Unity comes not through schemes and meetings but through heart-to-heart relationships.

Jesus prays, 'As you, Father, are in me and I also in you, may they also be in us.' The great gift of God to us is that we dwell in him and he in us. We are never without the presence of God, for in him we live and move and have our dwelling. This is expressed well in the 'Prayer of Seven Directions' (a good prayer to start and end each day with):

> God before me: God behind me.
> God on my right and God on my left.
> God above me: God beneath me.
> God, this day within and about me.

Because God is greater than we are, there are six directions saying that we are in God and one direction saying that God is in us.

We are more God-possessed than possessing God! This is the Glory and the love that we share: we can meet God in others and be God to others. The unity that we have is God-given. The joy we have is from our indwelling and it is something we need to take time to know and enjoy.

Illustration

There is an old story about God and the humans after the Fall. Because man had separated from God through disobedience, God decided to hide from humans. He asked his angels where he should hide. 'Hide in the heights of heaven,' said the first angel. God replied, 'The humans would expect me to be in the high places and they will find me in their own high experiences.' The second angel said, 'Then why not hide in the depths?' God replied, 'Again, all human beings descend into the depths from time to time and they will discover that I am there.' One little angel had bided his time and he saw the mistakes of others. He said to God, 'Why not hide in the human heart? They will never find you there.' God smiled and said, 'How true', and from that day hid in each human heart. Yet there are so few humans who seek his presence in their lives.

Pentecost

Aim

To know the Spirit as our strength and our guide.

Readings

Acts 2:1-21* or Genesis 11:1-9
Psalm 104:24-34, 35b
Romans 8:14-17 or Acts 2:1-21*
John 14:8-17 (25-27)

** The reading from Acts must be one of the readings today.*

Thought for the day

The disciples had shared in the ministry of Jesus. They had experienced his healing miracles and his teaching. True, they had suffered the trauma of the crucifixion, death and burial, but they had also seen the risen Lord. He had appeared to them two or three times, assuring them of his love and his presence. In story fashion you would expect these men to be bold and able to do anything, but in fact we find them hesitant and fearful, once again behind closed doors. Not a very inspiring display, yet typical of much of human nature: locked in and afraid of life.

It seems the resurrection was not enough in itself to get the disciples going. This wonderful event did not seem to make them braver or stronger. There was still an emptiness within. Jesus had understood this well and told them to wait in Jerusalem where they would be baptised by the Holy Spirit (Acts 1:4, 5) and then they would receive power to become witnesses (Act 1:8).

What exactly happened at Pentecost we will never know. The disciples could only describe their experience in terms of wind and fire, two of the strongest elements of the world. Their emptiness was changed and charged with power. The sound, the Spirit, filled the house. It was as if each received a flaming light and the Spirit filled each of them (Acts 2:1-4). The God who seemed to be outside of them was now also known to be within. In the first 13 chapters of Acts there are more than 40 references to the Spirit. The Spirit is experienced as power from on high (Acts 1:8, 4:31, 13:9). The Spirit is experienced as guidance (Acts 8:29, 10:19, 11:12, 11:28, 13:2-4, 15:28, 16:6, 20:23). Through the indwelling

Spirit the disciples are changed for ever and it is the selfsame Spirit that fills the Church of today and each of us. Let us wait upon the Spirit each day for strength and guidance.

Illustration

There are lots of ancient stories about werewolves and creatures that come in the night and steal away your life powers. You wake in the morning feeling drained and half-dead. Well, you might not believe such tales but it is still possible to awake short on energy and resources, and the more we try to put it right, the more in danger we are of becoming exhausted. When our batteries run low we need a charge from outside of ourselves. Too many of us think we are self-sufficient, able to go in our own strength, when we need to learn to wait upon the Lord for renewal and for guidance. Just as we would not drive around all day with a flat tyre, so we should make sure we begin the day filled with the power and love of God.

Trinity Sunday

Aim

To rejoice in the presence and power of Father, Son and Holy Spirit.

Readings

Proverbs 8:1-4, 22-31
Psalm 8
Romans 5:1-5
John 16:12-15

Thought for the day

There are some things that we cannot put into words no matter how skilled we are. It is difficult to capture a sunset in words, though it is not hard to enjoy the sunset. A meaningful relationship cannot be tied down by a description, yet it is still good to say why some relationships are meaningful to us. Love cannot be fully expressed in words – it is beyond mere expression – but it would be a sad world if we gave up trying to tell of our love. In the same way, when we try to explain the Trinity we find that words fail us. The mystery of Godhead cannot be contained in a neat formula or grasped by our minds. The majesty of God is beyond our comprehension. Yet we need to communicate our experience and tell of the things of our heart. Often what the mind cannot comprehend the heart can grasp.

The word 'Trinity' does not appear anywhere in the Bible, yet the Bible is full of accounts of the Creator, Redeemer and Comforter. The reading from Proverbs hints at 'wisdom' being God's co-worker from the beginning: 'I was beside him, like a master worker; and I was daily his delight, rejoicing before him always, rejoicing in his inhabited world and delighting in the human race' (Proverbs 8:30, 31). For God to have a personality there needs to be at least another personality to relate to. Personality is of the utmost importance because it is of the essence of the Godhead. The way we reflect God's image is through our personality.

In Romans, St Paul tells us, 'We have peace with God through our Lord Jesus Christ' (5:1). A little later St Paul declares, 'God's love has been poured into our hearts through the Holy Spirit that has been given to us' (5:5).

In St John's Gospel we have Jesus talking of the 'Spirit of truth' who 'will guide you into all truth' (16:13). He also tells us of the Father and how he had given all to his Son (16:15).

There are only hints and expressions of the Trinity but there is no doubt that our God is a triune God. We believe in God the Creator who made the world and all that is in it. God created the world out of his own love and for his love. We believe that God revealed himself to the world in Jesus. Jesus is God incarnate. When the world strayed away from God and got lost in sin and death, Jesus came to redeem the world through his love and to bring us to eternal life. Once Jesus ascended into the heavens, the Holy Spirit of God came to us and gave us strength and guidance. The Spirit is ever-present and fills us with his power and his love. The Holy Spirit is God. Yet there are not three Gods separate from each other but One God. Hard to grasp with the mind, but the heart will begin to understand if we give our attention to each person of the Trinity.

Illustration

To understand the Three in One is quite difficult. St Patrick suggested the shamrock with its three shapes that made one leaf. Clover is much the same. Others have suggested the human being as made up of body, mind and spirit: three parts that you cannot fully separate and yet one being.

You might like to think of the sun. You can see it in the sky and yet it is too bright to look at. In its glory you may like to compare the sun to God the Father. Even when the sun is hidden we know it is still there.

The sun provides the world with light. This light gives life to the world and in the light we can live and move. Let the light remind us of Jesus who is the Light of the World. Even on the dullest of days the sun still provides us with light.

The sun also provides us with warmth. Without the warmth the world would be cold and dead. In the warmth we grow and live. Let the warmth remind us of the Spirit.

Glory, light and warmth – we can talk of them as separate things and yet they are bound together. One would not exist without the other.

Proper 4

Sunday between 29 May and 4 June inclusive (if after Trinity Sunday)

Aim

To encourage people in their use of intercessory prayer.

Readings

1 Kings 18:20, 21 (22-29) 30-39
or 1 Kings 8:22, 23, 41-43
Psalm 96 or Psalm 96:1-9
Galatians 1:1-12
Luke 7:1-10

Thought for the day

Capernaum means 'the village of compassion'. Here Jesus has shown compassion for Peter's mother-in-law, for the man with the troubled spirit in the synagogue and for the ill people who were brought to him.

In Capernaum there was a centurion who asked Jesus for help. A centurion is like a company sergeant major. He would look after a hundred soldiers. He was a man used to authority and to being obeyed. We know he was a man of means for he had built a synagogue for the Jews in Capernaum. He was a Gentile but obviously had a good relationship with the Jews. Not all Roman soldiers or their leaders were disliked. The centurion was a man of compassion for he was concerned for one of his slaves. Under Roman law a slave was not counted of any value. The owner of a slave could discard a useless slave. He could actually kill a slave of his own and would incur no charge. Often a slave who was ill or old was thrown out to die. We are told the centurion valued his slave highly and was concerned that he was ill.

In his compassion for his slave, the centurion sent word to Jesus through some of the Jewish elders, asking him to come and heal his slave. He was used to delegating authority and asked the Jewish elders to intercede on his behalf. Perhaps the centurion did this because he knew that a strict Jew had no dealings with Gentiles and would not enter a Gentile house. Yet he was sure Jesus could heal his slave.

When the centurion saw that Jesus was on his way to his house he sent a message through friends, saying, 'Lord, do not trouble yourself, for I am not worthy to have you come under my roof; therefore I did not presume to come to you.' Here you see the humility of the man in his respect for Jesus and the high regard he had for the power of Jesus. The messengers continued with the words of the centurion, 'But only speak the word, and let my servant be healed. For I also am a man set under authority, with soldiers under me; and I say to one, "Go", and he goes, and to another, "Come", and he comes, and to my slave, "Do this", and he does it.' The centurion had others to intercede for him and he believed that Jesus could heal without having to go to the person: distance was not a barrier. The centurion believed he had only to ask and he would receive. This Roman soldier knew about the power of prayer and of others interceding on behalf of him and his servant.

Such a deep understanding and faith amazed Jesus. Here was a Gentile who put to shame so many who called themselves believers. Jesus said, 'I tell you not even in Israel have I found such faith.' Faith does not belong to a certain group or nation. Faith is revealed in the living relationship that a person has with God. Faith is not restricted to Jews or Christians. It is no use claiming to be part of the Church unless we show a living relationship with our God. The centurion put his faith in Jesus. He believed that Jesus would respond and could heal. He did not have to see Jesus but he believed in him and his power. Without ever meeting Jesus, through his own faith and the intercession of others, the centurion had the joy of seeing his servant healed.

Illustration

Martin's father was a tribune in the Roman army. This meant he was a man of authority and had charge over six centurions and 600 men. When Martin was 10 years old he went to church and declared he wanted to learn the Christian faith. His pagan parents were not well pleased. The church was attractive to this young mind as the church often is to young folk. By the time he was 15 Martin was often engaged in church work. Not long after this the recruitment age for the Roman army was lowered to 16. Martin's father saw this as an opportunity and got the recruitment officer to call. He came unannounced and with manacles to take Martin off to the army. Now he would have to spend the next 25 years as a soldier. This was not a barren time for Martin.

Here he would learn of discipline, obedience and orderliness. He would learn of the need to travel lightly without too many possessions, and because they were often on the move celibacy was the ideal. As the son of an officer he was soon given a commission and was allowed a servant. He shocked others by taking it in turns with his servant to clean their boots. He gave his money to the poor and cared for the needy. It was at the city gates of Amiens that Martin cut his cloak in half and gave half to a beggar.

That same night in a dream he heard Christ say to the angels in heaven, 'Look what Martin, who is still a catechumen, has given to me this day,' and showed them the cloak. Only later would Martin be baptised. Here was a Roman soldier who showed a living faith and a vital relationship with Jesus.

COMPLETE COMMON WORSHIP

Sermon Illustrations

Proper 5

Sunday between 5 and 11 June inclusive (if after Trinity Sunday)

Aim

To show Jesus is the Lord of life.

Readings

1 Kings 17:8-16 (17-24) or 1 Kings 17:17-24
Psalm 146 or Psalm 30
Galatians 1:11-24
Luke 7:11-17

Thought for the day

Jesus has left Capernaum and gone to Nain. This is a day's journey of about 25 miles. Nain is not far from Nazareth and not far from Shunem where Elisha brought a child back from the dead (2 Kings 4:18-37). As Jesus, the Lord of life, and those with him approached the gate of the town, they met a procession coming the other way. Leading the procession out was a group of professional mourners, playing instruments and weeping and wailing. A man who had died was being carried out on a bier. The bier was like a wicker basket and open so that the body was visible. The dead man had been the only son of a widowed woman. In this sentence we hear of a double if not a treble tragedy that is still common in many countries. The woman had lost her husband. That was hard enough but now she had lost her only son. What pain there is when a parent loses a child. To make matters worse, because the economy was based on men, the woman was likely to face isolation and poverty. She would become one of the marginalised people of the world, and so would her daughters if she had any.

Once again we see the compassion of Christ. When the Lord saw her he had compassion for her. The word St Luke uses to describe compassion means 'being moved to the depths of his heart'. This is not a God without feeling or a Christ beyond our pain. He feels our sorrows. 'In every pang that rends the heart, the man of sorrows has a part.'

Jesus said to the woman, 'Do not weep.' Then he approached the bier and touched it. For a Jew to touch a dead body made him unclean. The bearers stood still. Jesus had halted the procession towards death. The Lord of Life stood in the way of the grave. Now he spoke to the man and said, 'Young man. I say to you, rise!' The dead man sat up and began to speak. Jesus gave him to his mother. Death had taken the young man but the Lord of Life gave him back to his mother. Here is the mission of Jesus: he came that we should not perish (John 3:16); he came that we should have life and life in all its fullness (John 10:10). He is the Good Shepherd who rescues us from death. St John says of Jesus, 'In him was life, and the life was the light of all people' (John 1:4). By his death he destroyed death, and by his rising to life again he opens to us the way to life eternal (Hebrews 2:15).

Illustration

Pasha lived in India and his world was slowly getting darker and darker. This was hard enough to bear because his oncoming blindness meant he was losing the ability to enjoy the light of day. Even worse than this, however, was the fact that he would soon be without work due to his loss of sight. Not only Pasha but all his family would suffer. They would join the many poor and marginalised people of India. Then one day it was announced that an 'Eye Camp' was coming to his village. This was run by Sight Savers and was producing wonderful results all over India. Pasha was accepted for what was a relatively simple operation. Afterwards his eyes were bandaged for a few days and, in a sense, he felt worse off. Then came the wonderful moment when the bandages were taken off and he could see. Not only had his sight been saved but also his family had been rescued from poverty. The healing was one for the whole family and they were able to live a fuller life once more.

Proper 6

Sunday between 12 and 18 June inclusive (if after Trinity Sunday)

Aim

To encourage people to make contact with Jesus.

Readings

1 Kings 21:1-10 (11-14) 15-21a
or 2 Samuel 11:26–12:10, 13-15
Psalm 5:1-8 or Psalm 32
Galatians 2:15-21
Luke 7:36–8:3

Thought for the day

Because the story of the woman who anoints the feet of Jesus is given a different emphasis in all four Gospels, it is important to see what Luke is trying to tell us.

We are told it is the house of Simon, a Pharisee. In Mark, Simon is described as a leper. Luke uses the story to criticise the Pharisees, as he was doing in 7:30-35. The scene is likely set in a central courtyard. Maybe there was a fountain. In good weather meals were often eaten outside in the courtyard. It was the custom that when a rabbi visited a house such as this, people from round about came and listened to him. This explains the presence of the woman – although Simon was not pleased that she was there. Luke calls the woman a sinner to make a point about forgiveness and possibly about contact, for Jesus has just been described as 'a friend of tax collectors and sinners' (7:34).

Simon invites Jesus but when Jesus comes Simon seems to ignore him. When a guest enters a house three things are normally done. The visitor is welcomed with a kiss of peace. In the case of an important visitor or rabbi, this would not be omitted. Because roads were dirty, water was poured over the feet of the visitor to cleanse them and to cool them from the heat. Then it was usual to burn some sweet-smelling incense or to place a few droplets of attar of roses on the visitor's head. Simon did none of these things and obviously did not instruct his servants. Jesus was in his house; Simon could boast of a visit by this interesting rabbi. But Simon did not really make any contact with Jesus. Jesus was there but Simon ignored him.

The woman was just the opposite to Simon. As Jesus reclined at the low table, she came and stood over him. She stood there weeping, and large tears were dropping on to the feet of Jesus. Jesus was aware of this and did not move. The woman loosened her hair and used it like a towel to rub the feet of Jesus. By now the righteous people were scandalised. There was still more to come. The woman had a phial of sweet-smelling scent. She broke open the scent and anointed the feet of Jesus with the perfume. Jesus accepted all of these actions and the contact the woman had made with him. Simon could not hold back any longer. He said to himself, 'If this man were a prophet, he would have known who and what kind of woman is touching him – a sinner.'

Jesus was aware of this and talked to Simon about forgiveness. Obviously this was a subject that Simon found hard, yet he did understand about forgiveness. Simon had kept his distance from Jesus and from this woman. Jesus then asked Simon to look at his actions and the woman's. 'You gave me no water for my feet, but she has bathed my feet with her tears and dried them with her hair. You gave me no kiss, but from the time I came in she has not stopped kissing my feet. You did not anoint my head with oil, but she has anointed my feet with ointment.' Simon was told how he had avoided making contact but the woman had made immediate contact. Simon did not show love or respect towards Jesus but the woman did. Jesus turned towards the woman and said to her 'Your sins are forgiven.' Those at the table began to ask, 'Who is this who even forgives sins?' They were talking about Jesus rather than to him. There was an answer. He is the Christ, the Saviour, but many would not accept this. The woman made contact – a living relationship with Jesus – and that is what you call faith. Jesus said to her, 'Your faith has saved you. Go in peace.'

Illustration

Someone was described as 'a self-made man worshipping his own creator'. Think about this for a moment. Often what keeps a person from God is the illusion of self-sufficiency. Some say they have grown up and do not need such a Father figure. Yet none of us will survive without God. The strange thing is the closer someone comes to God, the more aware they are of their own weakness and sin. St Paul spoke of sinners and said, '. . . of whom I am the chief'. St Francis said, 'There is nowhere a more wretched sinner than I.' God can deal with those who are aware of their sins. He can reach out to them in forgiveness. He can reveal his love in accepting the sinner. The self-righteous and the self-sufficient set up their own barriers and are far harder to approach. Those who come to God aware of their sin and weakness are the ones who discover his power in their lives and his love.

COMPLETE COMMON WORSHIP

Sermon Illustrations

Proper 7

Sunday between 19 and 25 June inclusive (if after Trinity Sunday)

Aim

To show that Christ is the Prince of Peace.

Readings

1 Kings 19:1-4 (5-7) 8-15a
or Isaiah 65:1-9
Psalms 42, 43 or Psalm 22:19-28
Galatians 3:23-29
Luke 8:26-39

Thought for the day

The disciples have just been in a storm at sea and think they could have perished. Jesus stills the storm and also their fears and anxieties. Possibly the storm had driven them off course. They landed on the south-eastern edge of the lake. Perhaps they were hoping for a rest, a peaceful time. As Jesus stepped on to the land a madman met him.

The man's mind was in constant turmoil. He thinks he is a whole Legion, an army of demons. People have driven him out of the city and he lives among the tombs. He has been chained up but in his fury he broke the chains – perhaps they are still partly attached to his wrists and he waves them about like a weapon. Because he is not allowed to be with the living, he has made his home with the dead. A madman having lost contact with others now lives alone with his demons. His life is a mini-hell – though for him it is hell. He rushed towards Jesus. I am sure that gave the disciples yet another feeling of turmoil. He shouted at the top of his voice, 'What have you to do with me, Jesus, Son of the Most High God? I beg you, do not torment me.' He may have been mad but he recognised Jesus and that Jesus had power.

In contrast to the man, Jesus is quite still – Jesus who stills the storm, who calms the wind, who is the bringer of peace. Can the Lord who brought order out of chaos do anything for this man? We ask with Macbeth: (Act 5 Scene 3):

> Canst thou not minister to a mind diseased,
> pluck from the memory a rooted sorrow,
> raze out the written troubles of the brain,
> and with some sweet oblivious antidote
> cleanse the stuffed bosom of that perilous stuff
> which weighs upon the heart?'

Jesus can and he will. He asks the man his name.

The man replies, 'Legion.' Perhaps he feels he has a legion of demons in him, or maybe in his early days he suffered a trauma brought on by the atrocities of a Roman legion. The man pleaded for his 'army' and asked that they were not sent to the abyss. Jesus agreed to this and told the man the demons had entered a herd of pigs which were hurtling towards the sea. Perhaps the loud crying of Legion had frightened the pigs. The man was healed, he was clothed and in his right mind when people came out to see Jesus. The man wanted to follow Jesus but Jesus said to him, 'Return to your home, and declare how much God has done for you.' For many of us the telling of the wonderful story of Jesus should begin in our homes and among our friends.

Illustration

We cannot create peace but we can accept it. Peace is a gift from God to us. We can accept it by living in a peaceful way. The mind can often be in turmoil like a raging sea and yet God is there and offering us his peace. Peace is not an absence of activity but rather a working in harmony with the world around us. Peace comes through a right relationship between others and us, but, above all, between God and us. Peace is God's gift and will help us to get back in tune with everything, but if we persist in staying out of tune with others or the world it is hard for God's peace to get to work in us.

Proper 8

Sunday between 26 June and 2 July inclusive

Aim

To show that Jesus calls us to follow him and asks for our commitment.

Readings

2 Kings 2:1, 2, 6-14
or 1 Kings 19:15, 16, 19-21
Psalm 77:1, 2, 11-20 or Psalm 16
Galatians 5:1, 13-25
Luke 9:51-62

Thought for the day

Elisha's calling is described in both of today's readings from Kings. His vocation is progressive in that he is called first to be a servant and disciple and later to be Elijah's successor. This is the normal pattern of many vocations where there is a time of apprenticeship, training and learning before we enter into the fullness of our calling. In the Kings stories the cloak is important, as it is a sign of authority and power. When Elisha takes up the cloak, he is taking on the work that God gave to Elijah.

In Luke we have the words of Jesus to would-be followers. We hear of three who come to say they will follow him. Jesus does not say it is easy but warns there will be difficulties. To the first man Jesus is simply saying, 'Count the cost. To follow me is a way of hardship and denial.' Jesus did not want people to come under false pretences: He would offer no easy way, nor freedom from persecution. Jesus respected the person by telling him of the high demands. We need to know that being a member of the Church is demanding, and to follow God's call is not easy. But it will be a great adventure.

Jesus' words to the second man seems really harsh. It is likely the man was a little like St Augustine of Hippo when he said, 'Lord, make me a saint, but not yet!' He was putting off following. In all probability the man's father was not dead, and not thinking of dying. The man was saying, 'Wait until I have no ties' – well, that will never happen.

Jesus is saying there is a crucial moment for us all and if that moment is missed, we may not get another opportunity. The man had stirrings in his heart but could not escape the grip of his surroundings. We must act when the heart is moved: if we put off until tomorrow, it is not likely to happen.

The last comments of Jesus seem hard. The man only wanted to say farewell to those at home. Jesus knew that there are many things that can tie us and hold us back. Many a vocation has been hindered by members of one's own family or by looking back over what has been. Looking backwards to the 'Good Old Days' is often a danger of the Church. Vocation is a call for us to act now. In the words of God to the people through Moses, 'Tell the people to go forward.' Jesus calls us to move forward in faith with him.

Illustration

Dietrich Bonhoeffer was a German Lutheran priest who was executed by the Nazis for his resistance to their evils. He says this concerning the cost of discipleship:

> Cheap grace is the deadly enemy of the Church . . . cheap grace is the preaching of forgiveness without requiring repentance, baptism without church discipline, communion without confession, absolution without contrition. Cheap grace is grace without discipleship, grace without the cross, grace without Jesus Christ, living and incarnate.

Proper 9

Sunday between 3 and 9 July inclusive

Aim

To explore the mission of the seventy.

Readings

2 Kings 5:1-14 or Isaiah 66:10-14
Psalm 30 or Psalm 66:1-9
Galatians 6:(1-6) 7-16
Luke 10:1-11, 16-20

Thought for the day

The mission of Jesus needs to grow to be successful. The whole Church is in the growth business. Jesus does not work alone: he chooses twelve disciples. Then, as his mission grows, he appoints another seventy to be sent out in twos and prepare for his coming to other places that he intends to visit.

Seventy was a symbolic number. When Moses found he could not cope alone and needed helpers, seventy members were chosen for the twelve tribes of Israel (Numbers 11:16-25). Seventy was also thought to be the number of nations in the world. As St Luke was thinking of the outreach of Christ, it could be he was thinking of the day when every nation and person would be given the chance to know and love the Lord and be ready for his coming to each of us.

Jesus is aware that there are many souls to save: 'the harvest is plentiful'. Sadly the harvest could be lost because the 'labourers are few'. We still need to pray that the Lord will send more labourers who will be willing to say, 'Here am I Lord. Send me.'

Let us look at the instructions Jesus gave to the seventy and see how they still apply to us. His first word to them is 'Go'. So much of mission fails because we do not get going. We never start, never move from out of our security and comfort zones. We need be aware that there are dangers and we will often be like lambs among wolves.

Jesus asks us to travel light. Often we do not get started because our lives are so full of clutter that prevents us. Too often we become possessed by our possessions.

Do not be side-tracked. It is easy for small talk and trivialities to stop you. (See Elisha's instruction to Gehazi in 2 Kings 4:29. This is not a call to be aloof or discourteous but rather to remember our priorities.)

Ask God's peace on what you are doing and offer that peace to others. If they do not accept the peace of God, you have not lost it.

You do this not for what you can get out of it in the way of praise, money or food, but for the sake of the mission of Christ.

Know that you are to bring the wholeness and healing of God. You are to bring his peace and well-being to the sick in body, mind and spirit.

Let people know that the kingdom of God is very close to them. Their God is not a God who is far away but who is close to each of them and loves them.

This is the outreach of Christ through the Church, and you are called to share in it once you know the Christ and his love.

Illustration

Picture coming home on a dark night. All the lights are out in the whole area. There must have been a power cut. Everyone is in the dark. The only glimmer of light comes from the church. You are a bit nervous and you go in. There is someone sitting in the sanctuary and he is surrounded by light. You sneak forward and see that he has nail marks in his hands and feet. You know it is the Christ but his feet are fastened by chains and his hands are tied. The Christ is unable to move. You come close and ask, 'Lord, your feet are fastened and your hands tied – why?' The Christ replies, 'My feet are fastened and my hands tied because my people do not pray regularly. They do not reach out to others in love. They do not share in my saving works. I have entrusted my work to them and they have not accepted the light I have offered them. Things will only change when you share with me: when you see Christ in others and be Christ to others.' Suddenly you are aware of this truth, and lights start coming on all over the place.

Proper 10

Sunday between 10 and 16 July inclusive

Aim

To explore the question 'Who is my neighbour?'

Readings

Amos 7:7-17 or Deuteronomy 30:9-14
Psalm 82 or Psalm 25:1-10
Colossians 1:1-14
Luke 10:25-37

Thought for the day

The nature of teachers and students of the law is to question what they are told and to seek clarification from others. This is as true today as it was in the time of Jesus. The lawyer asks, 'What should I do to inherit eternal life?' Jesus asks a question in return: 'What is written in the law?' The reply of the man is part of what is written in a little leather box called a phylactery that is strapped on his wrist. He quotes from Deuteronomy 6:5 which says, 'You shall love the Lord your God with all your heart, and with all your soul and with all your might.' To this the Scribes added Leviticus 19:18 which bids a person to love his neighbour as himself. The rabbis sought to define who was a neighbour and at their worst limited this to fellow Jews; Gentiles were not counted as neighbours no matter how closely they lived to Jews. The parable of the Good Samaritan is a challenge to our limited care.

The story begins with a man on the downhill road from Jerusalem to Jericho. With his back to the Holy City, he is making his way towards a place that was known for its vice and corruption. Some have seen symbolism in these images. The man is going downhill and alone. Now this road was notorious for robbers and brigands, and it is foolish to travel alone, especially if you have anything precious. Is not life precious? The man is mugged by a band of robbers, stripped of his possessions, his dignity and his health. He is left half-dead and before long he will be three-quarters dead and then finished.

Lucky man: here comes a priest. Help is at hand. But when he sees him, the priest passes by on the other side. Well, if the priest had gone over and touched the man and the man was dead, it would make him unclean and he would not be able to perform his duties for seven days (Numbers 19:11). It would seem the priest was concerned with ceremony rather than charity. You could hear the common cry: 'It's more than my job's worth.'

Well, the next one who comes along is a good churchman, a Levite. Surely there is hope there. The Levite perhaps is frightened that the robbers are still near and the man on the ground is just a decoy. He could use the same excuse of the priest for not making contact. The law was more important than love.

Then comes the Samaritan – a non-Jew. Surely he won't bother. But he does because he is moved with pity for a fellow human being. He goes over to the man and pours oil and wine on the wounds – normal usage for both, though also symbols of peace and joy. He then lifts him up and puts him on his own animal, brings him to an inn and takes care of him. The next day the Samaritan pays the innkeeper and says, 'Take care of him; and when I come back, I will repay you whatever more you spend.'

Jesus then asked which proved to be a neighbour. When the lawyer replied, 'He that showed mercy', Jesus said, 'Go and do likewise.'

We are challenged to accept as our neighbour and to show concern for those we try to avoid; those who get into trouble through their own fault; those who are racially or religiously different; all who are in need or in trouble.

In John 8:48 the Jews called Jesus a Samaritan. Maybe we should heed the words of the Good Samaritan and interpret them as Jesus speaking to us: 'Take care of him; and when I come back, I will repay you whatever more you spend.'

Illustration

There is a story about Martin, a cobbler. He looked forward to the coming of the Lord and felt he would soon come to visit his shop. He busied himself getting ready, but he was often interrupted. He saw a child getting into trouble in the market place, so he went out to help him. Then he saw a poor woman who was in need of better shoes. He called her into the shop and saw to her needs. After this there was an old man who looked frozen. He invited the man in and gave him a warm drink. Martin would have liked to have prepared more for the coming of the Lord but he ran out of time. Martin reached out to all who came his way. That night Martin had a dream in which he saw the Lord. The Lord told him how he had visited him when the child needed help, when the woman needed shoes and when the old man wanted some warmth. In caring for his neighbour, Martin met the Lord.

Proper 11

Sunday between 17 and 23 July inclusive

Aim

To show the need for stillness and to be receptive to our God.

Readings

Amos 8:1-12 or Genesis 18:1-10a
Psalm 52 or Psalm 15
Colossians 1:15-28
Luke 10:38-42

Thought for the day

Only Luke tells this story of Martha and Mary. Other stories tell us they had a brother called Lazarus and that they lived in Bethany near to the Mount of Olives and on the ascent to Jerusalem (John 11 and 12:1-8; Matthew 26:6-13; Mark 14:3-9). Luke does not mention Bethany. Martha invites Jesus to her home. This fact and her busyness in the house suggest that Martha is looking after the house and its occupants. Perhaps their parents were already dead and, as was the custom, the oldest daughter took on the responsibility for domestic affairs.

This was a place Jesus was really at home. It was a good base when he was visiting Jerusalem for festivals. Here he was obviously fed and most likely given accommodation. This is the house we hear of most near Jerusalem. Martha is busy. Well, she would be – she has a guest to look after. Mary sits at the feet of Jesus as a pupil would for a rabbi. Mary is giving Jesus her attention and listening to him. Martha really could do with a hand. 'Lord, do you not care that my sister has left me to do all the work by myself? Tell her, then, to help me.' But Jesus does not command Mary to get up. He speaks kindly to Martha. 'Martha, Martha, you are worried and distracted by many things; there is need only for one thing. Mary has chosen the better part that will not be taken away from her.' You cannot help but feel at this stage that Jesus is lucky that Martha does not wallop him with a cooking pan! We must look deep into this event, for Jesus did need feeding.

Martha was distracted and anxious and no doubt she had good cause. Very often the lady of the house has to work hard when there is company while others sit having a drink and being waited on. Sometimes we need share out our tasks better, and sometimes we need to realise that our guests are there to spend time with us and not just to be fed.

Many of our troubles and anxieties occur because we do not spend time in quiet with Jesus. Many churches are hyperactive, doing all sorts of activities but spending little time in prayer. God is our priority. If we make God our priority, then he will send us out. God does not want things from us; he wants our love and us. The same could be said of many who come to us as friends. We miss healing relationships if we are too anxious or busy.

O what peace we often forfeit,
O what needless pain we bear,
All because we do not carry
Everything to God in prayer.

Listen to St Paul: 'Do not worry about anything, but in everything by prayer and supplication with thanksgiving let your requests be made known to God. And the peace of God, which surpasses all understanding, will guard your hearts and your minds in Christ Jesus' (Philippians 4:6, 7).

It is because our sympathies are with Martha that we need to learn more from Mary.

Illustration

The greatest danger of television is that it encourages us to switch off from one another. This is true of iPods and personal CD players. They all help to shut us off and enclose us in a world of our own. But we do not need any of these to be inattentive. A child comes in with an important message but the father is filling in his tax forms and the mother is busy preparing the dinner. 'But . . .' says the child and is still not given attention. The parents have not listened and the child is left feeling alone. The generation gap is often created because we do not listen to each other. The child goes out and wonders who will look at the washing machine that is overflowing!

Proper 12

Sunday between 24 and 30 July inclusive

Aim

To explore the Lord's Prayer.

Readings

Hosea 1:2-10 or Genesis 18:20-32
Psalm 85 or Psalm 138
Colossians 2:6-15 (16-19)
Luke 11:1-13

Thought for the day

The Lord's Prayer belongs to the Jewish tradition of talking with God. This prayer is based on confidence in God, openness to God and the belief that not only will God provide but will also bring in his kingdom. These are all exciting themes and become part and parcel of the life of the person who prays the Lord's Prayer with their heart and mind.

The start of the prayer is surprising in its intimacy. The Aramaic word 'Abba' is the word behind 'Father' and it means 'Daddy'. We need to see that we are made by God and belong to God. We need to know he created us out of his love and for his love. God wants a living relationship with us. It is good to spend a part of each day knowing God has made you and God loves you.

To speak to God is to recognise his presence and so come before him in awe: 'Hallowed be your name.' May we make God's name holy in our lives by recognising his love and his kingly rule. God's kingdom will come in us if we seek to do his will. If we want to be part of the kingdom, we have to live by its rules. We are called to hallow God's name in the world.

In asking for our daily bread, it is easy to forget that millions are still starving in our world. We all need feeding and we need more than food. This request is for nourishment upon which our whole being depends: that is, nourishment for our mind and spirit as well as our bodies.

It is thought that Luke 11:4 changes Matthew's 'debts' (Matthew 6:12) to 'sins.' Both are about being released from our past and set free in the kingdom of God. We are expected to forgive as we are forgiven. We must think very carefully about this when we pray the Lord's Prayer.

The 'time of trial' is thought to be the troubles at the end of the world. We all have to face the end of our world at some time, and we need to ask God that we are well prepared. To know God and his love, to be aware of his power and his presence, to rejoice in his kingdom and the promise of eternal life totally transforms all we have to face.

Illustration

When we turn to God in prayer we acknowledge his presence: that God is with us always and that he listens to us. You are actually in the presence, in God. We are in God in the same way as fish live in water and we in air. Listen to these words by the poet Francis Thompson from the poem 'No Strange Land':

> Does the fish soar to find the ocean,
> the eagle plunge to find the air –
> that we ask of the stars in motion
> if they have rumour of thee there?

We cannot search for God but we can open ourselves to his presence, and a good way of doing this is by speaking to him quietly each day.

Use the Lord's Prayer and pause between each phrase to be aware of the fullness and wonder of the words and of your God.

Proper 13

Sunday between 31 July and 6 August inclusive

Aim

To look at the relationships we have with our possessions.

Readings

Hosea 11:1-11
or Ecclesiastes 1:2, 12-14; 2:18-23
Psalm 107:1-9, 43 or Psalm 49:1-12
Colossians 3:1-11
Luke 12:13-21

Thought for the day

The story that Jesus tells today arises out of a sad situation, a family row after the death of parents. It is amazing how many people have fallen out over a piece of furniture or an ornament. The father has obviously died and there is no clear indication of who should have what: each wanting to own, to possess and to say, 'That is mine'. At least one of them was being greedy. As people today resort to law, so the rowing parties come to Jesus as they would to a rabbi. Jesus refuses to tell them what they should do – they need to live by grace and graciously rather than under the law. Jesus warns the crowd, 'Take care, be on your guard against all kinds of greed; for one's life does not consist in the abundance of possessions.' Then he tells a story in three acts.

Act one is a bumper harvest. The land produced abundantly. The barns are full and bursting at the seams. Carpenters are at work building bigger and better barns. Lucky rich man – he deserves this reward for hard work. God must love him. Most would admire him and some would envy him.

Act two and the farmer is in his den totting up his books: Haven't I done well! I can take it easy now. I have enough for many years. I can eat, drink and be merry. I can relax and look after myself. Lucky rich man – most people would not mind swapping places with him. Go and enjoy yourself, you deserve it.

Act three. If you do not like unhappy endings, you had better walk out now. If you do not want a challenge, do not watch this act. The rich man has died – poor rich man. He has left behind his farm, his barns, his leisure time. All that he possessed and counted upon has gone, poor rich man. He stands in the presence of God who says, 'You fool!' In no way was he prepared for this. He was rich to human eyes but poor in the eyes of God – poor rich man. He had cared about possessions but not about other people or God. He was rich in things but poor in the important relationships – poor rich man.

Notice in this story how in three verses the word 'I' appears six times. This was someone who was full of himself. God does not measure by what we have as much as by what we share. Riches are measured by what we can give away; the rest are possessions, and many are possessed by their possessions. Riches are to be shared with the community and in this way the poor and the marginalised are cared for. As an old proverb says, 'He who has bread is responsible for him who has none.'

Illustration

When John Wesley was at Oxford he lived by a rule that he set himself: 'Save what you can and give away what you can.' At first Wesley had an income of £30 a year. He then lived off £28 and gave £2 away each year. When his income rose to £60 a year he lived on £28 and gave away £32. As his income rose to £60 and then to £120 a year, he still lived on £28 and gave the rest away.

The Accountant General for Household Plate (a sort of tax collector) asked for a return from Wesley supposing he should have a good deal to show. Wesley replied, 'I have two silver teaspoons at London and two at Bristol. This is all the plate which I have at present; and will not buy any more, while so many people around me want bread.'

Proper 14

Sunday between 7 and 13 August inclusive

Aim

To encourage people to trust in God and to invite him into their daily life.

Readings

Isaiah 1:1, 10-20 or Genesis 15:1-6
Psalm 50:1-8, 22, 23 or Psalm 33:12-22
Hebrews 11:1-3, 8-16
Luke 12:32-40

Thought for the day

The times that Jesus lived in were troubled times. There were wars and rumours of wars, people suffered from famine, from acts of violence or from illness. In fact, in many ways the times were like our own. We are still being troubled: by global warming, wars, acts of violence and by illness. Many people are anxious and fearful about the future.

Today's Gospel begins with Jesus saying, just as God said to Abraham at the beginning of today's Old Testament reading (Genesis 15:1), 'Do not be afraid.' Someone counted that the Scriptures have the words 'Do not be afraid' scattered throughout them 365 times: that is one for each day of the year. God does not want us to be overcome by fear or anxiety, even in troubled times. Here are some wonderful words spoken by God through the prophet Isaiah (43:1b-3a): 'Do not fear, for I have redeemed you; I have called you by name, you are mine. When you pass through the waters, I will be with you; and through the rivers, they shall not overwhelm you: when you walk through fire you shall not be burned, and the flame shall not consume you. For I am the Lord your God, the Holy One of Israel, your Saviour.'

We need to know that even in times of trouble God is with us, and God cares for us. It is God's pleasure to give us the kingdom. He gives us the kingdom not through our own efforts and merit but freely through his own grace and goodness. Our lasting treasure is to be part of God's kingdom.

We need to be alert to the fact that God is with us, God cares for us and God seeks entry into our lives. God will not force himself upon us. He stands outside our lives waiting to be let in. We must open the door and invite him to come in. In the book of Revelation (3:20), Jesus says: 'Listen! I am standing at the door, knocking.' You need to spend time each day inviting God into your life. In this way you will not only discover God is with you, you will know his peace and his love. You will know that nothing can separate you from the love of God in Christ Jesus. (See Romans 8:39.)

Illustration

Look at Holman Hunt's painting 'Light of the World'. Here Christ is at a door knocking. The lack of a handle on the outside of the door shows it can only be opened from within. The weeds around the door show that it has not been opened for a long time. The apples lying on the ground remind us of the fall from grace in the Garden of Eden. Through sin, people and God become separate. Jesus comes to unite us again with God if we will let him into our lives.

Proper 15

Sunday between 14 and 20 August inclusive

Aim

To show we need to be active in our faith and that we need to practise.

Readings

Isaiah 5:1-7 or Jeremiah 23:23-29
Psalm 80:1, 2, 8-19 or Psalm 82
Hebrews 11:29–12:2
Luke 12:49-56

Thought for the day

Picture a large crowd of people in some great amphitheatre or football stadium. Every seat is taken so that the crowd can watch what is going on. Look closely and you will see the saints, men and women who have given their lives in the service of God. There are holy people who dedicated themselves to prayer. There are martyrs who died for the faith, crowds of men and women who proclaimed the gospel and witnessed to the power of God. All are watching the arena and the race that is taking place.

It is an important race, for much of what they lived and died for is at stake. The one sitting at the end of the track is the King. He also watches, for his kingdom is in some ways dependent on these runners. If the runners do not give themselves and dedicate themselves to the race, then the kingdom could be lost to the earth. The spectators know that if the runners do not win, much of what they have laboured for will have been in vain. This is a terribly important race.

Now look at the runners. You should recognise them for you are among them. It is we who are in the arena: we are fighting to win. It is a battle for our eternal soul, and more: it is the only way the kingdom can be established on earth. The saints depend on us for their work not to be lost. We are called to witness and to proclaim the gospel. Christ and the saints rely on you: 'They would not, apart from us, be made perfect.'

We need to realise that the battle for the world and to win it for God goes on, and it is now our turn. The good advice from Hebrews is to 'look to Jesus' who has already won the battle. In him, though we lose round after round, victory is assured as he has triumphed over evil.

Illustration

There were two brothers. Both were runners. One was very good and won most races when he was small. He always used to beat his brother. Because he could run well, he decided he did not need to train. It was more fun playing computer games and going out with his friends. He thought practising was a waste of time. The other brother knew that he had to improve his style. He practised often. He practised sprinting and long-distance running. He did exercises to increase his breathing powers and his physical ability. He was seen on the track most nights. His brother said he was wasting his time. By the time they were in their teens, the brother who had been the best now lagged far behind. He was paying the price for not practising and keeping his eyes on what he could do. His brother was now winning competitions and all sorts of prizes. If asked how he became a better runner, he said, 'By a lot of practice and by being willing to dedicate myself to the job.'

Proper 16

Sunday between 21 and 27 August inclusive

Aim

To show that coming to Jesus gives us a glorious freedom.

Readings

Jeremiah 1:4-10 or Isaiah 58:9b-14
Psalm 71:1-6 or Psalm 103:1-8
Hebrews 12:18-29
Luke 13:10-17

Thought for the day

I would like you to look at two people today and compare them. One is a woman who is terribly bent and the other is a man who is very unbending.

The woman has a curvature of the spine. It sounds like some crippling form of arthritis. We are told she has suffered this way for 18 years – definitely a chronic illness. Every movement is difficult and she needs a stick to walk with. It would be so easy for her to fall over. Yet she still made the effort and came to the synagogue on the Sabbath. Her suffering made her look in towards herself. This is often the danger of illness: it makes us inward-looking.

The man was the leader of the synagogue, an upright citizen, a man of good standing and rather unbending. He did not suffer fools gladly and he was quick to point out when people did wrong. He made sure that people kept the rules of their faith and did not stray. He was a law-abiding citizen and we need such as him – except that he was so unbending.

Jesus was in the synagogue where the man was the leader. Jesus was teaching in the synagogue on the Sabbath. Sadly this is the last time we hear of Jesus in the synagogue on the Sabbath. No doubt the leader was listening to Jesus and trying to take in what he said. Then the woman arrived. Jesus saw her struggling and as she came near he invited her to come closer. Jesus said, 'Woman, you are set free from your ailment.' Then Jesus laid his hands upon her back and she was able to stand up straight. She was able to look upwards and outwards. Jesus had given her a new vision of life. Jesus had freed her from being in a locked position. The woman was thrilled and immediately began praising God; the God in whom she trusted.

You would think everyone else would be thrilled. The leader of the synagogue was not pleased; in fact, he was indignant. He was annoyed because Jesus had healed the woman on the Sabbath. It was a day of rest when no one should work and Jesus had done work by healing this woman. The man could not bend: the law is the law. He kept saying to the crowd, 'There are six days on which work ought to be done; come on those days and be cured, and not on the Sabbath day.' He looked like a free man but he had become bound with a narrow outlook on what God requires. He was caught up in law rather than love. Such an attitude often binds people fast.

In life it is easy to become bound by rules and regulations or to hide behind them. People get stuck in routines, in watching television, in sport, in front of the computer – and all out of habit. We often think we have no time and it is because we have bound ourselves to certain patterns. It is easy to trap ourselves and lose the freedom that God wants us to have. Let Jesus touch your life. Come to him for he invites you. Come close and spend time with him. Break your routine and make space in your life for God – let him set you free.

Illustration

Robert was in prison for repeatedly breaking the law. He was a violent person. Taking drugs fuelled his violence. He was an addict – and that made him a prisoner as much as being in jail. He was not a likeable character and had few friends. Whilst in jail he went regularly to a rehabilitation unit to cure him of his dependence on drugs. Slowly he was freed from the habit. Whilst this was going on he had a regular visit from the prison chaplain. At first Robert rejected him and refused to listen but then he accepted a Bible. One day when he was reading St Luke the tears began to flow. When the chaplain came later Robert showed him the story of the crippled woman and said, 'Jesus has done the same for me. He has set me free.'

Proper 17

Sunday between 28 August and 3 September inclusive

Aim

To think about how God sends his messengers to us and comes himself in others.

Readings

Jeremiah 2:4-13 or Ecclesiasticus 10:12-18
Psalm 81:1, 10-16 or Psalm 112
Hebrews 13:1-8, 15, 16
Luke 14:1, 7-14

Thought for the day

Hospitality was a very important issue in the Holy Land. When Abraham gave hospitality to the three visitors, he was not only visited by men but also, through them, by angels and by God (see Genesis 18:1-16).

The sun was at its height and, as is the custom of the desert wanderer, Abraham rested in the shade of the tent door. As he looked out over a land of shimmering heat, three shapes came towards him out of nowhere. As they got closer, Abraham saw that it was three men. He offered them hospitality and provided them with good food. They were ordinary men who were dusty and hungry – but they had a message for him. They were messengers of God – angels. In this visit Abraham and Sarah his wife encountered God and angels.

It is with this story in mind that the writer to the Hebrews (13:2) said, 'Do not neglect to show hospitality to strangers, for by doing that some have entertained angels without knowing it.' What a marvellous disguise: God comes to us through other people. God sends his angels to us through the people we meet.

Throughout his ministry Jesus was dependent on the hospitality of many people and you often hear of him sharing a meal. On this occasion he was in the house of a leading Pharisee and he noticed how guests were trying to find the best seats where they would be seen. These people were full of themselves. They invited each other to parties because they would be invited back.

There was little room for a stranger and certainly no room for the poor and the outcasts. Yet if God comes to us in the other person, they would miss out on meeting God by their own exclusiveness and narrowness. God often comes in the most unexpected way and person. Do not neglect to show hospitality to strangers, for by doing that some have entertained angels without knowing it.

Who knows when God seeks to come closer to us? Who can tell which messenger of God is sent to bring us peace, joy or love, or to open our eyes to his presence? Often God seeks to change our life through an encounter with another. It is only when we are sensitive to others that we can be truly open to the great Other who is God. God sends his messengers regularly to us. Remember the word 'angel' means messenger. By being insensitive to others we often fail to hear the angel of God.

Illustration

Sadhu Sundar Singh was the first Christian Sadhu. He suffered great persecution in his missionary travels in Tibet. Often the sadhu declared that he was rescued by angels. The following tells of such an occasion.

The sadhu was arrested for entering Tibet and preaching Christianity. The Lama condemned him to death. The sadhu was thrown into a deep dry well. The well was covered and locked. The key was kept around the Lama's waist. The remains of others who had met a similar fate were in the well. The sadhu could not see this because there was no light. For two days and nights he was without food and water. On the third day, when he was exhausted, a wonderful thing happened. He heard the key turn in the lock and the cover was removed. A rope was lowered. It had a loop in the end for the sadhu to put his foot in. He was then gently lifted to the surface. He helped his rescuer to put the cover back on the well. When the sadhu turned to thank him, he was gone. It was only some time later, when the sadhu resumed his preaching, that the Lama discovered what had happened. Yet the key was still fastened at his waist.

I am sure it was a caring human being that rescued the sadhu. Just as I am sure and agree with Sadhu Sundar Singh that it was an angel of God that set him free.

Proper 18

Sunday between 4 and 10 September inclusive

Aim

To know we are in the hands of God and that he can restore and renew us.

Readings

Jeremiah 18:1-11 or Deuteronomy 30:15-20
Psalm 139:1-6, 13-18 or Psalm 1
Philemon 1-21
Luke 14:25-33

Thought for the day

Jeremiah saw that there was trouble ahead for Israel. The Babylonian Empire was rising and Judah was caught between Babylon and Egypt. The old securities were being broken down and there was danger that even Jerusalem could face a break-down. As he watched a potter at work, he realised that in the hands of God such breaking down of the nation could lead to its renewal.

Enter the potter's shop with Jeremiah. Have a look around. In one corner is a large pile of unused clay. It looks like useless lumps, dirty and not very attractive. But we know that in the hands of the potter it can be transformed to something of worth and beauty.

Look at the lovely things that the potter has made from the clay. If he can do that with clay, think what the Creator could do with you – even if you feel like an unattractive, useless lump! Look at the potter: he seems to be in difficulty with a lump of clay. It is not going as it ought to go. For a while the clay seemed all right but then it got a wobble. The potter seeks to form it but it still has a wobble. The potter stops the wheel. What will he do? He could throw the clay away and get another piece. Instead, he takes it in his hands and gently shapes it, or, if necessary, he breaks it down so that it can be rebuilt. A piece may be broken down two or three times but the potter is patient, and as long as the clay remains malleable, he will make something of it.

It is easy to see how we are like the clay. How many men and women have been counted worthless or have felt like a useless lump until they have put themselves in the hands of God? God says to us, 'Just like clay in the potter's hand, so are you in my hand' (Jeremiah 18:6).

We need to see that breakdowns are not always bad – they can be warnings that we are going in the wrong direction. Nervous breakdowns, business breakdowns, health breakdowns can change in the hands of God. In his hands a breakdown can become a breakthrough into a better life and a stronger life. All things are possible with God if we do not become too set in our ways.

We fear death as the ultimate breakdown. You can see it in a new way. The potter is taking you in his hands, planning to give you a new and more glorious shape and purpose. Remember God's words: 'Just like clay in the potter's hand, so are you in my hand.'

Illustration

In the saleroom there was a violin. It looked battered and neglected. One or two people picked it up and pulled the bow across it but the sound did not seem good. The auctioneer wondered why it was in the sale. He thought it should have been scrapped. It looked a sorry sight. Most people never even noticed it. It would probably sell for a few pence.

Just before the sale an elderly gentleman came in. As the seats were filling up he went over to the violin and retuned it. Then he started to play. The music was wonderful. The capabilities of the instrument were amazing. In the master's hand, the poor-looking instrument was transformed.

When the violin was put up for auction the bidding was brisk. People realised it was a precious instrument and that it had great potential. It is amazing how things can be changed in the hands of the master.

Proper 19

Sunday between 11 and 17 September inclusive

Aim

To show how God delights in all who turn to him.

Readings

Jeremiah 4:1-12, 22-28 or Exodus 32:7-14
Psalm 14 or Psalm 51:1-11
1 Timothy 1:12-17
Luke 15:1-10

Thought for the day

The Pharisees believed that they could keep themselves and their religion pure by being exclusive and keeping out anyone they thought of as a sinner. Tax collectors were among the wrong sort of people because they worked for the Romans and had regular contact with Gentiles.

The Pharisees complained that Jesus welcomed sinners and ate with them. No doubt they included Matthew the tax collector and Mary Magdalene among the sinners. The Pharisees were lucky not to need repentance! There is nothing as off-putting as the self-righteous to those thinking of becoming believers.

Jesus does not suggest that there is no need for repentance. He wants people to see that law-keeping by itself is not enough. Negative goodness, where we say what we do not do, is not enough. What do we do to fulfil God's ways and reflect his love in our lives?

In Luke 15 Jesus tells three stories in a row about returning to God and the delight it gives. In each story there is a party. God, the Father, delights in those who return. But in the last story the sad thing is he cannot get the self-righteous son to come in and join them.

The sheep gets lost through its own foolishness. How often we err and stray like lost sheep. The sheep followed its appetite, looking for new food and for fresh pastures. It never noticed it had entered a danger zone and could perish. The shepherd missed it and sought it out. He sought to bring it back. When he found it he was delighted. Because it was exhausted he carried it.

When he got home he threw a party to express his joy. The party could have cost more than the sheep but the sheep was more valuable to him than money.

The coin got lost through no fault of its own. It was a victim of circumstance. That which fastened it to others had broken loose. It just dropped off without a sound. But the woman missed it because it was of great sentimental value to her. She loved it and it was an expression of her love. She would search for it until she could find it. When she found it she was delighted. What a joy! She threw a party and invited friends to share in her joy. The party might have cost more than the face value of the coin, but the coin could not be measured by its face value because it was precious to her.

Jesus says that every time a sinner repents there is delight and joy in heaven. Every time someone turns to God the angels rejoice. We need to know that God seeks us and waits for us to turn to him. God delights in our love and offers us his love and life eternal. He will not force any of this on us but he will seek us and our love for ever. He could replace us but does not because we are precious in his eyes.

Illustration

A letter from God

When you awoke, I was there, waiting upon you. I wanted to share in your love.

At breakfast you listened to the radio and rushed your breakfast. You had no time to speak to me. I waited but you did not turn to me.

Though you travelled by rail you spent your time on your laptop and reading the news. You did not once give me a thought. And I waited for you to turn to me.

During your work there were lots of small gaps. There was more time at lunch. But you did other things and had no time for me. Yet I waited for you to turn to me.

At the end of the day you watched the television and played a game. For a while you dozed before you had your last drink of the day. And I waited for you to turn to me.

Now, I thought, you will have time – just before you go to sleep. Instead, you read until you were tired. You worried about tomorrow and at last fell asleep.

I will surround you with my love this night. I will wait for you tomorrow and if you do not remember I will be there the day after. I will wait until you turn to me.

All my love, God.

Proper 20

Sunday between 18 and 24 September inclusive

Aim

To see where our priorities lie and how we give our time to God.

Readings

Jeremiah 8:18–9:1 or Amos 8:4-7
Psalm 79:1-9 or Psalm 113
1 Timothy 2:1-7
Luke 16:1-13

Thought for the day

Today's story is a strange one in that it is about a rogue. To understand it, we need to know a little of the background. On one level it is obviously about possessions and our use of them, but beneath that there is something deeper.

Money often shows what we are like: mean or generous, shrewd or silly, to be trusted or not to be trusted. What we have gathered around us reveals the sort of person we are.

The Jews were forbidden to lend money at interest. They often got around this by lending in kind. Two common commodities for lending were wheat and oil. They were also ways of paying rent to the owner of the land. It could be that the steward had been lending his master's materials in kind and at extortionate rates. What he deducted from the bill was the interest, which had a lower rate on wheat than on oil. It would appear the interest rate on wheat was 25 per cent and on oil the rate was an extortionate rate of 50 per cent. If he reduced the bill, his master would not lose anything and his debtors would be delighted.

No doubt the unjust steward was trying to buy friendship in these actions. One way or another the steward had cooked the books and used for his own gain what was not really his. Yet he had assured for himself some sort of future. Not a silly man but a shrewd dealer.

Jesus sees us as stewards of God's world. We are not the owners. It is not ours to possess: we cannot keep it for ever. It is ours to use for the benefit of others and for the praise and glory of God. Yet, like the steward in the story, we tend to use most things to our own ends. We invest more time and energy in gaining and keeping than we ever do in thought about our spiritual life and our future. Most of us have chosen to serve the world and its ways first and God only second. If you doubt this, look at how much time you invest in work, in sport, in recreation and how much time you actually spend in prayer. It is amazing how many Christians never mature in their faith. They learn all sorts of complex things in life but remain unskilled and weak in their relationship with God.

The steward is called to account. We will all be called to account. Those who are found faithful and trustworthy in small things will be trusted to be responsible for greater things. If we have misdirected our worship to things of the earth and neglected the things of the spirit, we will have to account for this.

Illustration

Richard became a junior in the sales department of a large firm when he left school. It was soon discovered he had a flair for sales. In time he became chief salesman, and at that stage he negotiated a percentage of each sale for himself. He was becoming well-off. He had a wonderful home, two expensive cars and a good deal of shares in the business. He was made head of the sales department and then a member of the board. All was wonderful and he was rich indeed. Yet something told him all was not right. One night, returning from a sales conference, he was involved in a serious accident and nearly lost his life. Whilst unconscious he said he was aware of some being in white saying, 'Pity he has not done so well in the things that matter. This man is still a child in spiritual things.' When he recovered he went back to work for a while. His 'visitation' bothered him. He started going to church with his wife and realised he had a lot to learn and that he was poor in spirit. But he gave himself to this as he did to his work. After a year he offered himself to train for the ministry. He was ordained and after two curacies, moved to Africa with his wife and family where they worked for a relief agency. When asked about his wealth, most of which he had given away, he would reply, 'I was never as rich as I am now.'

Proper 21

Sunday between 25 September and 1 October inclusive

Aim

To encourage a greater sensitivity towards each other and to the poor.

Readings

Jeremiah 32:1-3a, 6-15 or Amos 6:1a, 4-7
Psalm 91:1-6, 14-16 or Psalm 146
1 Timothy 6:6-19
Luke 16:19-31

Thought for the day

Today's parable arose from Jesus noticing those who loved money. Money is not evil but to give it our love is to misdirect our vision and our passion. It can turn our love away from God and from others. Today's parable is about insensitivity.

There are three scenes. Scene 1 shows a rich man. He is clothed in purple and fine linen (same as the High Priest). His clothing probably costs about three years' pay of a labourer. The rich man is looking after himself. He dines sumptuously: he is a gourmet and loves exotic dishes. Jesus never tells us his name, though he is often called 'Dives', which is Latin for 'rich'. At his gate is a poor man covered in sores and he is hungry. He hoped for crumbs from the rich man's table. The rich man never seemed to notice him – well, there are a lot of poor people. Today this scene could be a family tucking into a good dinner whilst watching the starving of Africa or India on the television. (Does it not at least put you off your food?)

In Scene 2 the poor man has died – well, he would, wouldn't he! Now he is with Abraham in heaven.

The rich man dies and is buried – he took nothing with him. The rich man was in Hades and was in torment. He looked up and saw Abraham and Lazarus far away. He issued a request and an order. He asked for mercy and that Lazarus should come with water and cool him. So he had noticed Lazarus; he even knew his name. The rich man is told it is not possible.

Scene 3 is like scene 2. The rich man thinks of his five brothers and asks that Lazarus be sent to warn them of what could happen to them. Abraham replies that they have Moses and the prophets and that they should listen to them.

The rich man suggests that if someone – Lazarus – goes to them from the dead, they would repent.

Abraham replies, 'If they do not listen to Moses and the prophets, neither will they be convinced even if someone rises from the dead.' And so the curtain closes.

There was no suggestion that the rich man was a wicked man or that he did not keep the outward observances of the church. But we do know he was insensitive to the needs of Lazarus. Jesus says: 'Truly I tell you, just as you did not do it to one of the least of these, you did not do it to me' (Matthew 25:45).

Illustration

I know a planet where there is a certain red-faced man. He has never smelled a flower; he has never looked at a star. He has never loved anyone. He never does anything in his life but add up figures. And all day long he says over and over, just like you, 'I am busy with matters of consequence,' and that makes him swell with pride. But he is not a man; he is a mushroom!

A what?

A mushroom.

(From *The Little Prince* by Antoine de Saint-Exupéry.)

His insensitivity made the man less than human.

Proper 22

Sunday between 2 and 8 October inclusive

Aim

To seek to deepen our relationship with God.

Readings

Lamentations 1:1-6 or Habakkuk 1:1-4; 2:1-4
Lamentations 3:19-26 or Psalm 137 or Psalm 37:1-9
2 Timothy 1:1-14
Luke 17:5-10

Thought for the day

The disciples have decided that their faith is weak and ask the Lord, 'increase our faith'. Jesus realises that it is not a great faith they need but faith in a great God. We need to distinguish between faith and belief. When it comes to belief, we are told that even the devil believes with fear and trembling. Belief is to do with how our minds work and how we see the world. Many people believe in God but are weak in their faith. Faith is about a loving relationship with God, with a great and powerful God. Faith is not just to know with our mind but also to experience in our lives and in our heart. Faith is allowing God to work in us and through us; it is to experience his love for us. For this to happen we have to build up a relationship with God. Say with the writer of Lamentations, 'The steadfast love of the Lord never ceases, his mercies never come to an end; they are new every morning; great is your faithfulness' (Lamentations 3:22, 23).

You might like to express it in the words of the hymns 'New every morning is the love' or 'Great is thy faithfulness'. Both of these hymns express the abiding presence and love of God towards us.

It is interesting to note that a baby lamb or any small creature thrives better by being looked after by its mother than by humans. The relationship is as important as the food it needs. Many modern psychologists would say that a living relationship – love – is the power that enables people to thrive and to live to the full. A baby can go through hell if it feels it has been left on its own. Teenagers often get into trouble when they have been given everything they wanted but not love. When relationships break down it affects our whole way of living. This is as true about our relationship with God as our relationship with each other. Jesus suggests that faith, that relationship with God, is the most powerful thing in the world.

That which seems impossible by ourselves becomes possible with faith; faith can move mountains. Much that is not possible on our own becomes possible by our relationship with God. We have no power of ourselves to help ourselves.

We have to be clear about this relationship. We cannot put God into our debt. It is God who has made the world and us. We owe all to him. Our creation, salvation and preservation all are gifts from God. When we say we do something for God it is only our duty and our joy.

> Were the whole realm of nature mine,
> that were an offering far too small.
> Love so amazing, so divine,
> demands my soul, my life, my all.

It may be possible to meet the needs of the law but love knows that we can do more than the law asks. Our service to God is not to appease him or to repay a debt, though we are greatly indebted to him, but to give our love to him who gives his love to us. To say we are 'worthless' before him means we cannot demand but only ask of his love. And to live by that relationship is to live by faith.

Illustration

George Matheson looked forward to a good life. He was studying for the ministry. He was preparing to marry the one he loved. Then he began to go blind. His world began to go into darkness. He lost many of his friends, and his loved one decided she could not cope with a blind man and left him. His world was shaken but not his relationship with God. George Matheson wrote the hymn 'O Love that will not let me go'. The second verse is 'O Light that follow'st all my way' and the third 'O joy that seekest me through pain'. George had faith in a great God. The final verse 'O Cross that liftest up my head' affirms not only his steadfast relationship but God's relationship with him. Now that is faith.

Proper 23

Sunday between 9 and 15 October inclusive

Aim

To encourage an attitude of gratitude and to make people aware of the needs of lepers.

Readings

Jeremiah 29:1, 4-7 or 2 Kings 5:1-3, 7-15
Psalm 66:1-12 or Psalm 111
2 Timothy 2:8-15
Luke 17:11-19

Thought for the day

Leprosy was one of the most feared diseases. If you caught leprosy, you were asked to leave your home, your community and to live out in a desert place. You may never see your loved ones again. Leprosy was like having a death sentence. It was believed that leprosy was infectious and, as a safety measure, lepers were asked to keep their distance and to live 'outside the camp' (Leviticus 13:45, 46).

Jesus was in a remote area between Galilee and Samaria. Here in this barren land lived a group of lepers brought together by their illness. Even here the lepers had heard of Jesus and his power. As required, they kept their distance. They call out, saying, 'Jesus, Master, have mercy on us.' Jesus simply tells them to go and show themselves to the priest and as they go, they are healed. Only one returns to Jesus. They all did what he asked but one returns praising God with a loud voice and prostrating himself at the feet of Jesus. Leprosy often affects the vocal cords, so the loud voice was a sign he was cured. That he could come so close to Jesus was also a sign of his cure.

It is worth noticing again that all the lepers did what they were asked. But in this life keeping the rules is not enough. There are some very severe rule-keepers. The Samaritan does more than keep the rules; he comes before Jesus in love and in gratitude. He appreciates what Jesus has done for him. He praises God for his well-being. Such thanksgiving is always a sign of joy. It is very hard to be sad and grateful at the same time. Today many people demand their rights by law but it gives them no joy. Thanksgiving and appreciation are what fill us with joy, and that is a sign of a greater healing than just the body.

We should promise this day that we will not take our friends, our life, our God for granted.

Illustration

Richard was diagnosed as having a serious cancer. He had a brain tumour and if nothing was done, he would die. He was a rich and powerful man and also a man of prayer. The first thing his illness did was make him appreciate all that he had and what was precious to him. Amid the fear of what lay ahead a new joy had entered his life and his home. Each time he went for treatment he committed himself not only to the hospital team but also to the love of God. He was sure, whatever the outcome, he would not be separated from God and his care. Richard was fortunate and he was cured and given a good few years to live. He never ceased to show his appreciation for life and all that was around him. He gave thanks to God each day for all he was able to do. On top of this he gave a proportion of his income each week to Cancer Research in thanksgiving for what had been done for him.

Proper 24

Sunday between 16 and 22 October inclusive

Aim

To show that we need to persevere in our prayers.

Readings

Jeremiah 31:27-34 or Genesis 32:22-31
Psalm 119:97-104 or Psalm 121
2 Timothy 3:14–4:5
Luke 18:1-8

Thought for the day

In many homes there are objects that were bought with the intention of using them. These can range from an exercise bike to a piano, from a piece of knitting to a box of paints. They are there in case we may use them one day. Think of something you started but did not finish, like taking up a gym routine or practising the piano. Some people have done this with churchgoing or with their daily prayers. Francis Drake, that great sailor and explorer, once wrote, 'There must be a beginning of any great matter, but the continuing unto the end until it be thoroughly finished yields the true glory.'

Jesus was well aware that some people give up easily in their prayer life and that it is just too possible to lose heart (Luke18:1). One of the great weaknesses of the Church is that many of its people are not really praying people. If we do not pray regularly, it is a sign that God is not among our priorities. Prayer is not always easy but we can even express this to God. It is important for our own health that we keep in contact with our God.

Jesus told the parable of a widow who sought justice. The judge was used to giving sentence in favour of the one who could impress him most. He feared neither God nor man. This sort of fear is about awe rather than dread. Maybe Jesus was hinting he was not a wise judge for, as the people knew, 'The fear of the Lord is the beginning of wisdom' (Proverbs 1:7). Many of the judges decided in favour of the one who could pay them the most. For this reason, they were known as 'robber judges'. Being a widow was usually a sign of being poor and defenceless. She had no resources, nothing to offer, so could not hope for justice. But she did have a weapon: she was persistent; she pestered the judge until he gave in. The widow was praised for chutzpah, her nerve, the fact that she did no lose heart or give up.

If the woman persisted with her plea to the judge, how much more should we persist in prayer to the God who wants us to live our lives to the full? It is easy to stop saying our daily prayers but without them we lose a vital link with God. Make sure that God is your priority and that you keep your prayer life alive. Sometimes prayer is difficult and we have to wrestle with it, as Jacob wrestled with God. Yet a relationship with the loving God is always rewarding.

Illustration

St Teresa of Avila showed a great enthusiasm for life. In the front of her prayer book these words were written:

> Let nothing disturb thee,
> nothing affright thee,
> all things are passing,
> God never changes.
> Patient endurance
> attaineth to all things.
> Who God possesses
> in nothing is wanting.
> God alone suffices.

These are deep words indeed and should be thought about with care. (Make copies available – as a bookmark – to all who would like to think about the words.)

Proper 25

Sunday between 23 and 29 October inclusive

Aim

To make God the centre of our prayers and to rejoice in his grace and goodness.

Readings

Joel 2:23-32 or Ecclesiasticus 35:12-17
or Jeremiah 14:7-10, 19-22
Psalm 65 or Psalm 84:1-7
2 Timothy 4:6-8, 16-18
Luke 18:9-14

Thought for the day

This Gospel reading is the follow-on from last week and it is still about prayer. This week's story would be funny if it were not so serious. Too often there are still people with the attitude of the Pharisee. We must not stereotype all Pharisees as bad; as in all groups of people there are good and bad. The rabbis themselves listed all sorts of Pharisees. (1) There was the God-loving Pharisee, who lived by faith and was full of good works. There were many of these. (2) There was the Fearing Pharisee who was worried about the wrath of God and knew little of his love. (3) Then there were the Bleeding Pharisees. No Jewish rabbi was supposed to speak to a woman in the street, not even his wife or mother. The Bleeding Pharisees took it further by closing their eyes in the street so as not to see a woman. As a result they were always bumping into things and hurting themselves. (4) Then came the Hump-backed Pharisees who walked bent almost double in pretend humility – like Uriah Heep. (5) The Wait-a-while Pharisees always found an excuse for putting things off to another day. (6) The Shoulder Pharisees were those who wore their religion to be seen and to gain praise. (7) The last group were the Ever-reckoning Pharisees who added up their good deeds and struck up a sort of balance account with God – as if they could put him into debt.

Jesus told the story of the Pharisee and the tax collector to warn those who thought they were righteous and held others in contempt. Jews said their prayers three times every day at 9am, at noon and at 3pm. It was thought that it was better to pray in the Temple.

It would seem the Pharisee in the story was of the last two groups. Sadly we are told he prayed with himself. (Many translations have 'with himself' rather than 'by himself'.) We are able to see how self-centred he is: 'God, I thank you am not like other people . . . I fast . . . I give.' This man was the centre of his prayers, not God. He was the subject of the sentences and God the object. It was as if he was declaring God to be in his debt.

From the beginning of the story many would wonder about the tax collector being in the Temple praying. Who did he think he was? He had made himself unclean and unworthy by working for the Roman army. He is lucky no one kicked him out! This man did not dare look up to heaven (And rightly so, thought some of the hearers.) He could only beat his breast and say, 'God, be merciful to me, a sinner.' God in his grace and goodness is in control. God is the active party in the request. God is the subject of the sentence and the man sees himself as the object – the object, however, of God's love and mercy.

Jesus kept the punch line until the end: 'I tell you, this man went down to his home justified rather than the other, for all who exalt themselves will be humbled, but all who humble themselves will be exalted' (Luke 18:14).

Illustration

The outside of the house looked well in the twilight. The white-washed walls seemed to shine and even more so in the moon-light. Then during the night it snowed and we awoke to a bright morning. How shabby the outside of the house looked against the brightness of the snow and the sunlight – it certainly needed a coat of paint. How we are depends on what or whom we compare ourselves with. When we are placed before the grace and holiness of God, all that we can truly say is 'God, be merciful to me, a sinner.'

All Saints' Day

1 November or Sunday between 30 October and 5 November inclusive

Aim

To rejoice in the communion of saints.

Readings

Daniel 7:1-3, 15-18
Psalm 149
Ephesians 1:11-23
Luke 6:20-31

Thought for the day

At this time of the year, from All Saints' Day (1 November) until the Sunday before Advent when we celebrate Christ the King, we are asked to rejoice that we are part of God's kingdom, and not only us but the whole Church in heaven and on earth. We are part of the communion of saints. We are in communion with the Church Triumphant in heaven because we are all in the heart of God. We are called to be saints – that is, to belong to God, to witness to him and to help to bring in his kingdom.

When Paul writes the Letter to the Ephesians he addressed it 'to the saints in Ephesus'. In the same way he addressed his letter to the Corinthians as those 'called to be saints' (1 Corinthians 1:2). In the same way Paul would have addressed us as the saints in (Name). It should make you think if you are addressed as the saints who are faithful in Christ Jesus. Do you see yourselves as dedicated people, for that is what you are?

Paul now lists some of the hallmarks of the Church – to show if it is the genuine article and not some dull copy.

'You are sealed with the Spirit.' Paul knew that when anything important was sent off it was sealed to show whom it belonged to and that it should arrive intact. In baptism you were sealed with the Spirit, called to be holy, a people dedicated to God. Paul calls this sealing with the Spirit a 'pledge', and by this he means a deposit laid down, a first instalment, with the guarantee of much more to come. We have a far greater inheritance offered to us.

'I have heard of your faith in the Lord Jesus and your love towards all the saints,' says Paul (Ephesians 1:15). Another hallmark of our calling is love, love towards God and towards each other. Love cannot be healthy if we fail to love God or each other.

Paul prays that we might have wisdom, the gift that is more than just knowledge, as it involves discernment and is a gift of God. We have to be a thinking and a sensitive people.

Paul prays that we may come to know God; that we may see with our hearts as well as our heads; that we may know what is the hope, and the inheritance to which we are called. Paul asks that we may experience the power of God, and that we may know the resurrection of Christ.

He continues to ask that we may know that Christ rules over all and is all-powerful.

Then he reminds us that we are the body of Christ, that Christ works in us and through us. We are to work with him and for him.

These are enough hallmarks for anyone to think about. When you go home, quietly read today's Epistle – Ephesians 1:11-23 – each day this week.

Illustration

Aman presented himself to the minister leading the service once it was over. 'I would like to become a Christian.' The minister enquired what had brought him to this decision. Was it a sermon, a book or some event in his life? The man was a little embarrassed at this point and said how he read little and hardly ever attended church. 'It's my boss at work – he is a real tough chap and we are a hard bunch of men – it's the way he deals with us. I wanted to know what made him so sensitive and caring, what made him strive to be honest and fair to all. He told me it was because he was a Christian. If that is what a Christian is like, that is what I want to be.'

The best advertisement for God and for our faith is the way we live and witness to what we believe.

Fourth Sunday before Advent

Sunday between 30 October and 5 November inclusive; for use if the Feast of All Saints was celebrated on 1 November and alternative propers are needed

Aim

To know that Jesus comes to where we are and seeks to help us to rise with him.

Readings

Isaiah 1:10-18
Psalm 32:1-8
2 Thessalonians 1:1-12
Luke 19:1-10

Thought for the day

Jericho is at a strategic crossing of the river Jordan. It is an oasis in the desert, a place of palm forests and balsam trees. The smell from the balsam and the gardens of roses travels for miles. It has a perpetual supply of fresh water from a spring. There has been a city on this site for 10,000 years! It is one of the oldest cities in the world and it was a wealthy place with a great income. One of its strange features is that it is 400 metres below sea level – the lowest city in the world, and it lived up to this by its decadence. It was here that Jesus healed blind Bartimaeus and he set the story of the Good Samaritan on the road from here to Jerusalem. It was here that Zacchaeus lived and worked as a tax collector. It was a very lucrative job in a rich city and he was the chief tax collector, in charge of the others and making more money than the others. He was a big name in Jericho, with a big income and a big house. In the world of commerce Zacchaeus was a big man. But he was little in the eyes of the faithful, he was small in stature, a traitor to his country; he was not popular and he was held in low esteem. Someone described him as the lowest man in the lowest town in the world – and you could hardly get lower than that.

Zacchaeus had heard that Jesus was in town and he wanted to see him. Zacchaeus heard that Jesus was a friend of tax collectors and sinners, and Zacchaeus certainly needed a friend. He had to see Jesus. But Zacchaeus was so small and hated the crowd squeezing him out. Why should he be allowed to see Jesus?

Zacchaeus, not to be put off, goes on ahead and climbs a tree. He peers through the leaves and wonders if he will be noticed. Jesus misses nothing. Jesus looks up and says to him, 'Zacchaeus, hurry and come down; for I must stay at your house today.' The crowd grumble: Why does he mix with sinners? Why does Jesus stoop so low? Why does he mingle with the dregs?

One day some would realise that Jesus descended into the depths to lift us up. He came to the lowest to raise them to the heights. Jesus came to sinners exactly where they are: not where they ought to be or want to be but where they are. So he came to Zacchaeus and he called him by his name! Jesus reached out to the lonely, money-grabbing, no-hoper Zacchaeus.

In turn, Zacchaeus becomes a changed man. He offers to give half of all his possessions to the poor, and if he has defrauded any, to give them back four times as much. Zacchaeus wanted to show he was a changed man.

Jesus reminds us this is the reason for his coming: 'to seek out and to save the lost'. Have we allowed Jesus to enter into the depths of our lives to make friends with us? Jesus descends to lift us up. As the Good Shepherd, he calls us by name and seeks for the lost until he finds them.

Illustration

John was put in prison for the third time. He had a good mind but he used it for crime. He was a robber and occasionally given to violence. Even his family had given up on him. He rarely had any visitors other than the official prison visitors. One day he asked the man who had been coming to see him regularly why he bothered. The man explained he believed that everyone was important and could change, even John. He also told him that he was a Christian and so believed everyone was precious in the eyes of God. This really made John think: a God that actually knew him and loved him, that he need not be condemned for ever. John began to read the Gospels and the story of Jesus. He said he had never felt such a love or known forgiveness up to that time. John became a changed man. When he was released from prison he got work with an aid agency through the help of his prison visitor. He became a trusted and hard worker and in time held a position of great trust. He never hesitated to explain how he had plumbed the depths and how Jesus had reached down to him.

Third Sunday before Advent

Sunday between 6 and 12 November inclusive

Aim

To rejoice in the resurrection and newness of life.

Readings

Job 19:23-27a
Psalm 17:1-9
2 Thessalonians 2:1-5, 13-17
Luke 20:27-38

Thought for the day

Jesus met with a group that denied the hope of resurrection. They are the Sadducees. The Sadducees were mainly the wealthy Jews who were friendly with the Romans. They were collaborators with the occupying forces – as rich groups often are because they have more to lose in any rebellion. They were conservative and fundamentalist by nature. In dealing with the Scriptures they looked almost exclusively at the five Books of Moses and only allowed a minimalist interpretation of the Scriptures. Because the resurrection is not in the early texts they refused to accept it. They were strong on tradition but not on relating new experience to it. (There are still people like this within the Church.) The Chief Priest and the High Priest were chosen from the Sadducees: they were the ruling class.

In their meeting with Jesus we see them offering a nonsense question as they did not believe in the resurrection. According to their law (See Deuteronomy 25:5ff), if a man's married brother dies childless, then he must marry the widow and so provide children for his brother. In many ways this was to protect the woman from poverty and loneliness. The Sadducees took it to a ridiculous length by suggesting that seven brothers married this woman and then died in turn and asked whose wife she would be in the resurrection.

Jesus saw this question for what it was: a trap that came out of minds that were not willing to accept change and newness. They were not like the poor; the Sadducees didn't have to worry about justice and fairness – they had the lion's share. Their life was rich enough not to worry about the future. Their thinking was limited to this world and a God that they contained within their own image. The God of Jesus is a God greater than us all, who is able to do whatever he wills. The world beyond what we know is beyond our limited minds and imagining, but it does exist: it is new and different, in the way an egg is different from a hen, a seed from a plant or a caterpillar from a butterfly. If we believe in a loving and Almighty God who is a God of justice, it brings us to think about the possibility of the resurrection. Jesus came partly that we might know that there is a resurrection.

Illustration

High up on the moors there was a group of men setting the old heather on fire. The plants had become gnarled and twisted with age: they had come to the end of their usefulness. No longer did they provide food for the sheep or the birds. So the heather was burned and you could see large flames rising. Later there would be no signs of heather, only blackened ground were it had been. These men knew what they were doing. They made sure it was a controlled burning. Under the surface, hidden from sight, were living roots. The heather would rise again: having lost its gnarled and twisted quality, it would be fresh and nourishing to the creatures.

And so it is with the resurrection of the dead.

Second Sunday before Advent

Sunday between 13 and 19 November inclusive

Aim

To show that, though troubles will come, our God is with us.

Readings

Malachi 4:1-2a
Psalm 98
2 Thessalonians 3:6-13
Luke 21:5-19

Thought for the day

Jesus was never one to promise us good times always. He was well aware of the troubles that beset our fallen world. There were some admiring the Temple and its beauty. This is not surprising. The Temple rebuilding had began 20 years before Jesus was born and it was becoming more and more splendid. The cloisters and the columns were made of pure white marble. There was a vine made of gold and each cluster was as tall as a man. Josephus, in his book *The War of the Jews,* writes of the Temple that its front 'was covered all over with plates of gold' . . . and at the first rising of the sun, reflected back a fiery splendour, and made those who forced themselves to look upon it to turn their eyes away, just as they would have done at the sun's own rays. But to strangers, when they were at a distance, the Temple appeared like a mountain covered with snow, for as those parts of it that were not gilt, they were exceeding white' (Book 5, section 5). No wonder it was admired. However, there is always a danger of worshipping the symbols of worship and not the true subject.

Jesus could sense the troubles ahead. In their attempt to make him a king, they would be showing the signs of political unrest. Jesus saw a disaster in the making with a head-on clash with the Romans. The temple was not finished until AD 64; by AD 66 strife had really begun and by AD 70 Jerusalem had fallen, the city and the Temple destroyed. Over a million Jews died in this conflict and a further 97,000 were taken away captive.

Jesus knew there would be wars and rumours of wars, earthquakes, famines and plagues – and the media still seem to glory in this sort of news! Christians will not escape; they will suffer persecution and imprisonments. But, says Jesus, 'do not be terrified' (21:9), use this as a time of witness (21:13). Jesus himself will be with us through all the troubles. He will give us the words we need and the wisdom to cope (21:15). Though we may be hated and killed, we will not perish (21:18): through Jesus we are not perishable goods. For us death is not fatal! Now that is Good News. We are not alone, our God is with us at all times – even in the dark days – and he gives us the power to endure through the gift of eternal life.

Illustration

Life was often bleak for the people who lived in the Hebrides. Sometimes the future did not seem to hold any promise and when the mists came down it did not help. Here is an affirmation prayer that faces the reality of the cheerless day but also a much deeper reality of the love of God and our future in him.

> Though the dawn breaks cheerless on this isle today,
> my spirit walks in a path of light.
> For I know my greatness.
> Thou hast built me a throne within thy heart.
> I dwell safely within the circle of thy care.
> I cannot for a moment fall out of thine everlasting arms.
> I am on my way to thy glory.
>
> *Alistair Maclean, Hebridean Altars*

Christ the King

Sunday between 20 and 26 November inclusive

Aim

To know that Christ is our King and wants us to share in his kingdom.

Readings

Jeremiah 23:1-6
Canticle Luke 1:68-79 or Psalm 46
Colossians 1:11-20
Luke 23:33-43

Thought for the day

At the end of the Church year we look at the end of Jesus' life as a travelling teacher. The Crucifixion is horrible and we think about it near the time when we are preparing for Christmas so that we may avoid a slushy sentimental faith. Our faith is rugged and hard and makes demands. We have an odd sort of king because he died for us. Most kings would expect us to be willing to die for them and to protect them. Jesus our King died for us: he died that we might have life eternal. In his final battle Jesus conquers death itself through his obedience to the Father. Evil powers seek to prevent Jesus doing God's will and to sway him from his purpose, but Jesus is faithful to the end. Most sufferers would call down curses on their tormentors. Jesus prays from the agony of the cross, 'Father, forgive them; for they do not know what they are doing.'

Nearly all Jews wore five different garments – an outer cloak, an inner tunic, girdle, sandals and a covering for the head. As four soldiers led him to the crucifixion, they each had one article of clothing as their perk. Then they gambled for the outer-robe, as it was the more precious of the garments.

The leaders mocked Jesus, saying, 'He saved others, let him save himself.' They did not recognise that Jesus' purpose was to save others, including them. He did not come to save or to look after himself; he came for us and for our salvation.

They continued their mocking with the word 'If' – 'if he is the Messiah of God, his chosen one.' This is a little word but very destructive. The devil used it at the beginning of Jesus' ministry, using almost the same words to go with it (Luke 4:3, 9). Often the way to defeat a person is to create doubt in their mind about their purpose. Jesus never wavered and he knew that it was for this he came. He came to do the will of the Father. The soldiers also mocked him, saying, 'If you are the King of the Jews, save yourself!' They did not understand that Jesus did not come to use force but love. He did not come to conquer but to win by love. We can accept him as our King or, if we choose to, we can turn our backs on him. The inscription over him read, 'This is the King of the Jews'. The sad comment by the chief priests to Pilate is 'We have no king but the emperor'(John 19:15). Too often we are all caught worshipping worldly power and might.

One of the criminals crucified with Jesus also taunted him but the other rebuked his fellow criminal, saying, 'Do you not fear God, since you are under the same sentence?' I wonder how often we realise Jesus shares our pains and our sorrows. Whenever there is distress, suffering or injustice, he is there alongside the sufferers. This criminal says, 'Jesus, remember me when you come into your kingdom.' You can view this as a recognition of faith, however small – or even a sign of penitence. Whatever, when a person turns to Jesus, Jesus willingly accepts him. Let us turn to Jesus and know that we can walk with him in his garden. In the quiet hear him say to you, 'Today you will be with me in Paradise.'

Illustration

In science fiction films there is often a scene when the earth or a space ship is hurtling towards disaster. No human could possible save it. Obviously they try everything they can but they just get more exhausted. Some lose hope altogether. Then a mysterious being enters the story, someone or something from beyond our world. He or she has powers beyond our wildest dreams and can change destruction and disaster into peace, calm and order. The world is restored: the being is thanked and then gone from sight.

This is a salvation story and, although fiction, understands something of our need for salvation. It knows we have no power ourselves to help ourselves. It tells of the love from a being far greater and more powerful than we are and of our salvation. There is such a story in the Gospels and it is not fiction. It is the greatest love story and rescue story of all time and yet we do not always make it our own.

Acknowledgements

The publishers wish to thank all those who have given their permission to reproduce the following copyright material.

YEAR A

Fifth Sunday of Easter

The following extract by Minnie Louise Haskins, taken from a collection called *Desert*, © Minnie Louise Haskins, 1908:

And I said to the man who stood at the gate of the year . . .

YEAR C

Proper 8

The following extract by Dietrich Bonhoeffer:

Cheap grace is the deadly enemy of the Church . . .

Proper 21

The following extract from *The Little Prince* by Antoine de Saint-Exupéry:

I know a planet where there is a certain red-faced man . . .

Second Sunday before Advent

Though the dawn break cheerless . . .
Hebridean Altars, Alistair Maclean, Hodder & Stoughton.

Every effort has been made to trace the owners of copyright material and we hope that no copyright has been infringed. Pardon is sought and apology made if the contrary be the case, and a correction will be made in any reprint of this book.